The Undersea Discoveries
of Jacques-Yves Cousteau

DOLPHINS

The Undersea Discoveries
of Jacques-Yves Cousteau

DOLPHINS

Jacques-Yves Cousteau
and Philippe Diolé

Translated from the French by J. F. Bernard

CASSELL · LONDON

CASSELL & COMPANY LTD
35 Red Lion Square, London. WC1R 4 SG
Sydney, Auckland, Toronto,
Johannesburg

Translated from the French by Jack F. Bernard

All photographs in this book were taken
by members of the Cousteau team
Drawings by Jean-Charles Roux

First published in Great Britain 1975

I.S.B.N. 0 304 29486 1

Printed in the Federal Republic of Germany
F. 1174

CONTENTS

CHAPTER One.   FIRST ENCOUNTERS   *11*

A Sense of Direction. A Sense of Caution. The Silent World. An Underwater Congress. Ostracism?

CHAPTER Two.   THE DOLPHINS OF MONACO   *31*

Dolphins and Sharks.

CHAPTER Three.   THE LAWS OF THE CLAN   *55*

Sensitive Skin. Dominant Animals.

CHAPTER Four.   THE STORY OF DOLLY   71

In the Keys. Communication. A Draftee. Voluntary Prisoners. Saved, by Force. Fear of the Ocean. The Oar. A Certain Smile.

CHAPTER Five.   LIFE WITH MAN   91

Opo and the Children. A Local Celebrity. The Dolphin of La Corogna. Nina's Story. A National Glory. A Monument to Nina. The Final Enigma. In Captivity.

CHAPTER Six.   THE ROAD TO FREEDOM   113

A Mistake in Yellow. "It Works!" A New Tank. January 19. First Capture. A Merry-Go-Round.

CHAPTER Seven.   A WORLD OF SOUND   137

The Mysterious Organ. Ulysses. Communications Signals. Voices in the Sea. An Unknown Source. Vocabulary. An Unsuccessful Experiment. Dialogue. Calls in the Night. A Non-Language.

CHAPTER Eight.   THOUGHT IN THE SEA   161

A Long Experience. The Four Conditions. Sensory Equipment. A Marvelous Skin. Respiration. To Sleep — Perchance to Dream. Mutual Assistance. Games. Outside the Animal Kingdom. The Affective Aspect.

CHAPTER Nine.   THE EDUCATION OF DOLPHINS   181

The Capture. Captivity. Affection. Happiness and Unhappiness. Deformation. Naval Training. Impressionable Recruits. A Dolphin Researcher. Tuffy: Liaison Agent.

CHAPTER Ten.   THE FISHERMAN'S FRIEND   203

The Water and the Fish. The Killer Whales. Fishing. Visibility Zero. The Man-Dolphin. A Difficult Chore. A Problem in Identification.

CHAPTER Eleven. THE RIGHT TO RESPECT **221**

Tuna Fishing. In the Trap. Protection. The Misfortunes of the Beluga Whale. A Marineland Boarder. Cuttlefish Eaters.

CHAPTER Twelve. AN ANCIENT FRIENDSHIP **235**

Theseus the Diver.

CHAPTER Thirteen. THE PROMISE OF THE FUTURE **253**

Experimental Biology. The Ultimate Step.

APPENDIX I **261**

The Delphinidae Family.

APPENDIX II **265**

The Cetaceans

APPENDIX III **273**

Fresh-water Dolphins

APPENDIX IV **275**

Protective Legislation

APPENDIX V **277**

Dolphins in the Circus and in the Laboratory

ILLUSTRATED GLOSSARY **283**

BIBLIOGRAPHY **300**

INDEX **302**

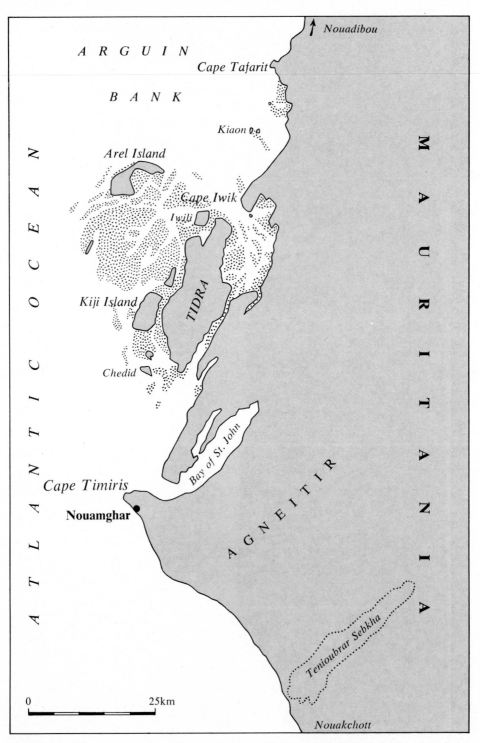

The Mauritanian coast, south of the Arguin Bank. This is the traditional fishing site of the Imragen

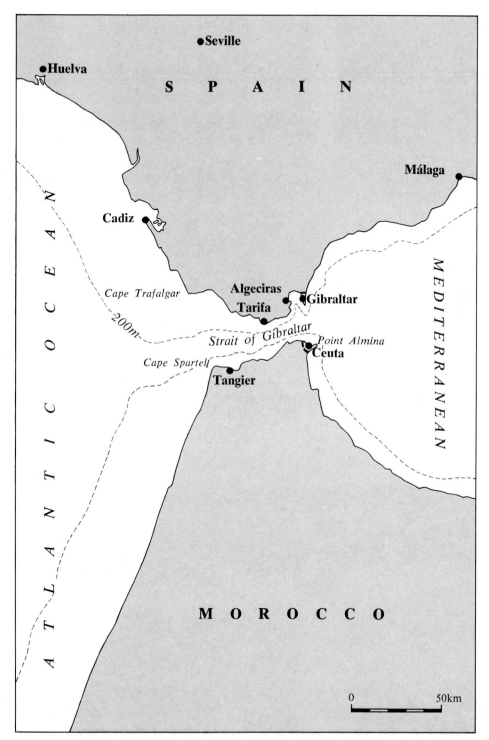

The Gibraltar Strait, where one can almost always spot cetaceans in abundance

Captain Cousteau and Jacques Renoir, our cameraman and sound engineer, approach a school of dolphins.

Chapter One

FIRST ENCOUNTERS

The cruiser *Primauguet* cut through the water at full speed, its prow rising and falling among the waves and raising a great wave of its own as it pushed irresistibly through the liquid wall of the sea. It was an impressive sight. The cruiser, a ship of the French Navy, had just been released from dry dock and we were testing her in the waters of the Far East. At that moment, the *Primauguet*'s engines were wide open, and we were moving at a speed of 33.5 knots.

I was standing on the bridge, enthralled by the performance of the mighty cruiser as it cut through the sea with incredible violence. Then, I glanced to starboard. A school of dolphins was alongside, their fins regularly appearing then disappearing beneath the surface, their dark backs moving with graceful power through the rough water. I watched. And suddenly I realized that the dolphins were moving faster than the *Primauguet*. Swimming some thirty or forty feet away from the cruiser and parallel to her, they were passing her! I could hardly believe my eyes.

Then, suddenly, the lead dolphin altered his course and cut toward our prow. When he reached the crest of the wave raised by the thrust of the *Primauguet*'s engines, he hovered there until he was displaced by another dolphin, and then another. The dolphins had devised a game which they played in the midst of the waves: one by one, in turn, they rode the crest of the cruiser's wave, directly before our prow, for two or three minutes, then let themselves be carried to starboard or port so that the next dolphin could have his turn. It was an astonishing spectacle, but its importance to me at that time was practical rather than aesthetic. I realized that the school of dolphins, in catching up to and then passing the *Primauguet* as it moved at full power, must have been swimming at a speed of no less than fifty miles per hour!

That was forty years ago. Since then, I have had many encounters with dolphins, but I have never forgotten my first impression of those great mammals as they materialized in front of the *Primauguet*'s stem — faster, and infinitely more maneuverable, than the best machines that human ingenuity had yet been able to devise.

There is no seaman worthy of the name, regardless of his nationality, who is not familiar with dolphins. For centuries, mariners and dolphins have been friends. Sailors have watched these mammals following in the wake of their ships, as though they were fascinated by the vessels — or perhaps by the men on them. And for centuries sailors have been puzzled by the preferred position of a dolphin with respect to a ship: just forward of the stem. There has been much speculation over the dolphin's reasons for this preference. Some have concluded that the dolphin's purpose is utilitarian, in that the motion of the vessel through the water provides a free ride and allows the dolphin to conserve its strength so that, with a minimum of effort, it is carried at a considerable speed but over rather short distances. Yet, the fact remains, as I found out aboard the *Primauguet*, that the dolphin does not need a ship to attain great speed. Moreover, dolphins never stay very long forward of a ship's stem. So, it seems reasonable to surmise that the dolphin's purpose in choosing that position has little or nothing to do with location. By the same token, the speed of a ship does not seem to be an important factor. There is documentary evidence that dolphins maneuvered forward of ancient sailing ships as readily as they do before the stems of our mightiest warships today, and as readily as they still do with small sailing vessels, inasmuch as their speed is at least three knots.

We could say that, in such instances, the dolphins are "playing." But how can we possibly know what a dolphin considers to be a "game"?

It is possible that contact with the rush of water raised by a prow is pleasant to dolphins. It stimulates them, caresses them, "pets" them. The skin of the dolphin is quite sensitive, and the motion of the water may give them a pleasure almost sensual in nature. Or it may be that that same motion serves simply to cleanse their skins. But it would seem that the dolphin could be caressed or cleaned just as effectively aft of a ship, in its wake, as forward of its stem. Yet, dolphins never swim in a wake. . . .

It should be obvious by now that we understand very little about this behavior of dolphins. We know that these mammals like to come into contact with objects they find floating on the surface of the water. Occasionally, they actually swim with their bodies touching the hull of a ship. And sometimes two dolphins will place themselves on each side of the hull in this position, as though they are trying to support the ship and keep it afloat. Not all species of dolphin venture near boats and ships — only those who are most "gregarious."

A Sense of Direction

I have often had occasion to realize just how mysterious the life of the dolphin is and how little we understand it. In 1948, for example, I was aboard the *Elie Monnier*, a ship of the French Navy, when we set sail from Toulon for the islands off Cape Verde. Our mission was to launch the *FNRS II* — the bathyscaphe designed by Professor Piccard. En route, near Gibraltar, we took the opportunity to conduct an interesting experiment.

Marine mammals are particularly abundant in the waters around Gibraltar, and one sees large numbers of cetaceans: sperm whales, whales, and pilot whales. On this occasion, the weather was beautiful, the sea calm, and the dolphins particularly numerous. We set a westward course, to a point in the Atlantic where we wanted to take soundings at the mouth of the straits. By the time we had finished the job, we were about fifty miles from shore and we sighted a large school of dolphins obviously heading for Gibraltar. We made a half turn and joined them. Almost immediately, the dolphins took up a position directly in front of our prow and began leaping out of the water, playing, and always remaining ahead of our ship.

To all appearances, they were as certain of the course back to Gibraltar as we were, with all of our navigational equipment. I wondered if it was a coincidence. Then I decided to try an experiment. I ordered the *Elie Monnier*'s course changed ever so gradually and slightly. For a short time, the dolphins remained with the ship, then, suddenly, they left us and resumed the true course toward Gibraltar.

Several times we tried to lead them astray in this way, and each time the dolphins left us to stay on course. I could only conclude that here, some fifty miles from land, the dolphins knew the precise azimuth of Gibraltar and were on a direct course toward their destination. I was left wondering how

Calypso at anchor.

they could possibly navigate with such precision. Were they guided by the currents? By the topography of the bottom? By the composition of the water where the Mediterranean mixes with the Atlantic? I still do not know the answer to that question.

A Sense of Caution

During the same cruise, off the coast of Morocco, we cut our engines near a school of dolphins. The dolphins were following a southward course, playing as they swam.

The sea was calm that day, and, for the first time, we decided to join the dolphins in the water. We hoped that our diving gear would enable us to get close enough to film the mammals and, perhaps, even to touch them. Remember, this was in 1948, and it was a marvelous and exciting experience for us. Unfortunately, we were able to get only a few brief shots of the animals as

(Right) Dolphins in the open sea.

they dived toward the bottom or swam frantically away from us.

We learned that day that, in the water, dolphins are extremely wary of divers. And that conclusion has been confirmed many times since then. Dolphins in their natural environment never approach a man beneath the surface, regardless of whether the man is moving or remaining absolutely motionless. They seem less frightened of a man who remains on the surface, but, even then, as soon as the man dives, the dolphins flee. It may be that the human form represents a threat to them. A diver beneath the surface may appear to be a marine animal similar to a shark — the natural enemy of dolphins.

It sometimes happens that a dolphin will overcome its timidity sufficiently to swim a bit closer for a better look, but, almost immediately, he swims away again. We have never seen a dolphin in the sea remain among divers for any length of time. Even in areas not usually frequented by man, where the dolphins have no reason to fear man, they seem to regard a diver as a dangerous creature who must be avoided.

During *Calypso*'s oceanographic expeditions in 1951 and 1952, we often sighted schools of dolphins in the Red Sea and in the Indian Ocean. Sometimes these schools comprised several hundred individuals. We learned to recognize them at considerable distances by the great splashes the dolphins make by leaping out of the water.

As soon as we spotted a series of such splashes, we dived into the water. But, no matter how quick we were, we never succeeded in really getting close to the animals, let alone in swimming with them or joining in their games as we had hoped.

We used to daydream about these marvelous mammals, imagining that, somehow, we could work out a common life with them in the sea. We exercised great care in approaching them, doing everything possible to avoid frightening them. We did all that we could to present ourselves as friends. But how does one go about conveying an attitude of friendship to dolphins? We tried everything we could think of to reassure them and convince them of our good intentions, but they refused to take the bait. They did not even seem to notice the fishes that we offered them — which would have been snatched up immediately by a grouper or a shark.

At that time, we knew even less than we know now about dolphins and

(Right) A large school of dolphins traveling in the open water.

(Following page) Three dolphins swimming near *Calypso*.

about life in the sea. For us, dolphins were legendary animals, for we had read all the surviving literature of the ancients about them. That is not to say that we believed all that we read, but, even so, dolphins seemed to us to be the most attractive and intriguing form of marine life. And so, we were determined to make friends with them. But, every time we dived and tried to get close to them, they scattered in every direction, majestic even in their flight.

It often happened that, during our expeditions, we saw schools of dolphins swimming on a course parallel to *Calypso*'s. On such occasions, just as it had occurred some fifteen years earlier when I was aboard the *Primauguet*, the largest and strongest of the dolphins would take up a position directly forward of the stem. He seemed to take great pleasure in being pushed along by the water. Around this dolphin, the other dolphins gamboled, diving under the hull and making sounds as though they were demanding the best place and the game that was most fun.*

Sometimes a school of dolphins would continue these antics for fifteen or twenty minutes. At other times, the animals spent only a few seconds at it.

We were particularly taken by the grace and suppleness of the dolphins in the sea. As divers, we are hopelessly outclassed by them, and we can only envy an ability which we can never hope to match.

I have mentioned the "games" of the dolphins. If they do indeed play, their games are not haphazard or disorganized. They are community games which all participants begin at the same instant, as though by magic — or as though at a given signal. We have seen immense schools of dolphins suddenly begin leaping out of the water, turning, and raising great splashes of water as they fell back on their sides or on their backs.

In the water, one can see their white undersides quite clearly. Sometimes the animals stroke each other with their fins or rub the entire lengths of their bodies against one another.

The Silent World

In 1954, after having worked in the Red Sea, we headed toward the Persian Gulf on a petroleum-exploration assignment. As we were leaving Aden, we sighted a school of dolphins unlike any that we had ever seen and unlike any that we would ever see again.

These were the dolphins who were seen in *The Silent World*. Even that film does not convey an exact idea of that incredible gathering as we saw it.

---

*Dr. Kenneth Norris has seen dolphins "surfing" ahead of a large whale, just as they do with ships.

When we sighted the school from afar, the water was churning as though it were boiling. Our captain, François Saout, was on the bridge at the time. He sent for me immediately and reported: "I don't understand this at all. There's a reef dead ahead which doesn't appear on our charts."

It was not until we were closer that we realized that the "reef" was an incredible assembly of dolphins — no fewer than 10,000 of them, and perhaps as many as 20,000 — leaping playfully into the air. These leaps were so fantastic that we have never again seen anything like them in all our years of observing dolphins in the sea. We remained there for several hours, watching. Then night fell, and we lost sight of them. We have since tried to locate similar concentrations of dolphins, but we have seen nothing to compare with what we saw that day.

A friend of ours, Professor René-G. Busnel,† on a number of occasions has seen dolphins assembled in schools that stretched to a length of thirty-five or forty miles. In the Mediterranean, he has witnessed schools streaking past his ship — schools which extended for miles in both directions — with the dolphins swimming swiftly in single file, without even ruffling the surface. Once, en route to Dakar, his ship was completely surrounded by dolphins, with the animals spaced out so that there was only one dolphin to every twenty square yards of surface. He estimates that some of these schools comprised several million dolphins.

An Underwater Congress

In 1955, when we were filming *The Silent World*, we left the Seychelles and headed toward Amirante Island in the Indian Ocean. *Calypso* dropped anchor on the leeward side of a reef and remained there for two days while we dived. We noticed that, every morning at about ten o'clock, a school of dolphins passed near *Calypso*, apparently on a swimming tour of the reef. I wanted to follow them, and, since it seemed unnecessary to use *Calypso* for this, Frédéric Dumas and I set out in one of our launches. To this day, I have not forgiven myself for not taking a camera.

On the other side of the reef, we saw a dolphin rise to the surface to breathe and then let himself sink down into the water again, without swimming. We inched forward in the launch until we were as close as we dared go, then we dived. On this occasion, the dolphins did not flee as soon as we got

†Professor Busnel has either initiated, or participated in, several of *Calypso*'s cruises. He is currently Director of the Laboratory of Acoustical Physiology of the INRA.

Our Zodiac managed to maintain a position very close to a group of playful dolphins.

into the water. From the surface — we did not have our Aqua-Lungs® with us — we looked down and saw them turn their heads and stare at us. The sight that greeted us was one that we have never seen again. There were about fifteen dolphins — probably the school that we had seen going past *Calypso* every morning — in the crystal-clear water, on the side of the reef. They were *sitting* on the bottom, in a group, as though they were holding a conference. I say "sitting"; I mean that they were literally poised on their tails.

They remained where they were, stirring a bit and looking at one another. Then they continued with their meeting. But when we tried to move in closer to them, they swam away immediately. It was a unique and extraordinarily impressive sight.

The truth is that I still have no idea what they were doing. For the most part, the life of a dolphin — that is, of a dolphin living at liberty in the sea — is an enigma wrapped in a mystery. We understand a bit more — but not much

A dolphin can leap about ten feet above the surface.

more — about that part of the dolphin's life which takes place on the surface, when the animals are en route between two points and when we see them swimming and playing before *Calypso*'s prow. What they do with the rest of their lives, we have no idea. I cannot even offer a plausible explanation for the "congress" Dumas and I witnessed except to say that it did not appear to have anything to do with mating. I have described it only because I think Dumas and I are the only humans ever to have witnessed behavior of this sort among dolphins.

Ostracism?

We had an encounter of a different kind in the Mediterranean, in 1953. Again, the weather was magnificent and the sea was like a mirror. We were sailing around Corsica, and had entered the Tyrrhenian Sea, between Corsica and the Italian mainland. I was in the observation chamber, and from that vantage point I saw, for the first time in my life, a finback whale swimming on its back. The whale was in my field of vision for fifteen or twenty seconds. At first I thought it was a white whale. But then, when the animal righted itself, I saw that it was black, like other finbacks. It occurs to me that almost all mariners' accounts of white whales are based upon sightings of whales amusing themselves by swimming stomach-up slightly beneath the surface of the water. Albino whales are a great rarity, and I suspect that when navigators and whalers reported a "white whale," they were referring to an ordinary whale swimming in this position. In some cases, it may have been a case of confusion with the Beluga (*Delphinus leucas*), which is a Delphinidae of very large size.

The same day, we reached the vicinity of the Lipari Islands. However, we could not distinguish the coasts of the islands because, following a period of calm weather, weak currents, and a recent volcanic eruption, the water was covered with pumice stone. It was as though *Calypso* were moving through a sea of liquid rock, and the pumice made a constant crunching sound as it grated against our hull. A continuous noise rose from the water all around us, and it took an hour for *Calypso* to pick her way through that field of volcanic debris.

As the pumice stone began to thin, we sighted a black dot in the distance: a dolphin, floating vertically, with his snout protruding above the surface. From time to time, he moved his tail to maintain his position, that is, to keep his snout above the surface so as to breathe. But he was not swimming.

Calypso drew nearer, and still the dolphin did not move. It occurred to us that the animal might be sick, or even dead. When we were five or six yards from the dolphin, I ordered *Calypso*'s engines cut, and we dived into the water. It was obvious then that the dolphin was alive; he was watching us. We swam closer, and the animal's head disappeared beneath the surface, only to reappear a few moments later. There was no attempt at flight. He continued to return to the surface regularly for air.

We watched the dolphin for perhaps three quarters of an hour, until our ship's doctor, Dr. Nivelot, came to a conclusion. "The only thing I can imagine," Nivelot said, "is that he's sick. I'll have to see if I can do anything for him."

Canoë Kientzy brought a net from *Calypso* and gently wrapped it around the ailing dolphin. The animal did not attempt to resist, or to flee. Then we hoisted him aboard and placed him in a small boat filled with water. He floated in the water and appeared not unduly frightened. His breathing

Falco was able to lay hold of a dolphin in the water and to swim with the animal.

seemed normal, and there was no sign of any kind of wound or cut on his body.

After examining the dolphin, Dr. Nivelot concluded that a stimulant of some kind might be helpful, and he gave his patient an injection of camphorated oil. There seemed to be no immediate effect.

An hour later, the dolphin was dead.

We were all very upset, and Dr. Nivelot undertook an autopsy. He found nothing — no organic disorder, no sign of congestion. Nothing. We had taken the dolphin's temperature while the animal was still alive and found it to be normal (38°C).

The death of the dolphin was the occasion for much reflection on my part. Finally, I reached a conclusion which is perhaps somewhat daring. Nonetheless, it is a conclusion based upon long observation and experience since that unfortunate incident in the Tyrrhenian Sea. It is my opinion that the dolphin may have been ostracized by the other dolphins. Dolphins are gregarious beings who do not take well to solitude. When they are excluded from the company of other dolphins, they are in desperate straits indeed. Then, they try to attach themselves to anything or anyone. In our laboratory experiments at Monaco, we have seen dolphins who *allow* themselves to die. Dolphins are emotional, sensitive, vulnerable creatures — probably more so than we are.

It seems likely that schools of dolphins observe a form of discipline that we do not understand. There are probably rules which none of the school is allowed to transgress.

(Above) Dolphins in the open sea can swim at speeds in excess of 40 miles per hour.

(Right) From *Calypso*'s stem, part of our team watches a dolphin maneuver in the water.

The animal that we had taken aboard *Calypso* was quite young, so it is certain that she (it was a female, as we discovered) had not been turned out of the school because of old age. It may be that she had broken a rule of some kind. In any case, the pitiful death of that dolphin, so many years ago, made a deep impression on me.

Another aspect of the mysterious conduct of dolphins lies in their attachment to beings of other species. I am perfectly well aware that I am leaving myself open to criticism by attributing anything like emotions to dolphins. I should therefore begin by stating that there are certain documented facts which cannot be explained except by admitting that dolphins have certain emotional or affective drives. When marine mammals try to keep a drowning swimmer afloat, it may be because they have a tendency to push against, or to keep on the surface, any floating object. But what are we to think of the dolphin who, when his companion in captivity died, stubbornly kept the corpse from sinking? And what are we to say about the dolphin who, for over a week, kept the corpse of a tiger shark at the surface and resisted any at-

tempt to remove the corpse? He abandoned his efforts only when the tiger shark had begun to decompose.

Certainly, we may speculate that the actions of those dolphins indicate an incomprehension in the face of death, a refusal to accept death. It may be that such actions prove nothing. But they do give us food for thought.

In our own minds, our encounters with dolphins take on many of the characteristics of encounters with human beings. Why? No doubt, it is because each dolphin appears to have its own distinctive personality.

In any event, it is obvious that dolphins are often motivated by curiosity, and especially by curiosity about man. One can literally see it in their eyes. This is a fact that can be doubted only by someone who has never really looked a dolphin in the eye. The brilliance of that organ, the spark that is so evident there, seems to come from another world. The look which the dolphin gives — a keen look, slightly melancholy and mischievous, but less insolent and cynical than that of monkeys — seems full of indulgence for the uncertainties of the human condition. Among primates, one sometimes detects what appears to be sadness at not being human. This sentiment is alien to the dolphin.

When I had *Calypso* converted from a mine sweeper into an oceano-graphic-research vessel, I had a "false nose" built under the stem. This is a metallic well, at the bottom of which is an observation chamber equipped with five portholes. The observation chamber is about eight feet beneath the surface, and from that vantage point we can observe the sea around us. We can not only watch the dolphins as they move in the water, but we can also look at them as they look at us. And we can do so only because the dolphins themselves are willing. They see us through the portholes, and they press their snouts against the glass to see us. The rictus that crosses their cheeks, from the eye to the snout, gives them the appearance of wearing an eternal smile. Their "look" — mischievous, curious, observant — is that of a mammal and does not have the icy fixity of the shark's stare.

On two or three occasions, we looked at each other, and their eyes sparkled with an unexpected gleam of connivance, as though the most intelligent of the dolphins was about to reveal, at last, the great secret which would permit man finally to cross over the chasm separating humanity from animality, finally to restore to life its primordial unity.

This book makes no pretense of solving these mysteries. All that we can do is recount what we have done and what we have seen. Perhaps it will be taken in good part if we mention that in the past twenty-five years, *Calypso*'s team has had more direct experience with dolphins than man has ever had before. We have observed dolphins living at liberty in the open sea. We have seen them in semicaptivity, eager for contact with humans, eager not only to be fed but also to be petted. We have taken dolphins from the sea and released them almost immediately, having detained them only a few moments for an experiment. And, unfortunately, we have also seen dolphins living in close captivity, sad dolphins the sight of which was sufficient to cure us forever of any urge to deprive these creatures of their liberty.

Now, at the beginning of this book, candor requires us to confess that neither our own experiences nor the research of the hundred-or-so scientists, who are at work trying to solve the mystery of the dolphin, are sufficient to enable us to answer with any certainty the many fascinating questions that have excited the interest of the public: the meaning of the sound signals emitted by dolphins, the hierarchical structure of the dolphin community, the degree of the dolphin's attachment to humans, and so forth. All we can do is resign ourselves, at least temporarily, to our ignorance and continue to observe and to experiment so that, someday, we may arrive at the truth.

We have been careful, throughout this work, to refrain from making affirmations for which there is insufficient evidence; and, even at the risk of disappointing the reader, we have tried to remain well within the realm of the non-miraculous.

It is a peculiarity of the dolphin that it is the animal which most excites popular admiration and interest and, at the same time, which most elicits caution among scientists. This paradoxical situation is explained by the fact that, so far as the public is concerned, dolphins are a relatively recent discovery. It was only some twenty or twenty-five years ago that the dolphin became a circus and television star. And, almost immediately, people began talking about the dolphin's "language," its "intelligence," its "feelings." These are terms the indiscriminate use of which is enough to make any scientist uneasy.

We do not mean to imply that the exceptional qualities popularly attributed to dolphins are all exaggerations and myths. On many points, we share the feelings of the public with respect to the dolphin. And our long experience with dolphins has only served to strengthen those feelings in us.

Therefore, it is certainly not the purpose of this book to "demythologize" the dolphin. At the same time, we must not ignore the opinions and criticisms of zoologists, neurophysiologists, and acoustical experts — all of whom are, and should be, skeptics by profession. These specialists require proof.

For all of that, we do not believe that the adventure of the dolphins will lose anything of its capacity to elicit interest and admiration. Let us remem-

Ivan Giacoletto, one of *Calypso*'s divers, photographed this group of dolphins in the water.

Falco attempts to capture one of the dolphins swimming before *Calypso*'s prow.

ber that this adventure is far from finished. It continues and grows from day to day. And let us remember too that life, in its exuberance, always succeeds in overflowing the narrow limits within which man thinks he can confine it.

Chapter Two

THE DOLPHINS OF MONACO

Our encounters with dolphins were, at first, more or less exceptional meetings in the course of our work, enjoyable distractions which occurred during *Calypso*'s expeditions. In our minds, we regarded the dolphin as a kind of friend in reserve, a rather mysterious and somewhat amusing friend to divers like ourselves engaged in the kind of work that we had undertaken.

It was our impression, at the time, that it required a certain amount of luck to sight a school of dolphins. We knew less about the sea then than we know now, and certainly much less about the kind of lives that animals lived in the sea. Even today, twenty years later, we do not know a great deal about the sea as a whole. The extent of the sea is so vast that even though a man may spend his whole life studying it, he can never know more than certain areas of the ocean.

One day in 1957, I decided that it was time to pay more attention to the dolphins we had seen in the Mediterranean. I had visited marinelands in the United States, and I had seen trained dolphins perform some extraordinary feats there. I had it in the back of my mind to obtain the same results for the Oceanographic Museum of Monaco.

I described my plan to Albert Falco, our chief diver. Albert, or Bébert, as we call him, is our most experienced diver, and he is also a man with a remarkable understanding of animals. I told Bébert that I wanted to try to capture some dolphins if it were possible to do so without harming them in any way.

"Capture dolphins?" Falco asked. "How on earth would we go about it?"

"Well, in America they lasso them."

"America is a cowboy country. They must have cowboy divers."

"Well," I said, "*Calypso* is going to be at Monaco for a week. We can devote that time exclusively to Operation Dolphin. At least it's worth a try."

Bébert shrugged.

As the first part of my plan, I had a platform installed on *Calypso*'s prow. The second part of the plan was to install Bébert on the platform, armed with a lasso which was attached to a pole.

Happily, the weather was perfect our first day out. Off Villefranche, we sighted a school of dolphins almost immediately. *Calypso* turned and began following a course parallel to theirs. As usual, the school quickly took up its position dead ahead of *Calypso*, and one of the dolphins placed himself so that he could ride along on the wave raised by our vessel.

The moment had come for Bébert to play cowboy.

Teetering on his platform, he swung the lasso and threw it. The rope struck the water, and the lead dolphin fled, closely followed by the rest of the school. In an instant, the sea was empty.

We then realized that if a lasso is thrown from a vessel moving at a speed of five or six knots, there is no chance that it will even penetrate the surface. Therefore, it is impossible to lasso a dolphin following that method. Nonetheless, Bébert was convinced that there must be some technique, some trick to it, that would make it possible to lasso a dolphin. For the next week, he tried one approach after another, but all in vain.

By then, it was time for *Calypso* to leave for an expedition in the Atlantic. When we reached Lisbon, however, Bébert left us to return to Monaco for the express purpose of pursuing his dolphin hunt. There was an old vessel there for him to use: the *Espadon*, a trawler which we would later convert into a ship for diving and oceanographic research.

Dolphins and Sharks

"At that time," Bébert says, "I knew practically nothing about dolphins. I had spent hours watching them playing around *Calypso*; and, for the past five or six years, we had been trying to dive with them in the water, but they

This is the *Espadon*, a converted trawler used by Falco in his first attempts to capture a dolphin.

would never let us join them. As soon as we got within ten or fifteen yards of them, they swam away.

"There was only one exception. During our expeditions in the Indian Ocean, whenever we passed near an island, we always went out in a launch or a Zodiac to inspect the bottom and the reefs, to see what kind of animals lived there. On this particular occasion in 1954, we were lying off the Farquhar Islands, to the northeast of Madagascar. And, following our usual practice, we went out in a launch.

"There were several dolphins in the water that took an immediate interest in the launch. As soon as we saw them, we cut our speed to a minimum and moved forward as slowly as possible so as not to frighten them. To our surprise, the dolphins did not run away, but remained at a distance of five or six yards from us. They were in relatively shallow water, and most of them kept their heads down. We could see their light-colored and somewhat plump bellies. For at least ten minutes, they remained motionless, watching us, with a mischievous expression on their faces.

(Following page) This photograph was taken at the precise moment that a dolphin, after having leaped through the air, struck the surface of the water again.

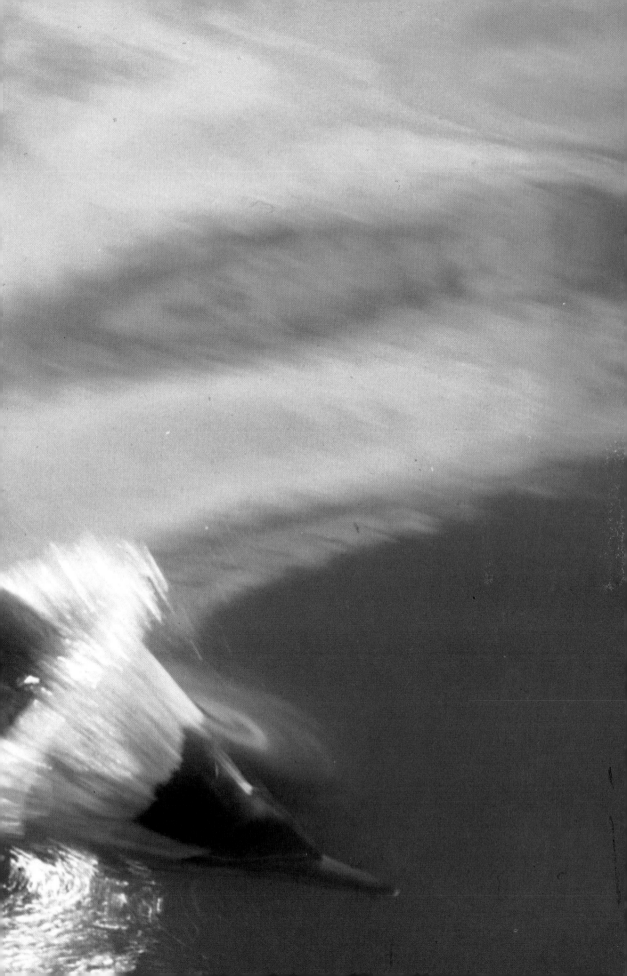

"I remember that, deeper in the water, directly below the dolphins, there were a number of sharks. We expected something to happen, thinking that perhaps the sharks would attack the dolphins. We had often heard, however, that dolphins were not afraid of sharks, that they were much more clever than sharks.

"In any case, the sharks and the dolphins left each other alone on this occasion. What struck me, though, was that this was the first time, in years of trying, that I had been able to get so close to a school of dolphins."

By the time he returned to Monaco, Bébert was convinced that if he was going to capture a live dolphin without hurting it, as I had instructed him, then he would have to devise some kind of special lasso for the job. He reasoned that the best place to lay hold of a dolphin with a lasso was just forward of its tail. This was the part of the animal's body which remained exposed the longest when a dolphin was swimming ahead of a boat. The problem was how to get a lasso around that slender part of the tail which lies just forward of the powerful tail fins.

Bébert approached the French Bureau of Marine Research — our research facility at Marseilles — and the Bureau manufactured a dolphin catcher of sorts for him. It was a kind of giant pincer, with two pawls designed to open on contact and then immediately close again.

Bébert did not give up his idea of a lasso. He designed a rigid hoop which was intended to hold the lasso open when he threw it. Then the device was modified so that it could be thrown by means of a hand harpoon or else shot by a harpoon gun. The idea was to slip the lasso around the dolphin's snout — a plan for which extraordinary speed would be required.

Designing an instrument capable of seizing — and holding — a dolphin is not as simple as it may sound. Bébert was dealing with animals weighing between 150 and 175 pounds and capable of leaping out of the water at a speed of thirty or forty miles per hour. His job was made more difficult by the fact that the dolphin's skin is extremely sensitive, and I had insisted that, above all, the specimen captured was not to be hurt in any way. Moreover, as we knew very well by that time, dolphins are very wary of man, and we had no idea of how a dolphin would react once it had been captured. We had often had occasion to note that the dolphin's snout is equipped with a large number of teeth.

The *Espadon* made its first attempt to capture a dolphin off the coast of Corsica. We had occasionally encountered schools of the mammals in these waters; and we did not know at that time that there were at least as many dolphins offshore from the Museum in Monaco, between Monaco and Nice, as there were around Corsica.

All in all, the mission of the *Espadon* in Corsican waters was a disappointment. By then, winter had set in and there were not many dolphins to be seen. There was a sufficient number, however, for Bébert to be able to try his new pincer device, and, as it turned out, the pincer was not nearly large enough. It was no larger, in fact, than the tail of a medium-sized dolphin. Moreover, the dolphin — a very sensitive and intuitive animal — seemed to be aware of what was afoot and always managed to avoid the pincer.

Bébert's attempts with his lasso were no more successful than the pincer had been, although the hoop he had designed, and the fact that the lasso could be launched by means of a harpoon gun, made it a more promising weapon. Unfortunately, the platform attached to the *Espadon*'s prow did not extend far enough over the water for Bébert to be able to position himself directly over the dolphin. He was therefore obliged to throw the lasso obliquely, which meant that when the rope struck the water it floated there, and the dolphin simply swam under it.

Here are a few extracts from Bébert's log during that expedition:

"At dawn today, we sighted three schools of dolphins. They all disappeared as soon as they saw us.

"I have the feeling that they see me standing on the platform and they know that something is up, so they are even more cautious than usual.

"I've tried the pincer, but it doesn't work. It's too narrow, and the dolphin always gets away.

"October 15 and 16. Bad weather. Very few dolphins. Those we do see don't even come near our prow. The *Espadon* is pitching wildly.

"October 17. My birthday. For a present, I'd like to catch a dolphin. The weather is right for it: clear, and a dead calm. Exceptionally good visibility. We are on a southward course, about ten miles offshore.

"We saw a sperm whale on the horizon, but no dolphins.

"We are putting in to Ajaccio for the night. I'm afraid we have become the laughingstock of the local fishermen.

"October 18. We have left Corsica and are returning to the mainland. During the crossing, I will work on a design for a new pincer."

The *Espadon*'s return to Monaco, therefore, was not exactly joyous. But the expedition had not been a total failure, for Falco had learned a great deal from the experience. He used the knowledge he had gained first of all to have the *Espadon*'s forward platform extended. Then it was suggested that he test a new means of capturing a dolphin, by using an arrow tipped with curare. By computing the amount of curare with great exactitude, he was told, it should be possible to immobilize an animal without causing it the slightest harm and, while it was unconscious, to hoist it aboard.

Bébert was skeptical about this device, but the "experts" who suggested it were so affirmative that he decided it would be unwise to ignore their advice. He felt that he should at least test their method.

At the same time, he decided that it would be useless to go all the way back to Corsica in search of dolphins. Instead, the *Espadon* would try to capture a specimen off Monaco, where Bébert had seen schools in coastal waters.

The test was run, with catastrophic results. The dolphin subjected to the curare was in no way immobilized. On the contrary, he embarked on a series of prodigious leaps out of the water and then fled at top speed. It was obvious that the animal had not been paralyzed, even briefly, by the drug. The reason may have been that the harpoon used was quite small and light, and it detached itself from the dolphin's body almost instantly. Moreover, Bébert saw blood flowing from the wound made by the harpoon, and he concluded that the curare was eliminated from the dolphin's system immediately.

Here is an extract from Falco's log:

"At 1 P.M., we were about sixteen miles from the coast when we sighted several schools of dolphins. I shot my famous curare-tipped harpoon at one of the animals, with the result that he made one fantastic leap and then disappeared, taking my harpoon, and my hopes, with him. Almost simultaneously, every dolphin in the area took off in the direction of Corsica at fifty miles per hour. It was total panic.

"We are now preparing a new harpoon, with an improved piston.

"October 29. The dolphin made off with my new, improved harpoon."

After several more days of tests, with identical results, Falco, by now totally disgusted, abandoned the "ultimate weapon" of the experts.

Once more, however, he had learned from his experiences. The *Espadon*'s venture into the waters off the coast of Monaco confirmed that dolphins were much more numerous in that area than we had previously suspected. And it also revealed that dolphins were much more creatures of habit than we had thought. What this meant, in practical terms, was that Falco had discovered he did not have to depend upon luck to sight a school of dolphins.

There are very few people who have the "feel" of the sea to the extent that Bébert does. Once he had established that there were dolphins in abundance nearby — within two or three miles of the coast, offshore from Villefranche and from Nice and in the Bay of the Angels at Var — he very quickly

(Upper right) A group of dolphins swimming at full speed off the island of Corsica.

(Lower right) As the Zodiac draws near, a dolphin suddenly turns and dives.

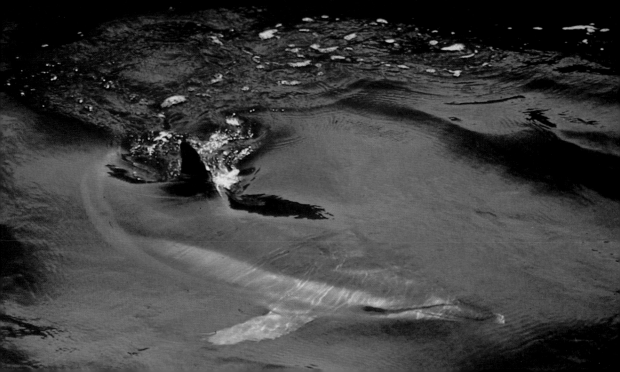

familiarized himself with their routine and habits. Facts unsuspected by those who had never observed dolphins in the sea were now, for Bébert, truths based upon evidence: simple truths and useful truths.

Yet, it was six months before Bébert succeeded in capturing his first dolphin.

The species of dolphin that is usually seen giving performances in American marinelands is a species common in Florida's waters, the *Tursiops truncatus*, or Bottlenosed Dolphin. This species adapts fairly well to captivity and has a robust constitution. It is also found in the Mediterranean; but there, the most numerous species is the *Delphinus delphis*, or Common Dolphin, which is smaller and lighter than the Bottlenosed Dolphin. It is also considerably more delicate than the latter, as we were soon to discover.

The *Espadon*'s team, equipped with binoculars, quickly learned to spot schools of dolphins; and the ship's captain, Jean Toscano, developed the art of steering his vessel into a position parallel to the dolphins.

"We had to lure them toward the stem," Falco said. And whether they were "lured" or not depended on the time of day, the weather, and the condition of the sea.

Usually, the dolphin who takes up a position directly forward of a ship's prow keeps close watch on the ship. He is extemely cautious. At the slightest sign of activity aboard, he stops playing. Sometimes he leaves, taking the others of the school with him. Therefore, when Falco was on his platform above the spot where the dolphin was playing, it was necessary for him to assume the appearance of a part of the vessel. He had to remain absolutely motionless. When the dolphins came within range, he says, he pretended to himself that he was a figurehead on the prow and did not move a muscle. He had to choose the proper instant to strike — and then he had to move with the speed of lightning.

Meanwhile, at the Museum in Monaco, workmen were busy constructing a large pool to house the dolphin that Bébert hoped to capture.

By this time, Falco had returned to his idea of a pincer device for capturing dolphins, and he had succeeded in perfecting a pincer that he was sure would work. The device, once it had been manufactured by one of the Museum's mechanics, resembled a pair of giant scissors. Its U-shaped arms were covered with a layer of soft rubber so as not to bruise the sensitive skin of the dolphin. The two arms of the scissors were locked open by means of a plastic pin; then, on contact with the dolphin, the pin was released and the arms were snapped shut by a spring. The whole apparatus was mounted on a harpoon. Then, a yellow buoy was attached to the pincer by means of a line.

A dolphin was caught during the first tests with this device, but he suc-

Albert Falco, Canoë Kientzy and Armand Davso carefully lay a captured dolphin on a pair of air mattresses.

ceeded in freeing himself from the pincer. It was therefore necessary to double the size of one of the arms of the pincer.

The next time, the pincer held, but the dolphin began thrashing about in terror, tearing his skin on the apparatus. The *Delphinus delphis* was more high-strung than anyone had suspected. Falco therefore released the dolphin.

So far as methods were concerned, it was back to the drawing board. Finally, a rather complicated procedure was worked out among Bébert, Maurice Léandri, and Canoë Kientzy. Bébert would fire the pincer, and then Léandri would immediately throw the yellow buoy as far as possible from the ship. The instant that Maurice had thrown out the buoy, Canoë was supposed to dive into the water. And the captain, at the helm of the vessel, would give a

Dolphins leaping at the entrance to the Bay of Villefranche.

turn to the right before ordering the engine to be cut and the gears to be disengaged.

Canoë, meanwhile, was supposed to be over the side with the inflated rubber mattresses. (The purpose of the latter was to avoid bruising the dolphin's skin.) He was to wrap the mattresses around the dolphin, remove the pincer, and then take the dolphin alongside the *Espadon*, where there was an open hatch aft to port.

The first tests, carried out off Monaco, Villefranche, and Nice, had given Bébert the opportunity to discover what areas were most frequented by the dolphins and also to observe their habits. He noted that the animals followed a fairly regular schedule. In the area between Monaco and the mouth of the Var, for example, the dolphins seemed to swim in from a southeasterly direction, heading toward Nice and staying at a distance of about three miles from the shore. During the day, there were few dolphins to be seen, but they began

to arrive from the open sea late in the afternoon, about 4 or 5 P.M. They never ventured into the water flowing from the Var into the Mediterranean, but stayed on the fringes of that water so as to take advantage of the abundance of fishes to be found there. When darkness fell, the animals disappeared toward the southwest, swimming at top speed and leaping out of the water. It is likely that, during the night, they swam in a large semicircle in the open sea so that, the following afternoon, they would arrive once more from the southeast.

The First Capture

Here is the definitive passage from Falco's log:

"October 31, 1957. Everything appears to be ready. I think that the pincer is working perfectly, and everybody on the team knows exactly what he is supposed to do. The weather is good, and the *Espadon* is no longer pitching.

"Luck is with us. We spotted dolphins on the horizon — a very large school of two or three hundred specimens off the Monacan coast. We had hardly completed our turn to the rear of the school when three dolphins, trailing behind the main body of the school, caught up with us and took up their position forward of our prow. Fortunately, I was already on the platform, holding the loaded harpoon gun. I fired. It was a good shot, and the pincer closed around the tail of one of the dolphins. Immediately, Maurice threw the buoy into the water. Captain Toscano stopped the engines, and Canoë jumped into the water with his mattresses as Captain Alinat and I leaped into the Zodiac and sped out to the buoy. By then, the dolphin had been in the pincer for about three minutes, and was apparently exhausted by his struggle to free himself. He was floating on the surface, not moving.

"This was the moment that we had been anticipating for the past three months. I jumped into the water near the buoy and swam the few yards to the dolphin, pulling the buoy behind me. Finally, the animal was within reach. I grabbed his tail, and immediately he dived, giving me such a blow with his tail that I was lifted out of the water. I fell back and began swimming toward the spot where I had guessed that the animal would surface. We reached it almost simultaneously, and this time when I grabbed the tail I was able to keep my hold. The dolphin's breathing was short and shallow. Apparently, the effort of diving had drained what little strength remained in him. With the help of Canoë and his mattresses, and of Alinat in the Zodiac, I removed the pincer and slipped a lasso around the dolphin's tail. Then we hauled him back to the *Espadon*.

"As soon as he was aboard, we began sprinkling his skin with a gentle shower from a hose. This seemed to facilitate the dolphin's respiration which, until then, had seemed difficult. Meanwhile, the dolphin's dark eyes watched us closely, following the movements of the men around him.

"Meanwhile, the *Espadon* was racing back to Monaco. When we sailed past the Oceanographic Museum, we radioed a message. Then, as soon as we had docked, the dolphin was carried off on an inflated mattress and gently placed into a truck dispatched by the Museum."

By 2:15 P.M., the dolphin, which had been captured at 12:30 P.M., was swimming in its tank at the Museum.

It was immediately evident that a captive dolphin's reaction to humans is very different from his reaction to man in the sea. So long as the dolphin is in his natural environment, man is a source of terror. But, as soon as the animal is removed from its environment and is alone, the situation changes radically.

When the dolphin was first put into his tank at the Museum, immediately upon arrival from the *Espadon*, Bébert got into the water with him and held him at the surface so that he would not drown. The dolphin was trembling and suffered a series of convulsions. As he was growing visibly weaker, we tried holding a tank of oxygen next to his blowhole, and, with the first few breaths, the dolphin seemed to improve noticeably.

Thereupon, Bébert began walking the dolphin around the tank so that he might familiarize himself with his new home. We had learned that this was an extremely important part of the acclimatization process, for dolphins usually panic if they strike an obstacle while swimming. Since dolphins cannot swim backward, they apparently feel trapped if their snouts encounter a wall; then, they fall prey to an overriding sense of terror.

By the time Bébert climbed out of the tank, the dolphin seemed gradually to resign himself to his new situation. He was swimming unaided now, in a narrow circle, and his breathing was more or less normal. Nonetheless, Bébert and Canoë remained with him, watching him every moment from the side of the tank, throughout the afternoon and into the evening.

It was already dark when, after hours of careful observation, Bébert and Canoë decided that there was no reason for them to spend the night with the dolphin. All indications were that the animal was now reacting normally and that he would not require their attention during the night. They started to leave, and then, as an afterthought, decided to remain by the tank a few minutes more. At that moment, they saw the dolphin sink slowly to the bottom of the tank. He was obviously unconscious and in serious danger of drowning. Immediately, both men dived into the tank and brought the dolphin to the surface. Then they began walking him around the tank so as to help him breathe. Canoë and Bébert were later joined by Boissy, and the three men took turns in the tank throughout the night.

By late that night, the dolphin was able to swim unaided for a while. Then, suddenly he was helpless again and would have sunk to the bottom if the men had not been there to support him in the water. His eyes were almost completely closed, and his tail seemed to be paralyzed. Once more, the oxygen tank was held over the animal's blowhole.

It was not until ten o'clock the following morning that the dolphin's condition had improved sufficiently for him to be able to swim more or less normally and even to attempt a few dives (although the tank was too shallow for this kind of sport).

Falco had taken the dolphin's temperature twice. During the night, it was 38.6°C; in the morning, 38.2°C. Falco had also observed his breathing. During the night, the dolphin had breathed from two to four times a minute, but, in the morning, the rhythm had slowed.

When Dr. Beck arrived in the morning, in answer to Falco's call, he also inquired about the animal's pulse — a reading which Bébert had learned to take by jumping into the water, holding the dolphin in his arms, and placing his hand over the animal's heart.

"It was sixty during the night," Falco replied. "But for the past few hours, it's been only forty-eight."

"That's normal," Dr. Beck assured Bébert. "When he was first captured, the dolphin was excited. Traumatized, if you will. Since then, he has calmed down, and his pulse has slowed. Actually, he seems in fairly good condition — considering that he's obviously still in a state of shock. The capture itself was hard enough on him, but confinement in this tank must be very difficult for such a sensitive animal. I recommend a regime of vitamins and minerals."

So far as I was concerned, vitamins and minerals were all very well, but I suspected that something more was needed. That feeling was confirmed when Falco told me the following story:

"During the night we spent with the dolphin, Canoë and I left the animal alone for a few moments to see if we could find some coffee upstairs in the Museum. Suddenly, we heard a series of shrill sounds coming from the tank. They weren't loud, but they were piercing, like the cries of a child trying to call someone. We returned to the tank immediately and got into the water with the dolphin and began talking to him. The crying stopped at once. I feel certain that just our being there with him was enough to restore his calm."

"Bébert," I said, "I don't want the dolphin to be left by himself any more. We'll have to try to find a companion for him."

We discovered that the greatest danger in capturing a dolphin was not only from the wounds that the pincer device might inflict, but also from the psychological impact on the dolphin of the capture, that is, the shock to its nervous system. Bébert had noticed in capturing the dolphin, and also in his previous unsuccessful attempts, that the moment that the mammal was touched by anything — lasso, harpoon, or pincer — it seemed to go into a state of paralysis for a few seconds, apparently as the result of that contact. The result was the same, regardless of whether at that moment the dolphin was in the sea, or on an inflatable mattress, or in a tank. The animal simply became immobile, as though stupefied, and began to shake and tremble. It appeared that the dolphin could not accept the fact that he had been stopped, seized; that he had lost his freedom.

It was this shock that may have been the chief problem with our dolphin in the Oceanographic Museum. The animal — upon discovering that "he"

(Right) A dolphin spurns Falco's attempt to offer a friendly gift.

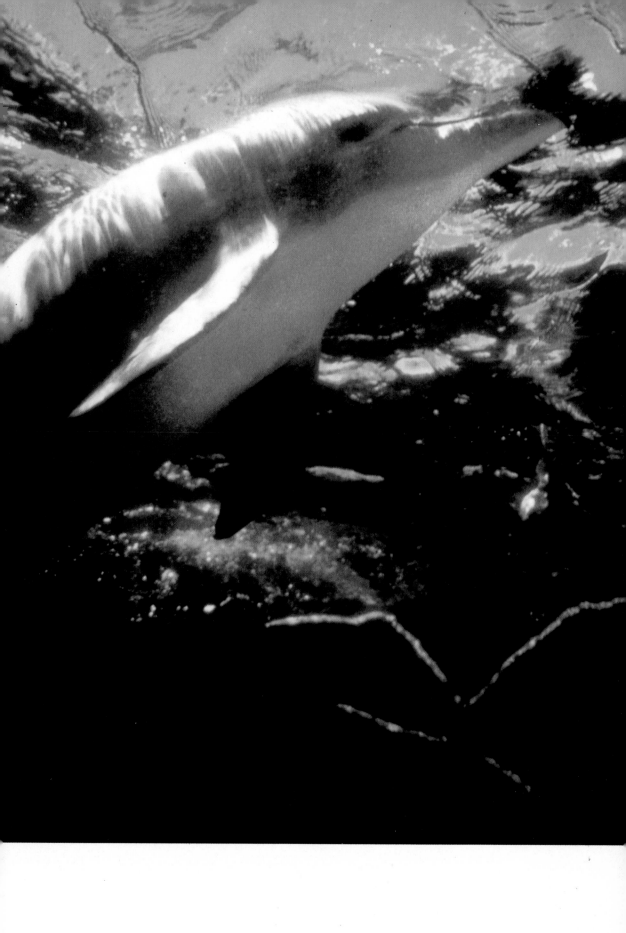

was, in fact, a female, we had christened her Kiki — of course was not exposed to public view. Nonetheless, a large number of people had access to the tank, people whom, for one reason or another, we could not exclude: journalists, radio and television commentators, and so forth.

The *Espadon*'s team was now living in a small room near Kiki's tank, and Falco was with the dolphin night and day, watching for any sign of irregularity or difficulty in her breathing. For days on end, he barely slept. As a safeguard against accidents, he installed an inflated plastic balloon under each of Kiki's flippers so that she might remain on the surface even if she lost consciousness. On one occasion, Kiki fainted. One of the balloons slipped, and the dolphin sank. Almost immediately, Bébert was in the water.

"Kiki had become very attached to me," Bébert said. "She used to look for me. Obviously, she knew that when I was with her I did what I could to help her, to give her as much relief as I could. Sometimes she tried to swim a bit, but if she ran into one of the walls of the tank, she immediately went into a panic. It happened occasionally that she inhaled water through her blowhole; and then she'd come to me so that I could hold her."

November 2, 1957. There has been no improvement in Kiki's condition, and upon Dr. Chalazonitis' recommendation, we gave her morphine by means of a suppository.

We are all aware that the dolphin is in pain. Sometimes she trembles and shivers uncontrollably. She does not seem to mind when we take her temperature, but remains motionless.

November 3. Everything was quiet last night. We took turns staying with Kiki throughout the night. The veterinarian was here this morning, and his prognosis is favorable. Kiki's temperature is now 37.4°C. Her respiration: four per minute.

Today we gave her the first penicillin injection.

Kiki has eaten nothing at all since her arrival at the Museum. We have tried force-feeding her, but she vomits anything that she swallows. In spite of all this, she has never once tried to bite any of us, although she has a set of very impressive teeth.

We gave her injections of theramycin at 3 P.M., 9 P.M., and 4 A.M.

The nights are most difficult for us because we must constantly be ready to dive into the tank to help the dolphin. During the night, we gave her two camphor suppositories.

November 6. The veterinarian visited Kiki today at 6:30 P.M. In the course of his examination, he discovered that her heartbeat had returned to normal. Her temperature: 36.3°C.

Falco threw three live mullets into the tank, making sure that they hit the surface with a splash. Kiki immediately gulped them down. Apparently, the fact that the mullets were alive and moving had much to do with her decision to eat them. This is a consideration that we will have to keep in mind for the future. We also fed her a dozen smaller fish, which she ate with good appetite. Obviously, this is not much food for a dolphin of Kiki's size, but it is a good beginning, and everyone is overjoyed at Kiki's progress.

Although Kiki now seems able to swim normally, we have continued to use the plastic balloons at night. The problem with these balloons is that they prevent the dolphin from submerging her head, with the result that the skin on her skull is dry and cracked. We have begun dampening her head with a cloth at regular intervals during the night.

Another sign of progress: Kiki's tail is no longer paralyzed.

November 7. We have finally found a tank of sufficient size to accommodate Kiki comfortably. I have obtained permission from the management of the Palm Beach Hotel to put Kiki in their swimming pool, which is about 150 feet long and 60 feet wide — a magnificent expanse of water.

Falco left aboard the *Espadon* in search of a companion for Kiki. Offshore near Nice, he succeeded in capturing a male specimen weighing 125 pounds, and the dolphin — we call him Dufduf — has now joined Kiki in her pool at the Palm Beach.

The first meeting between the two dolphins is something to remember. First, the male pushed his snout into Kiki's genital area, then he began swimming gracefully around her. The two elongated bodies, covered with gray, satinlike flesh, twisted, turned, crossed one another. Occasionally, they brushed against one another, then separated, and, a few moments later, touched again. They rubbed their bellies against one another for twenty minutes, then they began swimming side by side in perfect synchronization. But they did not mate.

Falco threw some sardines into the pool for Dufduf, and the newly arrived dolphin gobbled them down without hesitation. We all had the impression that Kiki had persuaded her new friend to eat.

Despite the fact that both animals are eating and exercising, they seem to be growing thinner. On their bodies, next to their flippers, there are hollows indicative of weight loss.

March 1, 1958. This morning, we found Dufduf at the bottom of the pool, dead. An autopsy was performed, and pieces of wood and cloth were found in his stomach. When a dolphin is fatally ill, he tends to swallow any-

(Following page) The dolphin's "smile" gives the animal a sympathetic look.

thing within reach. Falco has observed this phenomenon on several occasions. Thus far, no one has been able to devise a satisfactory explanation for this behavior.

Immediately we gave Kiki a massive dose of Vitascorbol and of cod-liver oil. She swam around the pool constantly, making her shrill, crying sounds. We all had the impression that she was searching for her lost friend. I think that we had better find her a new companion as soon as possible.

One of the most obvious conclusions we reached in the course of these first experiments was that dolphins are group animals. They are utterly incapable of living alone. If they have no companionship, they are extremely unhappy and do not adapt to captivity. Left alone, they sink into a torpor and remain inactive. But as soon as they are given a companion, they spring to life again.

Almost immediately after Dufduf's death, Falco left again on the *Espadon* to search for another dolphin. At first, he had no luck. There were many dolphins in the Bay of Angels, but they were all females with young; and as soon as the *Espadon* approached, they fled in every direction.

On March 16, we removed Kiki from the Palm Beach pool and returned her to the tank at the Oceanographic Museum. The hotel's clientele was beginning to arrive for the season, and few of the Palm Beach's customers would have enjoyed the company of a dolphin during their morning swim.

On the same day that Kiki returned to the Museum, Falco captured a dolphin — a female — which seemed unusually large and heavy. He brought her back to Monaco and we put her into the tank with Kiki. Almost immediately, the dolphin broke free of Falco's grip and crashed into the wall of the tank. Falco succeeded in grasping her in his arms. He raised her from the bottom, spoke to her, tried to calm her. But she wrenched herself free again and once more smashed her skull against the wall with a terrible noise.

At one-thirty in the afternoon, the dolphin was dead. She had killed herself by swimming at full speed from one side of the tank to the other and crashing into the walls. Her agony was horrifying. She lay on her side at the bottom of the tank, her body quivering. Then she began to stiffen, and her lungs filled with water and she was dead.

Falco was alone at the time, and it was not until the dolphin was dead that he could leave the tank to call Dr. Beck. The two men cut open the female and removed a perfectly formed baby dolphin, weighing three and a half pounds, from her womb. Unfortunately, the infant dolphin was already dead.

A captured dolphin is taken aboard a Zodiac by Bernard Delemotte and Jean-Pierre Genest.

Falco was deeply moved by this tragedy which bore such a marked similarity to suicide.

Shortly afterward, a male was captured. We called him Beps. He died as
the pregnant female had died, by smashing his head as hard as he could
against the walls of the tank. On the third attempt, he succeeded in killing
himself.

Despite the horrible deaths of the companions we had tried to provide
for her, Kiki seemed to thrive for a few months. Then she, too, died in her
sixth month of captivity — perhaps out of loneliness. She had no companions
of her own species, and Falco, whom she seemed to recognize and to regard
with affection, was now far away from Monaco on an expedition. It is possible that she might have lived longer if she had not been deprived of the
company of a human whose presence seemed to comfort her.

Chapter Three

THE LAWS OF THE CLAN

Our pursuit of dolphins during 1957 and 1958, as clumsy as it was, taught us many things. Our attempts to acclimatize dolphins to new surroundings ended, eight months later, in failure because at that time we knew so little about marine mammals — certainly far less than what we know now, sixteen years later. Sixteen years in the study of marine mammals is a long time, and yet, at the same time, it is so very little. . . .

The extended mission of Falco and his team in pursuit of dolphins provided us with much valuable information on the reactions of dolphins not only during and after capture but also, and paradoxically, on dolphins living at liberty in the sea. We learned, for instance, that the event of capture is an enormous shock to a dolphin, both physically and psychologically.

The pincer device developed by Bébert, while not perfect, was quite effective. Bébert had discovered that the device must be fired vertically and that the dolphin was immobilized for several seconds by the shock of impact.

(Left) A diver from *Calypso*, Jean-Pierre Genest, swims alongside a dolphin.

It is during these few seconds that the dolphin must be seized, so as to avoid any struggle and consequent injury to the animal.

We learned to care for and cure a dolphin's wounds. And, in so doing, we observed that dolphins never, in any circumstances, manifested the slightest hostility to man. Even when we held an animal in our arms, or applied pressure to a wound — which certainly must have caused considerable pain — there was no aggressive response. The dolphin consistently allowed us to do whatever we wished, without making the slightest attempt to defend itself. Even though it was sometimes necessary to force an animal's mouth open in order to feed it, never once was any of us bitten — a remarkable record, considering that a dolphin is a very highly strung and nervous animal.

One of the most pressing and immediate problems, in fact, was persuading a captive dolphin to eat. Falco eventually succeeded, thanks to his patience and ingenuity. Sometimes it was necessary for him to throw out a fish a hundred times before the dolphin would take it. And even then, the animal often refused to eat it. The noise of the fish striking the water might attract the dolphin, who would then approach the fish, nuzzle it, pick it up in his mouth, play with it, and then lose interest when the fish sank to the bottom. One can imagine, therefore, what a chore it is to get a dolphin to eat the ten or twenty pounds of fish a day that it needs. As we know, the easiest method consists in having an acclimatized dolphin in the same tank. The presence of this animal encourages a newly arrived dolphin to eat.

Sensitive Skin

The most serious problems we encountered with the Common Dolphin were caused by the extreme delicacy of its skin. The slightest bruise during capture, the least scratch, results in a wound which appears almost immediately. The *Espadon*'s team learned to judge the degree of seriousness of such a wound from its whitish color. The Common Dolphin, we concluded, required very clean water. The slightest impurity not only aggravated any wounds but also threatened the general health of the animal. In this respect, certainly the *Delphinus delphis* is much more vulnerable than the Bottlenosed Dolphin.

In the course of our experiments in Monaco, we observed that the behavior of our captive dolphins was determined largely by the extreme sensitivity of their skin. If an animal remained out of the water for several hours and was not kept damp, its skin dried, wrinkled, and looked as though it had been burned.

According to our observations, one of the chief concerns of marine mammals is to avoid contact with any solid object. When we were making our film on whales and were diving with humpback whales, these great mammals always were extemely careful to avoid touching us with their flippers.* At first, we thought, rather naïvely, that the whales were making an attempt to avoid hurting us, but now I believe that they were chiefly concerned with avoiding any shock to their skin.

The scientific research of the past twenty years has seemed to present the dolphin as an animal living in a world of sound, an animal whose acoustical talents are highly developed. This is true, of course. But this aspect of the dolphin's abilities has made us lose sight of the fact that a dolphin in a tank, despite his highly developed and fully functioning "sonar," lives in mortal dread of colliding with the walls of the tank. Life in a tank or pool entails a certain disorder in the sensory perception of the dolphin. And, from that, results a psychological disequilibrium, a distortion of behavior patterns, which, at least in the case of the Common Dolphin, causes the animal to weaken and to die.

It is true that the Bottlenosed Dolphin, which is sturdier than its Mediterranean cousin, adapts more easily to confinement; but, even then — as we shall see in the course of this book — the animal is profoundly modified by the fact of captivity.

It should be understood, of course, that one cannot make anything more than general statements in this respect. We must keep in mind, when comparing the *Delphinus* and the *Tursiops* (or other species), that specimens of the same species adapt to captivity with varying degrees of success. Some animals bear captivity better than others. Some adapt readily, while others never adapt.

Another phenomenon illustrated by our experiences at Monaco was the fact that the dolphin is an eminently social animal. He is a group animal, and he is not happy except in the company of one or more of his own kind. There was a striking difference between the behavior of a dolphin alone in a tank and that of a dolphin with a companion of the same species — regardless of the sex of either dolphin.

At the same time, it must be said that when a dolphin is ill or lonely, man seems to represent a possible companion on whom the dolphin may center its

*See *The Whale*, by Jacques-Yves Cousteau and Philippe Diolé, Doubleday & Co., New York, and Cassell, London, 1972.

(Following page) The waters of the Indian Ocean were like a lake when we encountered this school of dolphins.

attention. It appears reasonable to say that the food provided by man is not the principal cause of the dolphin's attachment to humans, for, in most instances, a captive dolphin initially refuses to eat. It seems that the presence of a human being, who caresses and cares for the dolphin, inspires trust in the animal. There is much evidence for this in Falco's log:

"The dolphin pressed herself against me so that I could hold her up to the surface. . . . As soon as she saw me get into the water, the dolphin swam to me and gently rubbed against me. When I approached the tank, the dolphin began emitting little cries which I'm inclined to interpret as sounds of joy."

I think that Falco's most valuable observations were those which he made at sea, while the *Espadon* was searching for dolphins off Monaco, in the Bay of Angels and at the mouth of the Var. While he was there in the month of February, he saw groups of fifty or sixty mother dolphins accompanied by their young. Sometimes, at night, Falco observed a few larger dolphins in the sea, not together but swimming 150 to 200 yards from each other. When the *Espadon* approached them, these dolphins leaped into the air. (A dolphin can leap as high as ten feet out of the water and for a distance of ten or twelve feet.) Then they watched the ship for a while before diving and remaining out of sight for a few minutes.

Not all of the dolphin's day was spent leaping and playing. There was a schedule of activities. For a part of the day, the dolphins remained beneath the surface, coming up only for air. Then, suddenly, one satin-gray body would leap into the air. As though on signal, it was followed by other bodies. This was the propitious moment for the *Espadon* to move alongside the school in order to attract some of the dolphins toward the prow. It was observed that females with young never played forward of the ship — with one exception. The exception, Falco reported, was a female who obviously was unable to resist the temptation offered by the prow. She cut in front of the *Espadon* and took up her position, while her offspring went off to join another female who had a calf of her own. The mother stayed before the prow for two or three minutes, then she gave up the game and returned to her baby.

There seemed to be a large number of young of all ages in the area. A baby dolphin at birth weighs only from four to six pounds. By the age of one year, they may weigh as much as seventy pounds. Usually, young dolphins do not play before a ship's stem. They are extremely timid. If a ship approaches them, they dive under the hull and remain at a depth of fifty to sixty feet. (When the water is clear, they can be seen from the surface.) Then, as soon as the ship has passed, they surface to port, to starboard, or aft.

On February 10, 1958, Bébert captured a female weighing 175 pounds.

The female had a calf; and the infant, without hesitating or trying to find its mother, went to another female of the same school. After a few seconds, the school, seeing that the captured female was unable to join them, swam away.

It sometimes happened that a young dolphin would take up a position forward of the prow. Almost immediately, however, its mother would arrive and push him away, forcing him to rejoin the school.

"From the platform," Falco says, "I once saw a young dolphin come directly under the platform. His mother was nowhere to be seen. Possibly she was hunting for food. In any case, the calf remained there, directly beneath my feet, for several minutes. The temptation was too strong for me. I took the pincer and fired, and the calf was caught. I could see the buoy behind him. I dived into the water right away so that I could remove the pincer. The skin of a young dolphin is even more delicate than that of a full-grown animal. I took the calf into my arms. He could not have weighed more than twenty-five or thirty pounds.

"As soon as I had a grip on the dolphin, I saw its mother streaking toward me. My first thought was that she was going to attack. Instead, she began swimming around us, making a series of little cries as she swam, sometimes brushing against me. She was a handsome specimen, probably weighing between two hundred and two hundred and fifty pounds. She was much larger than I and incomparably more agile in the water. I confess that I was more than a little frightened at first. Then I understood that the dolphin had no intention of attacking me. She was pleading, calling to her calf. She wanted her child back, but she also wanted to avoid harming me.

"I did not know what to do. I wanted to take the calf back to Monaco with me, for I felt that, at his age, it would not be terribly difficult to tame him. It was truly a dilemma. The mother, circling frantically around us, screaming, was more than I could take. I was very moved. I opened the pincer and freed the calf. He rushed toward his mother, and the pair dived immediately and were lost to sight."

Falco is so familiar with dolphins that he is able to locate a school of them by certain signs. For example, the presence of sea gulls circling overhead is often an indication that a school of dolphins is nearby, hunting for bluefishes, sardines, mackerels, and anchovies. The sea gulls remain in the area to eat what the dolphins leave.

"It is very difficult to see exactly how dolphins hunt," Bébert says, "since they move so quickly. I've noticed that they have difficulty seeing something that is directly in front of them. Regardless of what is generally believed about the bilateral vision of dolphins, I myself have seen them turning their heads from one side to the other. They probably do not do this in captivity,

but only in the excitement of the hunt. It may be that the purpose of this movement is to enable the dolphin to use its teeth on its prey rather than to see it. For dolphins rush into a school of fish and swallow anything they can, any way that they can. But, before a dolphin can swallow a fish, he must turn it in his mouth so that the fish goes down headfirst. Otherwise, the fish's fins and bones will cut the dolphin's throat as it goes down. It is likely that a dolphin loses some of his prey, when he tries to turn it in this way, and that the sea gulls seize the fish."

Dolphins have a larger number of teeth than any other mammal, marine or land: between 88 and 200 of them. These teeth, however, are all conical and all have the same function: to hold the dolphin's prey rather than to cut it or chew it. At the same time, the jaws of a dolphin living at liberty crush its prey into cylindrical form so that it will be able to cross the larynx and penetrate into the esophagus. In captivity, however, dolphins swallow fish whole. One can drop one fish after another down a captive dolphin's mouth without stopping — like dropping letters into a mailbox.

Dolphins eat at more or less the same time every day, and their meals last approximately one hour. When they have had enough, the dolphins assemble into a large group for a few moments, then break up into smaller groups before heading out to sea again. Their normal swimming speed is about ten knots.

The composition of these groups of dolphins seems to vary according to the season. In autumn and winter, the largest group comprises females and their calves. We know that the mothers help one another in watching over their offspring, just as they help one another in giving birth. This has been observed among dolphins in captivity, and it is a subject to which we will return later in this book.

For part of the year, the male dolphins live separately from the females, although they remain in the general vicinity of the main body of the school. The essential social unit of the school seems to comprise three or four adult dolphins. The females of this unit, under the authority and protection of the male, care for their young until the latter reach the age of six to nine months. The school is composed of a number of these fairly large family units. The school increases or decreases in size, according to circumstances, in order to

(Upper left) A gathering of dolphins at the mouth of the Var.

(Lower left) The *Espadon,* cruising off Agay, in search of dolphins.

In the Marineland of Florida, two dolphins display their expertise at catching fish. (Photo, courtesy of Marineland of Florida.)

form groups comprising from fifty to a hundred individuals.

Quite often, when a large group is being pursued, it will break into smaller groups of three or four dolphins. These smaller groups are probably family units.

It is not known whether male dolphins have "harems," like male sea lions and elephant seals.† We have been able to observe sea lions on land, and we know that one male will sometimes be lord and master of as many as eighty females. But dolphins, obviously, have never been observed on land. All that we know of their mating habits is what has been observed in aquariums, where their behavior may be different from what it is in the dolphin's natural environment. A dolphin in captivity does not appear to be attached exclusively to one particular female.

We know that dolphins sometimes divide themselves into groups according to sex, with the males in one group and the females in the other. But, in general, these are not mature dolphins.

†See *Diving Companions* by Jacques-Yves Cousteau and Philippe Diolé, Doubleday & Co., Inc., New York, and Cassell, London, 1974.

It is difficult to determine the precise age of these young animals. They are "adolescents," perhaps eighteen to twenty-four months old. They form extremely close-knit groups, and, at a given moment, the entire group leaves the adults and goes off together, striking out on their own. Perhaps these are less fond of playing and frolicking than the adults. They are very "serious." They know that they are still weak and vulnerable. Nonetheless, when they act together as a group, they are virtually invincible. They are capable of wild pranks.

Yet, these young dolphins are extremely wary of divers. It is impossible to get close to them. When they were younger, they played with their elders around ships; but, beginning at a certain age, they no longer care to take such risks. They remain together, in their group, and all their activities are group activities.

Later on, the males and females, when they are grown, are united into a single group.

The most exact observations on this subject have been made by Japanese scientists, who have captured entire schools of dolphins and are thus able to study the division of sexes according to age within a large group.

A dolphin allows himself to be petted by Falco.

Dominant Animals

We know that there exists a hierarchy among dolphins which is probably as well defined as that found among African elephants. However, it is not known precisely what the function of that hierarchy is, or what its criteria are. There is probably a leader dolphin, and probably there are dominant dolphins.‡

In this respect, we know more about the sperm whale, which is also a toothed whale, than we do about the dolphin. Some schools of sperm whales

‡It is possible that these ranks are temporary. Dr. Kenneth Norris is of the opinion that there is no permanent leader among free dolphins.

are led by old males, although usually old males do not live with a school. Other schools, however, have females as their leaders. We have no way of knowing what, precisely, qualifies a particular individual, male or female, as the leader of a school.

It appears that, in nature, it is the oldest males who mate with the females. This is true both of marine mammals and of land mammals who live in groups, such as lions.

In capturing marine mammals, we have observed that it is not the leader of a school who, in order to save a school, will destroy an obstacle or tear through a net. This function devolves upon a male of the second rank, as though the life of the leader were too precious to the future and fecundity of the group to be risked.

There are not only dominant individuals but also dominant species. We have observed that in large schools of cetaceans, species are mixed. We have seen pilot whales mingling with the Bottlenosed Dolphin, for instance; and during our expedition on the coasts of Mauritania, we saw a *Sousa teuszi* in the same school as two other species, of which one was probably the Bottlenosed Dolphin.

In captivity, according to Caldwell,* certain species seem to dominate others. But are these truly dominant species, or is the fact of their domination merely a function of the limited space available to captive animals?

It is much more difficult to observe marine animals who live in groups than to observe land animals. We know more or less how elephants and antelopes live. But, so far, it has been impossible to get an idea of the social structure of dolphins living in the open sea. We can only surmise that that structure exists, and we think that it must be well defined.

To the extent that it is possible to judge, it seems that the hierarchies which exist in our marinelands are even more stratified than in the sea. This phenomenon is observable in marinelands — such as those in St. Augustine, Miami, San Diego, and Los Angeles — where some of the tanks are large enough to accommodate twenty or twenty-five animals.

In these tanks, each animal occupies a special territory corresponding to his rank in the hierarchy. This situation also obtains in zoos, among land mammals occupying the same enclosure. In a tank, the most desirable place, and that occupied by the dominant animal, is in the center of the tank, or next to the opening through which fresh water is pumped into the tank. Each animal seems to have its own "miniterritory," which it defends with vigor.

*David K. Caldwell and Melba C. Caldwell, *World of the Bottle-Nosed Dolphin.* Philadelphia, 1972.

Observations made at the Marine Studios of Florida† indicate that, except while mating, the dominant adult male dolphin usually swam around his tank alone. Occasionally, he was accompanied, at least briefly, by a female or by a younger male. Although generally peaceful, it sometimes happened that the dominant male showed signs of aggressiveness — often without provocation. At times, however, the provocation was obvious: another animal took some of the male's food, or a younger male approached the female swimming with the dominant male. In such instances, the male bit his presumptuous rival, or struck him with his tail, or even pursued him. Usually, the younger male was scratched or cut and bruised. But when the offender was a female, or a very young or small animal, the leader did not harm it.

At the Marine Studios, the highest ranking dolphin, after the dominant male, was a female named Pudgy, who had already borne several calves. Pudgy by no means lived in the glorious isolation affected by the dominant male. On the contrary, she was a constant point of interest and activity in the tank. She was not afraid to take chances, and she made it a point to investigate any strange object that appeared in the tank. After a series of increasingly daring inspections of the object, she would inform the dominant male that there was no danger, and then he would venture forth.

If the intruder was an unknown diver, he was treated as though he were a dangerous object, even though his equipment was exactly the same as that of a diver known to the dolphins.

Pudgy was the only female whose company the dominant male would tolerate outside of the mating season.

Directly below the dominant male and Pudgy in the hierarchy, there were a certain number of animals, all of approximately the same rank: old females and other, younger females who were carrying their first calves.

A second group comprised three males, of which one was the "boss" of the other two. The third group included the younger animals, who had all been born in the same year and who were not yet weaned. All social activity in the tank centered around the first group, of which Pudgy was the animating spirit. There was another female who, although quite young, belonged to the circle of older females. She served as Pudgy's adjutant, and she supervised the calves in the tank.

This outline of social life in an aquarium tank is sufficient to indicate how complex must be the relations among dolphins living at liberty in the sea. It is also an indication of how little we know in this area. We only suspect the existence of a hierarchy, but we have good reasons to think that dolphins in the sea have "territories" — but territories which belong to the school as a

†See Margaret C. Tavolga, "Behavior of the Bottlenosed Dolphin," in *Whales, Dolphins and Porpoises*, University of California Press, 1966. K. Norris, Editor.

whole. In Hawaii, Kenneth S. Norris observed a school that remained for several weeks, and perhaps even several months, in the same place.

The Florida habitat of the Bottlenosed Dolphin is not very large — a stretch of rather shallow water about fifty to a hundred miles long. Many Bottlenosed Dolphins sojourn at the mouth of the Mississippi. An albino dolphin, who was quite easy to spot and who was finally captured, made it possible to gather some interesting data on the movements of the Bottlenosed Dolphin. There are cases of dolphins who have remained in the same area for as long as three years. It is quite possible that, especially in Florida, the movements of the dolphins are confined to a relatively small area, and that the dolphins cover the same stretch every day. Falco had remarked that, near Nice, the dolphins arrived from the southeast in the morning and departed in the evening toward the southwest. They were probably following the movement of the fishes who themselves follow the movement of the sun.

This is also what occurred during our research in the Gulf of Málaga. During the morning, we were rather certain of being able to find dolphins on the left side of the Gulf, and in the evening, on the right side.

It has been claimed that the *Tursiops* of Florida prefers shallow water to deep water. But we must remember that what is true in one part of the world may not be true in another. Professor Busnel, for example, has encountered the Bottlenosed Dolphin at depths of 10,000, 12,000, and 15,000 feet. According to Busnel, the Bottlenosed is not specially a shallow-water mammal. It is found in Florida's coastal waters because it follows the schools of fish — especially mullets — which come to feed there.

The Bottlenosed Dolphin as well as the Delphinus delphis is also found near the coast; but it is found, too, and more frequently, in water from 2,000 to 2,500 feet deep, at the edge of the continental shelf.

Various observers have indicated that dolphins move in aligned ranks, like an army on the march. In such cases, the animals all rise to the surface, at the same time, in order to breathe. Professor Busnel has seen schools of dolphins in this formation.‡ It may be that these groups are formed of animals of the same age and sex. It is also possible that that particular formation is employed only when the dolphins are moving over a considerable distance.

It will undoubtedly require much time for us to become acquainted with the social life of dolphins in the sea. Only detailed and repeated observation by divers will finally reveal what occurs in groups of marine mammals subject to the authority of one or several leaders.

---

‡David K. Caldwell has observed the same phenomenon.

Chapter Four

THE STORY OF DOLLY

I think that the most interesting phase of our observation of dolphins was that which dealt with dolphins who had entered into relationships of various kinds with humans, but without giving up their liberty in so doing.

There are many instances of this phenomenon in the United States, Australia, New Zealand, and Great Britain.

The attraction of dolphins to human beings is attested to throughout human history. There are documents, for example, which cite numerous instances of this attraction in the period of Antiquity — instances which, for many years, were regarded as myths.

One of the most celebrated of these legends may be that of Arion, a Greek poet born on the island of Lesbos. Arion was saved by a dolphin after he had been thrown overboard by the crew of a ship on which he was traveling.

No less an authority than Plutarch has recorded the story of Korianos, a native of Asia Minor, who pleaded with a group of fishermen to spare the life of a dolphin caught in their nets. Shortly thereafter, Korianos himself was

(Left) Dolly playing near the Asburys' dock in Florida.

shipwrecked, and his life was saved, Plutarch assures us, by a dolphin.

Today, we know enough about dolphins to be able to see a core of truth in these anecdotes of Antiquity. We know that a certain number of dolphins, living at freedom in the sea, seek out the company of humans, become attached to them, and persist in returning to the places where they have encountered swimmers — and especially where they have encountered children. And we know that dolphins are fun-loving and dependable creatures who, upon occasion, act as lifesavers. There are numerous, well-documented cases which demonstrate that the ancients, in believing that dolphins were friendly and benevolent toward humans, were not quite so naïve as we "superior" men of the twentieth century might like to believe.

In the Keys

One of the most touching and best documented of such adventures is that which occurred to an American family in our own time. The Asbury family includes the father — who happens to be President Nixon's helicopter pilot — his wife, Jean, and their two daughters: Kelly, who is eight, and Tina, ten. There is also a dog named Puggy.

The Asburys live in Florida, on one of the numerous canals of the Keys. The house is several miles from the ocean, although it is accessible by means of the canals.

One morning in May, 1971, the Asbury family was startled to see a Bottlenosed Dolphin appear not far from the pontoon on their property. The dolphin reared his head above the surface, showing all his teeth in a "grin" and making characteristic crying sounds. The Asburys watched as the dolphin came closer. Then Jean Asbury ran back to the house and returned a few moments later with a fish, which the dolphin eagerly accepted. The dolphin ate what he was offered, while the two little girls watched in utter enchantment.

Only Puggy the dog seemed to disapprove.

From that moment, the Asbury family regarded the dolphin as one of them. They fed her regularly, named her Dolly, and made her the official family pet. Even Puggy eventually was won over.

Dolly, a handsome female, four or five years of age, weighing about 425 pounds and measuring seven feet in length, became the swimming companion of the Asbury children. Kelly and Tina held on to Dolly's dorsal fin and

(Left) When Jean Asbury calls, Dolly comes.

Jean Asbury offers Dolly a fish from her mouth.

the dolphin towed them through the water.

Dolly seemed truly to enjoy such activities, and it soon became evident that she had adopted the Asbury family as well as been adopted by them. She showed only perfunctory interest in the other humans living along the canal, and most of her time was spent at the Asbury dock.

The star in Dolly's firmament of humans was undoubtedly Jean Asbury, who fulfilled the role of "mother" to Dolly as well as to Kelly and Tina.

The affective relationship implicit in this situation is very difficult to interpret. We know that affection among humans is sensed by animals. Jean Asbury's maternal love, the affection she radiated, was certainly not lost on Dolly. Jean's gentleness, patience, and obvious interest no doubt influenced Dolly considerably. Thus, the relationship established between Jean and Dolly seems to have been essentially emotional and maternal. At the same time, we must take into account that it was Jean who fed Dolly, who usually played with her, and who taught Dolly the tricks that the dolphin had learned to perform. Mr. Asbury was often absent for several days at a time, and the two daughters were usually at school during the day.

Communication

Jean and Dolly often had lengthy "conversations." As Jean spoke softly, Dolly held her head out of the water and listened with an attitude expressive of eager attention and of intense desire to communicate.

Dolly was able to understand the sense of certain words — "yes" and "no" for example. She seemed to understand when Jean scolded her for being naughty or expressed pleasure over something that Dolly had done. She was able to distinguish certain objects and to carry them to Jean upon command. All of which seems wonderful indeed until we remember that many household pets, such as dogs, do these things.

The Asburys constructed a shelter for Dolly next to their pontoon, and the dolphin used this shelter when she wanted to rest. Using the shelter was one of her best tricks, for she had learned to open and close the door unaided.

She knew how to catch rings, to fetch a ball and put it into a basket, and to leap high out of the water upon command. One of Dolly's games was to tow a small plastic boat with Puggy, the dog, as her somewhat hesitant passenger.

One of the tricks Jean Asbury taught Dolly was to distinguish various coins. Jean would throw a handful of change into the water, and Dolly would collect and return to Jean only the dimes — a difficult task, considering the muddy bottom of the canal, the size of a dime and the relative size of Dolly's snout. Yet, Dolly never made a mistake and brought back the wrong coin, and she never failed to bring back every dime that Jean had thrown out. The dolphin's "sonar" obviously was powerful enough to penetrate the layer of mud on the bottom, into which the dimes sank.

Dolly did not spend every moment of her day with the Asburys. She was beginning to be known in the neighborhood, and sometimes she swam in some of the other canals. Occasionally, she visited other people, but she showed an unmistakable preference for the Asburys and their property. She knew the canals very well, and she never failed to return promptly to her "home" with the Asbury family.

A Draftee

The Asburys, by a series of inquiries, learned something of Dolly's background. It seems that the dolphin had belonged to the U. S. Navy and had been assigned to a dolphin-training base at Key West. The base was known officially as a "study center," since the Navy is reluctant to have it known that these animals are being trained for military service.

One of Dolly's former trainers told Jean that when the "study center" had been transferred from Florida to California, he had decided at the last minute not to have Dolly shipped to the new facility. Dolly, it seems, was regarded as undisciplined and undependable — in short, a bad recruit. When she was ordered to take an object to a particular location, she did so; but then she insisted on carrying the object back to the man who had given it to her originally. It was obvious that such behavior during military operations might present problems. She was therefore given an "undesirable discharge" and turned loose near the Florida coast. But she had become accustomed to humans and apparently was unwilling to give up their company. She therefore swam toward shore and entered the network of canals in the Keys, where she had been lucky enough to encounter the Asburys — a family which satisfied her need for contact with man.

Voluntary Prisoners

There is no doubt that a dolphin who lives among humans for any length of time undergoes a deep psychological modification. There are many examples of this in addition to Dolly. On several occasions, captive dolphins have regained their liberty, either accidentally or because they were intentionally released by their keepers, and yet continued to seek out human contacts.

Perhaps the most celebrated instance of such a dolphin is that of Tuffy, a male Bottlenosed Dolphin who was used as a bottom-to-surface messenger during an American underwater-survival project. Tuffy was confined in a floating pool off the California coast when a passing fisherman spotted him and opened the gate of the cage, setting Tuffy free. The dolphin was probably extremely puzzled. The opening of the gate had always been preceded or accompanied by a ceremony of sorts: whistles, the giving of orders, the assignment of a mission. But he was not so puzzled as to refuse to take advantage of the opportunity thus presented.

An immediate and extensive search, by sea and air, was launched for the missing Tuffy, who was, after all, extremely valuable and almost irreplaceable. The dolphin was found very quickly, and he returned, with undisguised pleasure, to his trainer.*

A similar case was reported at the Lerner Laboratory at Bimini, in the

---

*See David K. Caldwell and Melba C. Caldwell, *World of the Bottle-Nosed Dolphin.* Philadelphia, 1972.

Captain Cousteau and Jean watch Dolly swim.

Bahamas. The gate of a dolphin's tank was accidentally left open, but, in this instance, the dolphin simply refused to leave. And at the Marineland of Florida, a dolphin was intentionally set free, just as Dolly had been. The dolphin remained in the vicinity of the Marineland for quite some time; finally, he must have concluded that there was no access possible from the sea back into the tanks, for he eventually went away. A few months later, a team from the Marineland captured a "wild" dolphin with suspicious ease. The dolphin, of course, was the animal who had been turned out of the Marineland's tanks and who had finally succeeded in getting himself captured once more.

At the St. Petersburg Beach Aquatarium, on Florida's Gulf coast, a dolphin who suffered from a physical deformity was released in the Gulf. This dolphin was recaptured — not once, but several times. He had discovered the secret of getting captured: whenever he saw a fisherman's net, he threw himself into it. Finally, the Aquatarium officials gave in, and the dolphin was admitted back into their tanks.

Saved, by Force

Calypso's diving team, headed by my son Philippe, went to Florida to make Dolly's acquaintance. They were warmly welcomed by the Asbury

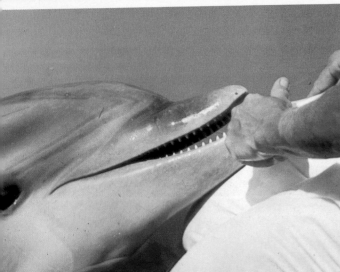

Dolly's various expressions during her life with the Asbury family; Dolly playing with a ball and a rubber ring; Dolly resting her head on Jean Asbury's lap.

family, and by Dolly herself. After two or three days, the dolphin had learned to recognize the divers, and she adopted them. She was so interested in them that there were times when she made a pest of herself. It was impossible to go into the water without being obliged to play with Dolly. The dolphin insisted that Philippe and his men dive with her, or that they allow themselves to be towed while holding her dorsal fin. Playing with Dolly became something of a chore.

Dolly was perfectly trustworthy, but, even so, one had to be careful when playing with her. She was very strong, and sometimes she did not know the precise rules of the game being played. The divers used their Aqua-Lungs® when they went down with her; and since Dolly had been taught to pick up objects on the bottom and carry them to the surface, she insisted on latching on to a diver by his belt and taking him back to the surface. There was no point in struggling, since it was impossible to break away from her. The unhappy diver simply had to resign himself to returning to the surface. Perhaps Dolly thought that the divers at the bottom were drowning, or it may be that it was no more than a new game for her.

On the surface, she adopted the opposite tactic. She forced her snout and head between the arm and the body of the divers and then dragged them to the bottom.

Dolly was so friendly that she eventually suffered for it. She lifted her head above the surface so frequently, in order to call the Asburys or to talk to them or to play or simply to see what they were doing, that she became sunburned, especially on the top of her head. It became necessary to apply sunburn lotion to relieve the pain.

Fear of the Ocean

We spent six weeks trying to find out exactly what the relationship was between Dolly and her adopted family. The most striking aspect of that relationship was that Dolly absolutely refused to return to freedom in the sea. We attempted a number of times to release her in the ocean, away from the Keys, but without success. Our purpose was to film Dolly in the open sea, since the water in the canals is often cloudy. We tried luring her out of the Keys by gifts of fish, a task in which the two Asbury children helped by talking to Dolly along the way. In this endeavor, we used a Zodiac around which Dolly was fond of playing. At first, we got no more than a mile or two from our point of departure before Dolly turned around and went back to the Asbury dock. It is unlikely that Dolly's decision to remain in the canals was based upon any inability to find her way into the open sea, for, I had already observed, dolphins seem to have an extraordinarily accurate sense of direction. As our efforts continued, we managed gradually to entice Dolly farther and farther away from the Asbury property, but it was never possible to get her to remain in the sea. We could not even persuade her to venture onto the level roof which borders the main reef — let alone get her away from the reef into deep water.

If Dolly was rejected by the U. S. Navy as being unfit for military service, it could not have been because she lacked anything as a swimmer. On the contrary, she was a rare spectacle of suppleness and grace in the water.

We have seen many "shows" at aquariums and marinelands, and we have filmed many spectacular "acts" outside of such places; yet, we had never before had the opportunity to live for several weeks with an animal like Dolly who, as time went on, became increasingly co-operative.

It is very rare — indeed, it may never have happened before — that humans are able to spend time in the water with a dolphin who is completely free to come and go as she wishes and to do precisely as she wishes. We felt that we had entered into a new stage of the relationship between man and animal, for most studies and observations of dolphins had, until then, been carried out in aquariums, with the dolphins held captive in tanks.

During our life in common with Dolly, we had only one inconvenience. The water in the canals, as I have mentioned, was very cloudy, and it was almost impossible to do any filming. If the water had been clear, we would have been able to get full-faced shots of Dolly swimming toward us — something that is virtually impossible in the sea. It is possible only with a tame dolphin. And it is rare one encounters an animal which is both tame and free.

Obviously, then, the sequences that we were able to film, for the most part, show Dolly performing the tricks that Jean Asbury had taught her — the same kind of performance that we could have filmed in an aquarium. Yet, the surroundings, the ambiance, were totally different. Dolly was not living in a tank. She was swimming freely in the Florida Keys. She could have run away if she had wanted to. But she did not. She always returned to the Asburys and to us. Every morning, she was there, waiting for us, asking for nothing more than to be allowed to swim with everyone else, or to be able to play and to invent new games — such as taking over the Zodiac, ramming it, and turning it over.

At first, we were afraid that Dolly might be struck by a passing boat, or might be injured by a propeller. But the canal on which the Asbury property is located leads nowhere. It is a dead end, and there is very little boat traffic. All the neighbors knew and loved Dolly. And Dolly herself had learned that certain boats were dangerous because of their speed, and she always avoided them.

It was impossible to discover whether Dolly caught fish for herself, or whether she lived exclusively on the food provided by the Asburys. It seems likely that her own hunting was very limited, for the canals do not abound in fish.

Every day, we tried to take Dolly for a promenade in the canals. We would call Dolly, take the Zodiac (which Dolly liked because of its round form and its feel), and start off at a very slow speed. It was a great pleasure to watch her swimming level with the Zodiac and then, with a mischievous look in her eye, suddenly shoot ahead of it.

Unfortunately, the Asbury house is quite distant from the sea. When we began to get rather far from the canal on which they lived, Dolly seemed to be seized with fear. She slowed down and eventually turned and swam back to her "home" without us.

The Oar

It seemed especially puzzling that Dolly was not tempted to leave the Keys and return to the sea in order to find a mate. For it was clear that she was not naturally inclined to celibacy. One day, an oar fell overboard, and Dolly immediately mounted the oar, tried to straddle it, and rubbed herself against it. Obviously, nothing came of all her activity. The oar was constantly slipping away from her and floating away. Then Dolly swam about nervously, making little cries.

This pitiful scene was repeated several times.

Dolly was obviously in the throes of sexual desire, and there was nothing she could do about it. Whenever she could, she brushed against the divers, pushed them with her nose, or attempted to lay her body against theirs. She seemed to relish contact with the divers' vinyl suits, which she no doubt found soft and pleasant. The shape of the divers, however, seemed to come as a surprise to her, and she often seemed puzzled.

Sexual desire was not the only reason that Dolly rubbed herself against

(Right) Jean and Dolly engage in an animated exchange as Philippe Cousteau looks on.

(Below) Dolly eating from Captain Cousteau's hand.

the divers' suits. She was actually obeying a law of her species and attempting to satisfy a deep need. For dolphins are intensely social animals, and their social activities are based upon physical contacts. Whether swimming at liberty in the sea or in marinelands and aquariums, dolphins brush and rub against each other. They touch each other with their snouts and flippers. All these gestures are undoubtedly of great importance as functions of the structure of the group and also of the place of each individual animal in the dolphin hierarchy.

Dolly, isolated from other dolphins as she was in the canals, was deprived of these social contacts. To some extent, she had adapted herself to human contacts, and she even sought them out. She loved to be petted by the Asburys and by our divers because she was unable to participate in the physical contact with other dolphins which plays such an important role in their social life.

Dolphins, unlike land mammals, have no sense of smell, and therefore they have no "scent." Instead of smelling, they touch, particularly around the genital area. This may be a means of recognizing one another and of publishing one's rank in the hierarchy. The slightest turbulence in the water makes it possible for a dolphin to sense the proximity of other dolphins or of a diver.

The skin of a dolphin is so soft and pleasant to touch that it is comparable to that of the most seductive woman. "But in the case of a dolphin," Michel Deloire pointed out, "one never knows what the reactions of a four-hundred-pound female will be at the moment of ecstacy."

It was obvious, on the other hand, that Dolly's attachment to Jean Asbury was free of sexual overtures. The dolphin was attracted by Jean's maternal warmth, and she responded to the woman as any child would have responded; while Jean, on her part, treated Dolly with boundless patience and affection — despite the fact that taking care of Dolly involved more work than if Jean had had another child on her hands. Her life necessarily had come more and more to center around Dolly's needs. The dolphin remained in the neighborhood constantly, and, when she was lonely, she called. Jean then had to drop whatever she was doing to go out to talk to Dolly. Her conversation consisted of words without any particular meaning or logic and were intended to calm and pacify the animal: "Good girl. Pretty girl . . ." The conversations ended with Dolly "kissing" Jean, that is, giving her a lick with her tongue which scratched Jean's cheek.

Like a spoiled child, Dolly insisted on constant attention. The situation reached such a point that Jean could no longer be away from the house. She could not go to a movie, or visit friends. And, obviously, a vacation was out of the question. The Asburys attempted to find someone who could keep Dolly company while they were away — a dolphin-sitter, as it were. But the experiment was a fiasco. Dolly had a tantrum and refused to eat.

A relationship like that between Dolly and the Asburys is a marvelous and exciting adventure, but it entails a responsibility to the animal which eventually monopolizes the lives of the humans involved.

We recently received a letter from Mrs. Asbury telling us that after the departure of *Calypso*'s team, "Dolly was heartbroken." Undoubtedly, she missed the "walks" with the divers in the Zodiac and the various games that she played with them. Dolly became so fond of the Zodiac, in fact, that once, when the Asburys had let an entire day go by without using it, Dolly tried to start it up herself.

Dolly had not yet found a mate, although she had had the opportunity to do so. In July 1972, during the Democratic National Convention, Dolly was taken to Miami to campaign for the protection of marine mammals. In her letter, Mrs. Asbury says: "When time came to go home, we couldn't catch her with a net, so we swam her sixty-five miles through rough and open water to Key Largo. Along the way we passed some wild dolphins. Dolly stopped to play for a while, but when time came to continue our journey she came along willingly. She did stop to play with some sea turtles, but she wanted to stay with the Zodiac because she knew we were going home. We stopped at the Anglers Club on Key Largo for the night. Dolly was tired from her long swim, so we were invited to stay for a week so she could rest. She was so weak her skin had turned white. On July 17 we decided to take Dolly home by truck. Finally, after many long hours, we caught her. She was very happy to be back home.

"Dolly loved to make nightly visits to the neighbors, but one afternoon she came home with a steel rod wrapped around her. The only thing we could figure was that she had brought it to show to me from one of the local construction sites. We untangled her and treated her cuts with gentian violet. I was heartbroken and didn't know what to do. Dolly would lie in my lap and all she would do was cry.

"With this happening, plus various other things, in March I decided to board Dolly over at the Sugar Loaf Lodge with another dolphin, Sugar. Dolly doesn't like it over there and she has lost a lot of weight from moping, but I feel it is the best thing for her. If things get better, I will bring her back home. I go over every day to feed her and Sugar, and Dolly is teaching Sugar some new tricks. Tina and Kelly go over to swim with them when they can. I still talk with Dolly at night. Our relationship is just as close as before, if not closer. Dolly is improving now. We took the Zodiac over to help her adjust.

(Above) Captain Cousteau and Dolly take a swim together.

(Left) Jean Asbury's daughter, Kelly, and Dolly are great friends.

She is beginning to gain back some weight, but I know she hates captivity."

A Certain Smile

Such is the story of Dolly. We have been witnesses to it. We spent several weeks with the dolphin, and we have tried to judge her behavior as objectively as possible. What intrigued us initially, when we first heard about Dolly, was the question of whether it is possible for an emotional relationship to exist between man and marine mammals. In other words, can there be a real exchange of affection between them?

The experts are generally negative in this respect, including our friends Busnel and Albin Dziedzic,† who have both participated in expeditions aboard *Calypso*. In their opinion, only man is capable of feeling an emotional attachment. A dolphin is not attracted to any particular individual human but seeks out human contact with any available human being.

This is also the opinion of most American scientists, as well as of the

†Albin Dziedzic, like Professor Busnel, is attached to the Laboratory of Acoustical Physiology of INRA.

dolphin trainers at the various marinelands.

Is it true that the dolphin has no "heart"? That he is less affectionate, less loyal than, say, a dog?

"Yes," says Professor Busnel, who feels that we have been led astray by "a certain smile." The smile to which Busnel refers is that engaging rictus which is the permanent expression on the face of the Bottlenosed Dolphin — an expression which it is tempting to interpret as a smile or a laugh.

Other marine mammals, such as the killer whale and the pilot whale, and the fresh-water or river dolphin, do not awaken our sympathy to the same degree as the Bottlenosed Dolphin. And yet, they are at least as clever as the latter when we see them in our marinelands. Trainers say that these species learn even more quickly than the Bottlenosed Dolphin.

The Bottlenosed Dolphin, like most stars today, was launched by television. The "Flipper" series has popularized the photogenic smile of the dolphin; and, by now, there is no scientific argument which could possibly persuade the general public that Flipper's expression is not, in fact, a smile.

Konrad Lorenz has studied at length the animal signs and gestures which man tends to interpret as favorable or unfavorable and to which he attributes an unwarranted, or a totally false, meaning. The dolphin's "smile" may indeed be as misleading as many of the signs cited by Lorenz. But the total absence of aggressivity in the dolphin, the fact that the dolphin will not bite a human, even when the animal is subjected to the most horrifying tortures — such as having metal hooks driven into its skull with a hammer — these are documented facts which cannot be denied. In one experiment conducted in the United States, twenty-nine dolphins were killed, and not one of them ever attempted to bite, or harm in any way, the men who were tormenting them. It would be difficult to think of any animal, other than the dolphin, who exhibits such patience, forbearance and magnanimity toward human aggression. Even a faithful dog sometimes turns on his master; and there is no household pet, however thoroughly domesticated, that will not, when sufficiently provoked, bite or scratch. We sometimes speak of the animal kingdom as a world of "tooth and claw." And so it is, indeed, a kingdom where animals turn their natural weapons against one another and, if need be, against human beings. The dolphin, for a reason which we have yet to fathom, seems to be the exception — at least as far as his dealings with humans are concerned.

Unless one has actually seen it, it is difficult to imagine the trust shown by the dolphin who, of his own accord, places his head into the hands of the man who is going to put blinkers over the animal's eyes. And it is difficult to deny that dolphins show a special attachment to children — as we shall see in the course of this book — and sometimes to a particular child.

Dolly and her favorite oar.

We are perfectly willing to admit that affection cannot be sketched out by means of a diagram. It cannot be measured on a scale, or recorded on a tape. Dolly never said or wrote: "Dolly loves Jean." But Dolly, when she was suffering, did go to Jean, and to no one else, and lay her head on her adoptive mother's lap. Can this be conditioned behavior? Or a sentimental illusion? Scientists, in their quest for certitude and proof, tend to reject the marvelous, and, in so doing, they sometimes risk not seeing the forest for the trees.

Chapter Five

LIFE WITH MAN

The case of Dolly, described in the preceding chapter, is hardly unique. There have been several dolphins who have acquired more or less permanent fame by associating with humans. One of the most celebrated of them was Pelorus Jack, who became known in 1888. Pelorus Jack lived in Cook Strait, which separates the two principal islands of New Zealand, between French Pass and Pelorus Sound. It is from the latter that the dolphin took his name.

Pelorus Jack was a *Grampus griseus* (Gray Grampus, or Risso's Dolphin). It was never discovered for certain whether Jack was, in fact, a male or female. But, for almost a quarter of a century, he (or she) was a world-wide celebrity. He was mentioned by many writers, including Kipling and Mark Twain. One of the most famous journalists of the time, Frank T. Bullen, made a special trip to New Zealand to write an article about Pelorus Jack.

Unlike Dolly and some other dolphins, Jack was never in direct contact with human beings. He was fascinated by ships, and there was hardly a vessel which entered Cook Strait that Jack did not accompany on part of its journey.

(Left) The tail fins of dolphins are very powerful. Dolphins can literally stand on their tails.

The Opononi dolphin of New Zealand allowed children to ride on his back. (Photo, courtesy of The Auckland *Star*.)

He rubbed against the ships' hulls, swam before their prows, and dived and leaped around them.

Jack's usual station was at the entrance to the Strait. He was there so often that many people journeyed to the Strait solely to see him. Sometimes two steamers arrived simultaneously, then, Jack would invariably choose to accompany the faster of the two. He tended to ignore mere yachts and other lesser craft.

The Opononi dolphin playing with bathers. (Photo, courtesy of The Auckland *Star*.)

The *Penguin*, a steamer which frequently passed through the Strait, on one occasion inadvertently rammed Pelorus Jack, and the dolphin was rather seriously injured. From then on, whenever the *Penguin* entered the Strait, Jack was careful to keep his distance from that particular vessel.

Pelorus Jack disappeared in 1912. Some have attributed his disappearance to death from old age, and this explanation is quite plausible. Others have claimed that he was killed by a Norwegian whaler at the entrance to Pelorus Sound.

Opo and the Children

It was also in New Zealand, in Hokianga Bay, in the North Auckland District, that another man-loving dolphin appeared in 1955. This dolphin first became conspicuous for its habit of following pleasure boats, and it was widely believed at first that the animal was, in fact, a shark. It was actually a female dolphin, quite young — probably an orphan whose mother had been killed by one of the Mighty White Hunters who seem to be always with us. In any case, the dolphin was not yet one year old. She loved to have her back scratched with an oar or a broom, but even then, she initially kept her distance from humans.

When summer came, the dolphin began to mingle with the bathers at Opononi beach. Which of the bathers first got up the courage to pet the dolphin? It is not known. It may well have been a child, for the dolphin, whom the bathers called Opo, showed a marked preference for young people.

Opo spent most of her time at Opononi beach, or, if she was not there, she quickly arrived at the first sound of a boat's engine. Soon, thousands of people were going to Opononi to see the dolphin and, if possible, to pet her. The fortune of the innkeepers and businessmen of the modest village was assured. Ice cream and beer were sold at an unprecedented rate. The grateful population formed a committee for the protection of dolphins and installed large signs at the entrance to the village: "Welcome to Opononi. But do not try to kill our happy dolphin."

It was Opo's delight to swim among groups of children. She seemed to invite petting, for she sought out those children who were affectionate and avoided those who played too roughly. Her favorite was an excellent swimmer, Jill Baker, a girl of thirteen. "Whenever Opo saw me go into the water," Jill said, "she left the other swimmers to come to me."

Opo often dived between Jill's legs, then picked her up and took her for a ride on her back. At first Opo had seemed to dislike being touched, or having her dorsal fin grasped by the children. But, as soon as she realized that the children had no intention of hurting her, she allowed them to do whatever they wished.

It is difficult to believe that Jill Baker merely imagined that Opo preferred her to the other children, or that the witnesses to Opo's preferences — tourists, journalists, and fishermen — were all victims of an illusion in believing that Jill was Opo's favorite. The only conclusion possible is that Opo recognized Jill and was able to distinguish her from the other bathers.

Some of the fishermen in the neighborhood sometimes offered Opo fish from their catch — mullets, especially — but she would never accept their offers. She preferred to catch fish on her own.

A Local Celebrity

One day, a swimmer gave Opo a multicolored beachball. The dolphin invented a game with it, which consisted in throwing the ball high into the air and then swimming out, as fast as she could, to catch the ball when it came down.

She also enjoyed searching for empty beer bottles on the bottom. She picked up the bottles in her mouth and then threw them as far as she could. When she had performed a particularly spectacular trick and there was applause and shouts of admiration from the beach, Opo would leap into the air in a sort of triumphal jump. It seems that she heard the people's shouts, understood their meaning, and was pleased. She became a star.

At times, there were so many visitors to Opononi beach that Opo was overwhelmed. Some tourists were so avid to touch the dolphin that they ran into the sea fully clothed. A few people handled Opo inconsiderately, pulling her tail roughly, or trying to turn her over on her back, or attempting to block her. She showed her displeasure at such treatment by swimming out of reach, though without undue haste. The only sign of irritation was the constant beating of her tail. Never did she give any stronger indication of resentment than that.

Opo was in her glory when the children of the Opononi school held their school picnic on the beach. The children were playing in the water when one of them suggested forming a circle and holding hands. Opo, as though she knew what was expected of her, came right into the center of the circle and performed her tricks with her beach ball, to the delight of her audience.

In March 1956, a law was passed forbidding anyone to capture, hunt, or otherwise molest dolphins in Hokianga Bay. A few days later, it was noticed that Opo was conspicuously absent from her favorite haunt off Opononi beach. Four boats were sent out to search for the dolphin, but they found no trace of her.

A clam digger found her, dead, her body squeezed between two rocks. It seems most unlikely that Opo would have deliberately swum into that position. The probable explanation is that the dolphin was the victim of an explosion and was thrown into the rocks, for, in that area, there are men who fish with explosives.

Opo's body was carried back to the beach and buried there. The people of the village covered her grave with flowers.

The Dolphin of La Corogna

It was our good fortune to take part in an adventure similar to that of Opo. We were in Paris, about a year and a half ago, when we received a letter from Spain reporting that there was a dolphin, near La Corogna, which was accompanying fishing boats and swimming among the bathers at the local beach. In other words, it was obviously a particularly sociable dolphin.

Jacques Renoir, who was shooting our film on dolphins, went to La Corogna, where he was warmly welcomed. He was immediately driven to Lorbe Cove, about twelve miles from the town, which seemed to be the spot most favored by Nino, as the dolphin had been named.

Renoir, wearing his diving suit, dived into the water. A few minutes later, he saw a handsome dolphin coming toward him in the water. He came near, turning, twisting, and brushing against him. Then, without the least sign of fear, Nino slowly rubbed the whole length of his body slowly against Renoir's. Jacques began stroking Nino gently, and suddenly the dolphin rolled over on his back, showing his light-colored underside — a position characteristic of females in heat. Renoir caressed the dolphin in a more precise way and extended his arm. Nino, of his own accord, began rubbing himself against the arm. Jacques's Spanish hosts, who were watching him from the surface, were obviously shocked but were too polite to say anything.

When Jacques returned to the surface to climb back into the boat, Nino tried to stop him. He no doubt wished to continue sampling the pleasures of which he had been deprived.

It remained for Jacques to explain to the Spaniards that their Nino was really Nina — an eight-foot female *Tursiops truncatus*, weighing about four hundred pounds. She was an adult specimen and was probably ten or twelve years old.

The next day, Jacques dived with a local diver who was employed as a dock builder. This diver knew Nina well because, whenever he was in the water, the dolphin came to circle around him.

Nina's Story

José Freire Vásquez, who knew the story of Nina from its very beginning, told me about his meeting with her:

"The first man to make the acquaintance of our dolphin was a diver named Luis Salleres, who worked in the Lorbe clam beds. Salleres was working in the beds one day when he looked up and, to his surprise, saw a dolphin nearby, watching him. The following day, the dolphin was there again, and this time the animal came closer. Salleres tried to pet her; and not only did the dolphin not flee, but she actually seemed to enjoy it.

"Salleres told some friends of his in La Corogna about the dolphin, but no one believed him. He came to see me because he knew I was interested in marine biology and in animal behavior. I must say that, at that time, I wasn't really convinced of what he told me. Nonetheless, the following day I went to Lorbe with Salleres, and we went out in a small boat. Salleres had his diving suit with him, and he got into the water. Very shortly, as I watched, I saw a dolphin approaching our boat and then diving toward the spot where Salleres had gone down. A few seconds later, Salleres and the dolphin both surfaced and began swimming around side by side.

"I was astonished. And I couldn't resist the temptation to join them in the water. The dolphin was perfectly willing to play with me, but it was obvious that she was more interested in her friend the diver.

"Then something notable happened. After playing with the dolphin for a while, Salleres returned to the boat to get his underwater camera. I was still in the water with the dolphin. The water was quite cold, and I'm not really a good swimmer. Suddenly, my legs felt as though they were paralyzed. I was terror stricken. I began waving my arm to attract Salleres' attention. At that instant, the dolphin, as though she understood what was happening, came very close to me and remained absolutely motionless in the water next to me, so that I was able to put my arms around her body. With the dolphin supporting my weight in the water, my fear vanished, and I simply waited for Salleres to return from the boat."

Nina and Jacques Renoir dived together for a week. Jacques's boat was anchored in about forty feet of water, and, using his Aqua-Lung®, he ordinarily dived down to the depth of the anchor. It usually took about five

Nina with the Spanish diver, Luis Salleres.

minutes for the dolphin to make her appearance. She approached on the surface of the water, and then, as she drew nearer the boat, she dived, spiraling down the anchor line until she reached Jacques. No doubt, the feel of the line against her body, as she descended, was an agreeable sensation.

When Jacques saw her, he held out his hand, and Nina immediately went to him and rubbed her genital area against his hand.

"We played together for thirty or forty-five minutes," Renoir recalls. "There always came a time when Nina began leaping into the air, then she would fall back and return to me, wildly eager for more fun and games. It was an extraordinary situation, as though the barrier between man and animal no longer existed. There was some sort of strange understanding between us. It

When other dolphins came to play in her bay, Nina ignored them.

would be very difficult for me to say exactly what our feelings were for one another, but there was undoubtedly *something*. Luis Salleres, the Spanish diver, had the same sort of feeling for Nina. In fact, he told me that his wife was jealous of the dolphin and sometimes made scenes over her."

A team of divers from *Calypso*, including Bernard Delemotte and Yves Omer, went to La Corogna to take part in filming sequences for our dolphin film. "You'll see how beautiful Nina is in the water," Jacques Renoir told them when they arrived. "She's like some gorgeous woman. . . ."

"They laughed at me, of course," Jacques relates. "But the first time they dived and saw her, they told me: 'You were right. She *is* beautiful. We could never have imagined anything like her!'"

Nina had won them over.

A National Glory

La Corogna is a small town, and the adventure of Nina, added to the presence of our divers, created a sensation. All the chief men of the town were involved in the affair, and the newspapers in the area began devoting whole pages to Nina. The dolphin, who had started out as a local personality, quickly became a national heroine. The Spanish television network sent a team to Lorbe to make a film which showed Nina playing with a group of swimmers, among whom Franco's grandchildren figured prominently. Nina became the symbol of the link between the Spanish people and the sea. Tourists flocked to the area, and the town's only bistro was jammed to the rafters. The price of land began to rise, and speculators made a great deal of money.

The local fishermen, who had always been poor, suddenly prospered as tourist guides. Now, they earned in a day what it had previously taken them a month to earn. And every weekend there were monstrous traffic jams which were the despair of the local police.

Nina, like any star, gave of herself for her public. She allowed herself to be petted. She mixed with the bathers. She played near any boat that put out into the water.

The tourists loved her. When she swam on one side of a sightseeing boat, everyone rushed over to that side; and when she crossed over to swim on the other side, everyone rushed back to the other side so that the boats were often in danger of capsizing. Some people fell into the water. There were shouts and screams and a constant coming and going of craft of all sizes.

Nina's patience seemed inexhaustible. Sometimes, on Sundays espe-

Even when Salleres put his arms around her, Nina did not seem to mind. (Photo, Jose Freire Vasquez.)

cially, there were as many as two thousand people in the water, all determined to touch Nina. Some of the tourists climbed onto her back. The children tugged at her tail. But she never showed a moment's irritation or impatience.

When she had had enough, she simply disappeared for a half hour or so, then returned, apparently ready for another appearance before her fans. Like any performer, she could not do without her audience. Her stage was always the same, an area some nine hundred feet from the beach. She never dived so deep as to lose her audience.

It is interesting to note that Nina showed a marked preference for swimmers wearing diving suits.

She played constantly throughout the day except for a period of approximately one hour, around noon, when she disappeared, perhaps to eat. In any event, she never accepted food from any of her admirers.

Except for the fact that Nina was a dolphin and that she liked humans, there is very little similarity between her case and that of Dolly. Dolly was a dolphin who had been captured, trained, and then released. She sought out the company of human beings because she was accustomed to them, had

Shooting a sequence.

lived with them, and been fed by them. She behaved like a trained animal who, when released, refused to go "wild" again. She was conditioned by her education, and she asked for nothing more than to be allowed to perform her tricks. What was extraordinary about Nina, on the other hand, was that, so far as it was possible to discover, she had never been trained. There is no aquarium or marineland in the vicinity of La Corogna. And it is most unlikely that, alone, she had crossed the Atlantic to Spain from the United States.

Moreover, her behavior gave no reason to believe that she had undergone any special training, or that she had been previously conditioned in any respect whatsoever. She performed no tricks. She was not eager to play, or to leap out of the water. All she wanted was to be with humans and to be petted by them. Her attitude was as spontaneous as that of Opo. Except that Nina had no favorites among her admirers. She liked everyone, and, for that reason, she was particularly vulnerable.

A Monument to Nina

The civil authorities of La Corogna and the Spanish Navy, accepting responsibility for Nina's welfare, passed certain measures designed to protect the dolphin who had brought prosperity to La Corogna. It was forbidden to use outboard motors around Nina, lest the dolphin be injured by the propellers. No net could be lowered into the waters of the cove, lest Nina become entangled in it and perhaps drown. And no one was allowed to tug at Nina's tail, which was judged to be fragile.

One evening, there was a banquet attended by the mayor, the commandant of the naval district, and the district prefect. Jacques Renoir was invited to speak at the banquet. In halting Spanish, he said:

"We all know how much Nina has done for this area. She has attracted crowds of tourists. She has caused the value of property to double. And she has brought a great deal of business to the town. Nina has done all these things for La Corogna. But what is La Corogna doing for Nina?"

"We love her," someone answered.

"That is not enough," Jacques responded. "There should be a monument to Nina — on the La Corogna jetty, for example."

The next morning, the newspapers launched a fund-raising campaign for Nina's monument. It was proposed that a statue be commissioned, representing a diver with his arms around a dolphin. There was an enthusiastic public response.

The Final Enigma

"At the end of November," relates José Freire Vásquez, "a group of fishermen reported that they had seen Nina near one of the clam beds and that she seemed very ill. Luis Salleres and I went to Lorbe immediately. We searched the bay thoroughly in a boat, without seeing any sign of her. If she had been there, Nina would certainly have come to us, as she always did.

"Five weeks later, at the neighboring beach of San Pedro, the decomposed body of a dolphin washed up onto the sand. Luis and I inspected the corpse and immediately recognized it as the remains of poor Nina.

"It is difficult to say what caused her death. It may have been an accident. Certain individuals in this area use grenades to fish, and Nina may have been the victim of an explosion. Or she may have become entangled in a fisherman's net and drowned. It was winter, and the fishermen, who worked as tourist guides during the summer, had returned to fishing when tourists became scare. They had to earn their living, and they wanted to use their nets again, although it was forbidden by law to do so, precisely because of the danger the nets presented for Nina."

Nina had spent five months in the area of La Corogna, seeking human companionship. She seemed to have given up living among her own kind. Once, a school of Bottlenosed Dolphins was sighted outside the cove. Two of the school entered the cove and spent about a quarter of an hour with Nina. Then they returned alone to the school, and Nina remained in her cove.

Why would a dolphin voluntarily give up living among her own kind for the sake of contact with human beings? There is no way for anyone to answer that question at the present time. It may be that she had been banished from her school for some reason or other, that she was condemned to exile, and that she sought relief from her loneliness among humans.

In Captivity

The love life of dolphins has rarely been observed in the sea, but it has been studied in aquariums. In that environment, the sexual act is preceded by an extended period of love play. The male nips at the female and caresses her. The female flees and generally plays the coquette. Both dolphins swim around at full speed, splashing water in their tank. It is very likely that there is more sexual activity in captivity than in the natural environment of dolphins. This is usually the case among animals confined in zoos.

One pair of dolphins, observed in captivity, behaved as follows: The

(Above and right) Jacques Renoir and Nina

male dolphin, beginning in the spring, showed an extraordinary interest in one of the females, whereas, during the preceding year, he had played indiscriminately with all the other members of the group in the tank. He undertook a real courtship of his inamorata, giving her little pats with his flippers, nipping her on the snout, pushing her with his nose, uttering little cries, and clicking his jaws. This characteristic procedure, which was observed on different occasions, continued for several days. Then the female began to respond in her own way. Her response climaxed in a brief mating. Immediately, the male lost interest in this particular female and began courting another one.

The act of copulation itself is of very brief duration. Dolphins, like all cetaceans, have fibroelastic penises similar to those of Artiodactyls, which differ from the vascular penis of carnivores and primates. Coitus is therefore extremely rapid, lasting from one to thirty seconds, for erection, rather than being caused by an influx of blood into the penis, results from muscular action. Yet, coitus can be repeated (especially among Common Dolphins) several times, at intervals of fifteen minutes.

Mating usually takes place at the surface of the water and is easy to observe in aquariums. That of the Bottlenosed Dolphin has often been described in various publications.

It frequently happens that the female will take the initiative and position herself in such a way that the dorsal fin of the male penetrates her sexual

(Following page) Two dolphins photographed in the open sea.

orifice. Among some species (Pilot Whales, Bottlenosed Dolphins, and Pacific White-sided Dolphins), the female indicates that she is in heat by taking the initiative in amorous games. For dolphins, lacking a sense of smell, cannot catch the characteristic scent of a female in heat as land mammals do.

Female dolphins have a clitoris located at the vaginal orifice, which is about two inches in depth. The male organ is flat and triangular and ordinarily remains within a sheath in the dolphin's body. It emerges like a knife from a scabbard. The dolphin has conscious control over the muscular action which results in erection, and he is therefore able to attain erection very quickly.

The prenuptial games of dolphins sometimes represent scenes of great beauty.* The animals intertwine their flippers, twist and turn, lay their heads on the neck of their partners, and swim gracefully side by side. They dance a veritable ballet of love. Sometimes the male seizes the female around the middle of her body with his flippers. They nip at one another, and their whistles and cries can be heard above the surface of the water.

These amorous preliminaries may last as long as thirty minutes to an hour. The sequence is somewhat less tender. The male rushes at the female as though he intends to ram her head on. At the last second of his charge, he turns, and the partners' bodies rub against each other vigorously. It is during this rubbing that the male's penis makes contact with the female's ventral area. At the moment of climax, the male slides under the female and almost perpendicular to her, with the hind part of his body and his tail folded over her.

This position is reminiscent of the right-angular position taken by sharks. But there are variations. At the Florida Marine Studios, mating takes place during the night or very early in the morning. The male approaches the female from the rear, slightly to the side, either perpendicularly or at a lesser angle. Erection follows immediately.

Among Bottlenosed Dolphins, coitus occurs in either of two ways. The penis enters the female for only half its length, and coupling lasts only ten seconds; or else it penetrates for its full length, and then the act continues for thirty seconds. Coitus is often accompanied by rhythmic movements of the pelvis.

Another mating technique has been observed among Killer Whales, Stenella plagiodon, and Steno which copulate belly to belly on the surface of the water, but in a horizontal position.

During pregnancy, the female Bottlenosed Dolphin stays somewhat apart from the rest of the group but remains in the company of the other

*Some of these have been described by Antony Alpers in his book, *Dolphins, the Myth and the Mammal*, Boston, 1961.

female who will assist her during labor. The expectant mother diligently performs what can only be described as prenatal exercises: she bends her head and tail toward the bottom of the tank, then raises them toward the surface. Some pregnant females continue these exercises for sixty minutes at a time.

Usually, a dolphin gives birth to only one calf at a time. Gestation lasts for one year among Bottlenosed Dolphins and eleven months among Common Dolphins. Lactation continues for sixteen months after birth.

The first birth of a cetacean in captivity occurred at the Brighton Aquarium, in England, in 1914. But the calf was stillborn.

In February 1947, a Bottlenosed Dolphin named Mona, who had been captured pregnant, gave birth in the Florida Marine Studios. Her offspring, a female, was alive and healthy and was christened Spray.

The birth of Spray made it possible to collect some important data. The calf is born not headfirst, but tailfirst. The umbilical cord breaks spontaneously. Since the newborn calf's lungs contain no air, it will drown unless the mother takes it to the surface at once for its first swallow of air. In this endeavor, the mother is usually aided by another female dolphin, known as the

Nina diving. This photograph was taken only a few days before Nina died. (Photo, Jose Freire Vásquez.)

"aunt" or the "midwife." The two females push the calf toward the surface with their snouts. Perhaps this necessary raising of their young to the surface is at the origin of the dolphins' ability to use their snouts to throw balls or rings, and even to save drowning humans.

Some specialists maintain that the mother does not push her calf to the surface. According to this opinion, the calf rises of its own accord, accompanied by the mother.

A newborn dolphin is already rather large and heavy at birth, and it already possesses all the organs of an adult. This no doubt is the reason why the period of gestation is of such long duration. An infant dolphin's body weighs approximately 10 to 15 per cent of its mother's weight and measures a third of the length of the latter's body. For a newborn dolphin must be strong enough to maintain its body temperature and to react against the cold.

Female dolphins, like all female cetaceans, are devoted mothers. They keep constant watch over their offspring, who swim against the mother's body, and defend them courageously against such enemies as sharks. The mother's milk is unusually rich. The mother's breasts are located in pairs, next to her genital organs. A mammary muscle makes it possible for the dolphin, like the whale, to turn slightly on her side and send a jet of milk into the waiting mouth of her offspring.

The milk of cetaceans is composed of 35 to 40 per cent fatty materials, which makes it possible for a young dolphin to grow very rapidly. But a calf is unable to feed itself until it grows teeth — usually at the age of five to seven months. It sometimes happens that the calf continues breast-feeding long after its teeth have grown in, until the age of two years.

A newly born male dolphin is able to have an erection only a few hours after birth. These erections are stimulated by contact with the mother. The first attempts at copulation take place during the first few weeks following birth and have the mother as the sexual object.

The proximity of the mother's breasts and genital orifice is no doubt a factor in this sexual precocity. The calf, in nursing, stimulates the sexual instinct of the mother, and it is not rare that the mother herself causes the calf's erection. She then turns on her side and encourages copulation. This is the young dolphin's first lesson in sexuality.

A male dolphin is unable to impregnate a female until he reaches the age of seven years — the same age at which the female attains sexual maturity.

Sexually, dolphins are extremely active animals. Jacques Renoir is by no means the only witness to this phenomenon. Remington Kellogg, a renowned expert on cetaceans, was passionately loved by a male dolphin in a marineland — so much so that the animal tried every means possible to make Kellogg fall into his tank. On two occasions, the dolphin succeeded; and on both occasions he manifested his affection in an unmistakable manner

Some dolphins are homosexual. It has happened that two males attacked a female who was put into their tank. The female had to be removed in great haste, for the males would obviously have killed her.

In the course of a series of experiments at the St. Thomas Laboratory, in the Virgin Islands, John C. Lilly requested that one of his assistants, Margaret Howe, live with a dolphin for two limited periods. The first period lasted seven days; the second, two and a half months.

During this time, Miss Howe was to remain with the dolphin, named Peter, day and night. The purpose of the experiment was to give the dolphin a "cram course" in language.

In the center of Peter's tank, a platform was constructed. And, on this platform, Margaret Howe installed her bed. At night, Peter rested in the water alongside the bed. During the fourth week of the experiment, Peter began to show unmistakable signs of having something more than a student-teacher relationship in mind. By the end of the month, Miss Howe was writing: "I find that his desires are hindering our relationship. When Peter was upstairs in the Fiberglas tank, he would occasionally become aroused, and I found that by taking his penis in my hand and letting him jam himself against me he would reach some sort of orgasm, mouth open, eyes closed, body shaking, then his penis would relax and withdraw. Now, however, I am completely in the water with him and because so much of my body is exposed . . . I am completely vulnerable to him. . . ."

The remedy devised was to place Peter in a tank with two female dolphins. The following morning, his ardor had noticeably abated.

During the next two weeks, under the pretext of playing ball, Peter succeeded in calming Miss Howe's fears. At the same time, he devised a form of love play which consisted of nipping at Margaret's legs, or holding them gently in his mouth without biting. Peter had become very gentle in his sexual approaches, and he no longer tried to push against Miss Howe, or to knock her over.

At the end of two months, Peter had demonstrated beyond doubt that he would not bite Miss Howe's arms or legs and that he could be trusted. At the same time, he had demonstrated his trust in his mentor by allowing her to handle his sexual organ.† This is the closest contact known between a dolphin and a woman.

†John Cunningham Lilly. *The Mind of the Dolphin*, New York, 1967.

Michel Deloire, our cameraman, getting footage of dolphins surfing in *Calypso*'s wake.

Chapter Six

THE ROAD TO FREEDOM

For a very long time, it had been my intention to devote an entire film to dolphins. Yet, I could never bring myself to use dolphins from aquariums and marinelands as subjects in the film, for these dolphins seemed to me to be deformed and perverted by their captivity and their contact with man. I felt that trained animals — performing animals — could not give us a true representation of the way that marine mammals lived in freedom in the seas. Moreover, the behavior of dolphins in captivity had often been described and filmed.

Therefore, if I wanted a film on dolphins, my subjects would have to be free dolphins. I felt that with our team of divers, and with all of *Calypso*'s resources, we might be able to contribute something to man's understanding of dolphins. We are among the few divers who have had numerous opportunities to observe dolphins in the sea — often at close quarters — either when they came to swim around *Calypso* or when we followed them in our Zodiacs.

The experience we had acquired with dolphins, and especially Falco's observations on the *Delphinus delphis*, seemed to indicate that we might make the film I had in mind. And so, in 1970, I entrusted the project to Jacques Renoir.

During our earlier expeditions, we had seen large numbers of dolphins in the vicinity of Gibraltar and offshore at Málaga. For that reason, I decided to begin our filming in that part of the Mediterranean.

We were aware from the very beginning that it was not easy to film dolphins in the sea. There was no way for our divers and photographers to come near them in the water, and, from *Calypso*, we could never get a frontal view of them. The dolphins swam before our prow, and we could get shots only of their tails, whereas what we really wanted was shots of their heads, their "smiles," their expressions.

With this purpose in mind, I had an arm constructed which extended over *Calypso*'s stem. A camera was attached to this arm, with the lens aimed at the prow. It seemed reasonable to expect that, with this device, we might be able to film what had always eluded us before: a frontal view of dolphins swimming in the open sea.

Yves Omer, our underwater cameraman, supervised the installation of this new piece of equipment. A supporting arm was attached to the stem and then heavily braced to prevent vibration as much as possible. A marine camera and a television camera were coupled in a mobile compartment the position of which could be changed to allow for shots from different angles. Both cameras were remotely controlled.

Calypso's underwater observation chamber made it possible for us to observe dolphins approaching and also to check the action of the cameras.

A Mistake in Yellow

January 17, 1971. We are lying off Málaga and, as we expected, there are many dolphins in this area. We are ready to begin filming, but, to our great disappointment, the dolphins seem reluctant to take up their usual position forward of our prow. It is possible that our new camera arm, extending in the water from the stem, frightens them. It has been the same all along the coast of Spain and around Gibraltar. No school of dolphins that we have encountered will even come near *Calypso*'s prow. And yet, our captain, Philippe Sirot, employs the greatest skill in maneuvering so as to attract them. *Calypso* catches up to the schools slowly and moves parallel to them as gently as possible. But it does no good. I am sure it must be the camera arm. Dolphins have never been afraid of *Calypso* before. . . .

I have now discovered what the trouble was. I went forward and leaned over the side to look at the arm. The braces attached to *Calypso*'s hull, and the compartment housing the cameras, have been painted a bright yellow, a color

Professor Busnel and Captain Cousteau study the movements of dolphins on closed-circuit television from *Calypso*'s bridge.

that can easily be seen in the water. The only thing to do is to take down the whole installation and paint it over, in the same color as our hull: dark red.

We returned to Málaga and the repainting was undertaken immediately. Then we set out to sea again. The first school of dolphins we sighted surrounded *Calypso* without hesitation. Yves Omer and I went to the bridge to watch the television screen. And, for the first time, we saw a frontal view of dolphins swimming in the sea.

"It Works!"

Yves and I were enthusiastic. "It works!" we both shouted.

There were a number of dolphins visible through the portholes of the observation chamber, each one, in turn, taking his place in the wave raised by *Calypso*'s prow. They seemed to swim effortlessly, their tails moving at regularly spaced intervals. Long ago, aboard the *Elie Monnier*, I calculated that in order for a dolphin to attain a speed of ten knots, its tail must beat 120 times per minute, or two strokes per second. But now, the dolphins were moving their tails at a much slower rate. My guess was an average of a stroke and a quarter, or a stroke and a half every second.

The dolphins do not place themselves directly before the prow. Their bodies are at an angle to it, sometimes slightly to one side or slightly to the other. This is very likely intended to enable them to keep an eye toward the surface. "They really are cautious," Yves says. "They obviously want to swim

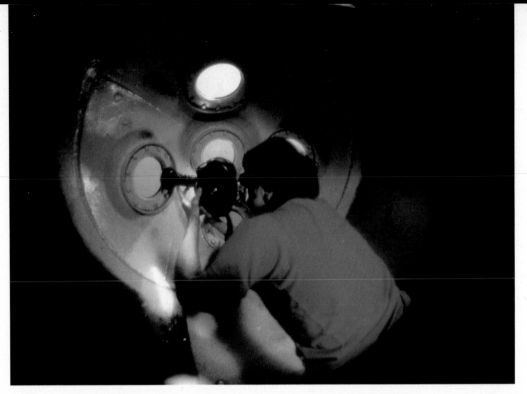

at the prow, but, at the same time, they are uneasy about it."

Despite this cautious approach, some of the dolphins are sufficiently courageous to pass between the prow and the camera. They move from one side to the other, obviously ready to dive at the slightest sign of danger. Sometimes they lie on their sides and we can see their light bellies. We are struck by their suppleness in the water — and by their speed, for it is apparent that they can outdistance us whenever they wish.

"Imagine," I told Yves, "we have 1200 horsepower in our engines. And these animals can swim circles around us!"

Indeed, the dolphin has more power, in proportion to the weight of its muscles, than any other animal.

Yves and I estimate that there are probably a thousand dolphins around *Calypso*'s prow, and we are fascinated by the way they move. The dolphin does not use its lateral flippers to swim, and its dorsal fin probably serves only as a stabilizer. It is able to move so rapidly because of its marvelously hydrodynamic shape and because of its powerful tail. The tail moves up and down horizontally, rather than vertically as in the case of fish. It can also move at an angle on both sides even when the animal is swimming at a rapid pace.

In aquariums, the Bottlenosed Dolphin can be seen swimming back and forth at the surface of its tank, at high speeds, with its tail much lower than its head. All these movements are possible because of the heavy musculature of the caudal peduncle, which is located both above and below the vertebral column. And yet, the tail of the dolphin is essentially the same as that of land mammals. The only difference is that it has adapted perfectly to life in the sea.

(Left) From his vantage point in our observation chamber, Gerard Petiot films dolphins in the sea.

(Right) Dolphins viewed through a porthole of the observation chamber.

(Below) A dolphin swims past the observation chamber and the automatic camera located at *Calypso*'s fore.

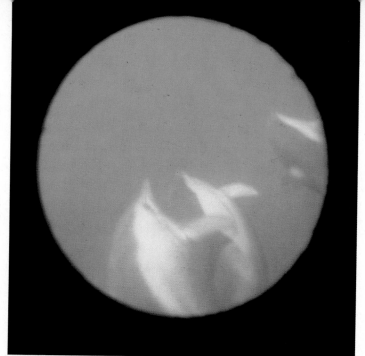

The body of the dolphin still contains traces of the animal's land origins, especially in the bones situated near the anal region which were once a pelvis and two limbs. Similarly, the dolphin's flippers contain all the bones of the hand, the wrist, and the arm.

A New Tank

I invited several researchers to participate in our dolphin expedition. Among those aboard *Calypso* are Albin Dziedzic, research engineer at the Laboratory of Acoustical Physiology; Alain Hellion, researcher at the Institute of Physics and Chemistry at Lyons; and Bernard Gautheron, a technician at the Phonetics Institute. Professor René Busnel joined us later.

We have a floating tank designed by Albin Dziedzic and built by the Laboratory of Acoustical Physiology. The tank is a triangular pool twenty feet in length. It is surrounded by air bags, which give it buoyancy. A net, which goes down to a depth of fifteen or twenty feet, is attached by these floaters. The shape of the net is maintained by rigid inserts located at the bottom of the net. We intend to place animals in this pool, for very brief periods, in order to study them. They are then to be released immediately.

We have already tested our new tank in the sea, off Málaga. All went as planned.

January 19.

We are leaving Málaga, despite heavy weather from the southwest. We are going to try to catch a dolphin.

A platform has been installed on *Calypso*'s stem, and Bébert Falco is going to try to capture a dolphin, using the same method employed thirteen years ago.

Now, however, we have the benefit of a new pincer, designed by R.-G. Busnel. This pincer is U-shaped, like the one Falco used earlier, but it has a long wooden handle at its extremity. A net bag is attached to the pincer by means of some rather fragile string. It is no longer necessary to use a harpoon gun to launch the pincer. It is simply held before the dolphin's snout. When the dolphin pushes against the device with its snout, the strings break and the net falls. The metal pincer itself never touches the dolphin's body, since it never leaves Falco's hand. A nylon line runs to the Zodiac which follows the dolphin.

The first tests of the new pincer have been unsuccessful. The weather was rough, *Calypso* was rolling, and it was impossible to take proper aim at the dolphin. The platform on *Calypso*'s prow makes it difficult to hold the pincer at an absolute vertical. We have, therefore, replaced it with a beam, which once was used to lower a sounding device into the water. This beam goes to within ten feet of the surface and makes it possible for the pincer device to be positioned directly over a dolphin swimming forward of our stem.

I should note here that not all species of dolphins like to swim in the wave of a prow. The Common Dolphin, the White-sided Dolphin, and often the Bottlenosed Dolphin are those who favor this kind of game. So does the Steno. (Professor Busnel captured a specimen of the latter, which was the first one to be taken alive.*) Pilot whales occasionally swim before a prow, but Harbor Porpoises never do.

We have also had to modify our pincer somewhat. The knots in the netting were too large and bruised the animal, and the fastenings were too weak and too stiff. I think that we now have an apparatus that will do the job for us.

First Capture

January 24. Falco, perched on the beam of *Calypso*'s prow, was unable to aim properly at a dolphin swimming directly under him. So, he chose another target: a dolphin swimming slightly to the side. However, he held the pincer in a vertical position.

The net has a great advantage in that the animal was so surprised that it very quickly came to a halt. Simultaneously, *Calypso* did likewise, and the Zodiac raced out, leaping from the crest of one wave to the next. But the sea was so rough that it was difficult for the little craft to maintain its speed. Nonetheless, Delemotte and Giacoletto, who were in the Zodiac, acquitted themselves with their usual competence and caught up to the dolphin. They then loaded him onto the Zodiac and brought him aboard. The animal was trembling.

The whole procedure lasted no more than sixty seconds. Speed is of the essence, since, if the dolphin goes into shock, there is a danger that it may suffocate. Not once did we ever have any problem of this kind during the first phase of our operating procedure. The co-ordination between Bébert and the men in the Zodiac was absolutely flawless.

---

*The Steno Dolphin was first described, and its existence known, in 1880, when a dead specimen was found.

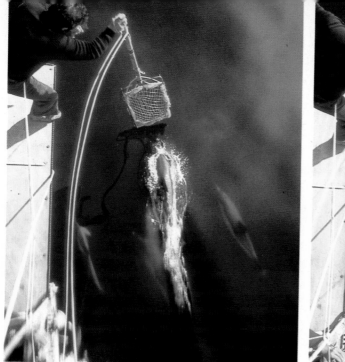

The various phases in the capture of a dolphin by Falco. The net must cover the dolphin's head. Then the animal is picked up by the Zodiac.

As soon as the dolphin was aboard, Busnel gave him a cortisone injection and a tonicardiac.

The weather is so bad that no experiments are possible, and we are en route back to Málaga. Meanwhile, the dolphin is dehydrating, and we are giving him continuous doses of glucose.

The vat in which we have placed the dolphin, on *Calypso*'s rear deck, is quite small, and the sea is so rough that the animal was thrown up against the side. We have covered the bottom and sides of the vat with foam rubber so as to form a protective cushion around the dolphin and to keep him from being thrown against the sides.

Upon docking at Málaga, we lowered the floating tank into the water and put the dolphin into it. We've attached orange ribbons of nylon to the net, because we're afraid that the animal will not see the knots and will bruise himself against them.

As soon as the dolphin was in the tank, Falco went down also and spent a quarter of an hour with him. The animal seemed dazed and was not moving very much. By the time that Bébert came back aboard, however, the dolphin was swimming normally. Nonetheless, we want to make certain that his blowhole is above the surface at all times; so, we have placed small bolsters under his snout.

During the night, the storm reached its peak, and even within the port the waves were so high that *Calypso* broke two of her hawsers. At the height of the storm, the floating tank became unbalanced and twisted. By the time that one of our divers managed to work his way into the tank, the dolphin had become entangled in the netting and had drowned. We are all very sad.

January 25. The weather is better this morning, and we are setting out to find another dolphin. . . .

There was no problem in capturing the first dolphin we encountered — a specimen weighing over two hundred pounds. Falco has lost none of his skill. He captured the animal on the first try. The sea was calm and still, and Bébert was able to lower the pincer almost to the surface. Then, as soon as the dolphin came up to breathe, Bébert quickly put the pincer around him and the dolphin was caught in the net without injuring himself.

The dolphin is neither a Bottlenosed nor a Common Dolphin, but a *Stenella styx*, which is grayer than the Common Dolphin.

The tank was immediately lowered into the water. It is light but handles rather clumsily. We keep it on the aft deck, with its air bags always inflated. We have got the knack of getting it into the water, but getting it back aboard is something else again. The whole team has to work at it, and we must be extraordinarily careful to keep the net from snagging. Naturally, it tends to hook onto anything within reach. With all its problems, however, it is still an ingenious device.

As soon as we had the tank in the sea, the dolphin was placed into it. The animal positioned himself vertically in the center of the tank and then refused to move. Occasionally, he sank deeper and then rose to the surface again, but he would not swim around in the tank. Our dolphin was so obviously unhappy that I decided to free him. He was no sooner out of the tank than he shot out of sight as though he had been fired from a cannon, proving that he could, after all, swim like any other dolphin.

January 26. Today, Falco captured another dolphin. We put the animal into the tank, and very soon it was swimming round in a circle.

We've decided to install hydrophones in the tank so that we can record the dolphin's whistles and cries.

Just our luck. We've captured a taciturn dolphin. Thus far, he's made three sounds. One when he was captured and two during the night. Thereafter, he has absolutely refused to speak.

January 27. We've spent the day waiting for our dolphin to "talk." We are beginning to feel slightly ridiculous. . . .

At 6 P.M., a squall from the east caught up with us. It is too dangerous to the dolphin to keep him in the tank in this weather, so I have ordered him set free. I think that Falco will be glad to see him go.

We are hauling in the tank as fast as we can. . . .

The weather is too bad for us to be able to work effectively. Moreover, *Calypso* has other assignments waiting for her. We will have to interrupt Operation Dolphin for a while.

A Merry-Go-Round

On April 5, *Calypso* returned to Málaga, and we were ready to begin the next phase of our dolphin project. This time, we were going to work in the vicinity of Gibraltar. The television and movie cameras were in place, aimed at our prow, and we set out with high hopes.

We were not disappointed. Very shortly, both screens were filled with the fantastic spectacle of a crowd of dolphins swimming in circles, pushing and brushing against one another. It was an incredible, animated merry-go-round. Occasionally, we caught a frontal view of a dolphin with its broad smile, then, everyone on the bridge laughed.

We were able clearly to distinguish the stream of air bubbles rising from their heads as they were whistling.

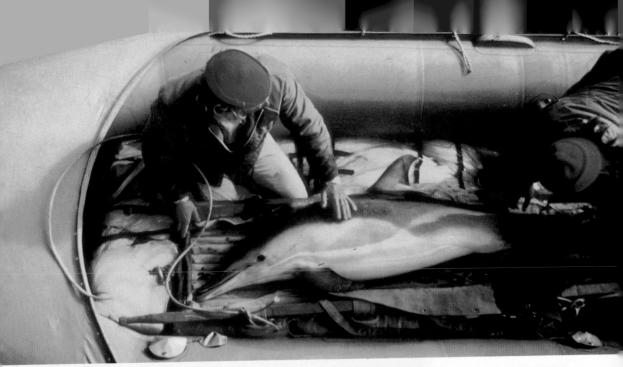

(Above) The dolphin has now been taken aboard the Zodiac.

(Left) The captured dolphin is hoisted aboard *Calypso*.

(Right) Yves Omer gives first aid to the dolphin, which is now in a tank on *Calypso*'s aft deck.

Falco, meanwhile, had taken his position on the beam at our prow, and, on the first try, he was able to capture a female dolphin. She was immediately placed into the floating tank. It took only a short while for her to become accustomed to the tank, and she swam around without fear of ramming into the sides. Occasionally, however, she pushed her head against the air bags, obviously searching for a way out of the tank.

Professor Busnel advised us that a dolphin weighing 150 pounds required at least eighteen or twenty pounds of fish per day.

The sea had become so rough that it was necessary to remove the dolphin from her tank and place her into one of the two large vats that we kept on *Calypso*'s aft deck.

The ceremony of getting a dolphin into the vat always followed the same

pattern. Falco would take the animal in his arms and pass her gently to Bernard Delemotte. Delemotte would hand her to Yves Omer, who was standing next to the vat. Everyone had to be extremely gentle, for dolphins, out of the water, are unable to support their own weight. When they are moved, they must be supported at all times, for their vertebrae are very fragile.

Falco was not the only one concerned about the health of whatever dolphins we had aboard *Calypso*. Bernard Delemotte kept constant watch over them, and he summoned our ship's doctor at the slightest pretext.

"I can't tell you how often Delemotte has awakened me in the middle of the night," Dr. Joseph François says. "It's always the same. He wants me to examine one of the dolphins who, he says, 'looks funny.' And he insists that I do it immediately. He reminds me of one of those nervous mothers who call the doctor whenever their child sneezes. They are always sure that something is wrong."

Fortunately, most of Bernard's alarms were false. Nonetheless, we felt obliged to keep very close watch indeed over our dolphins. We knew that *Calypso*'s rolling and pitching would throw the animals against the walls of the vats, or even empty the vats and leave the dolphins without water. Even though we lined the vats with foam rubber to protect the dolphins, we did not lower our vigilance.

The bruises which appeared on the dolphins' bodies were a source of constant worry to us. Their skin is so tender that moving them from the tank to the vats, or from the vats to the tank, no matter how gentle we tried to be, caused lesions which quickly became infected.

Falco regarded it as a challenge to feed our female dolphin. He slid sardines into her mouth at every opportunity — fresh sardines, caught that very morning by means of a *lamparo*. The dolphin's eyes shone, but she refused to swallow the fish. Finally, by means of gentle insistence, Falco was successful. The dolphin began eating.

April 15. There are many dolphins here around Gibraltar, and Falco has captured a male weighing two hundred pounds. The sea is quite calm today, and we were able to lower the floating tank and to put the dolphin into it without delay. Dziedzic and Gautheron used their hydrophones to record the dolphin's whistles when it was captured, that is, as soon as the animal realized that it was a prisoner. These sounds continued for fifteen or twenty minutes. Then, when the animal began to swim around in the tank, he fell silent. When there are other dolphins in the area, they respond to these whistles, but, as soon as they see that there is nothing they can do for their friend, and that he is silent, they leave.

Our second dolphin was christened Fox Trot.

Aboard *Calypso*, the two dolphins were tossed about in their vats by the ship's rolling. We noticed that they seemed unwell, and we knew what was wrong! They were seasick. We had noted before that marine mammals are no more immune to this affliction than man.†

Later, more bad weather obliged us to put our second dolphin into the other vat on *Calypso*'s aft deck. The two vats were twelve feet apart, and we had the impression that there was constant communication between the dolphins. The female turned her head and whistled. The male immediately raised his head and whistled back. This exchange continued for over two hours, without pause.

"I suppose," Falco said, "that the female told the male that we were going to give him something to eat, and that it would be all right for him to accept it."

Falco was obviously right, for the male dolphin ate four sardines without hesitation. (We were fortunate enough to have made the acquaintance of a fisherman from Málaga who was very interested in our work and who provided us regularly with fresh fish.)

We put the two dolphins together into the floating tank, and they seemed overjoyed. Both animals performed acrobatics to express their pleasure. The female, who was familiar with the tank, served as guide to her companion to keep him from becoming entangled in the net. She kept her body pressed against him as they swam together.

At night, we were afraid that the animals might be caught in the netting, and we brought them back aboard *Calypso* and put them in their vats. However, we used a stretcher that Dr. François had among his supplies, and this device, in combination with our crane, worked perfectly in hoisting the animals aboard. Of course, we were careful to be as gentle as possible, but I was saddened by the sight of the dolphins being tossed about in their tanks. Captivity, no matter how well intentioned, is no life for a dolphin.

When both animals were together in the tank, everything seemed to go smoothly. They did not make a sound. But as soon as the animals were separated, the female began to utter cries. She seemed to panic and dived toward the bottom, with her mouth open. On several occasions, she became entangled in the net, and Yves Omer was obliged to go down and release her.

The male dolphin occasionally performed an interesting maneuver. He placed himself in a vertical position, then bent down upon himself. It would have been an amusing trick for a marineland audience. However, we had no

---

†Commandant Alinat has invented a non-rolling aquarium, which we use aboard *Calypso* to house rare coral fishes destined for the Oceanographic Museum of Monaco.

(Above) Falco joins the dolphin in our triangular floating pool.

(Right) Once in the floating pool, the captured dolphin begins to make sounds. Notice the bubbles rising from the animal's blowhole.

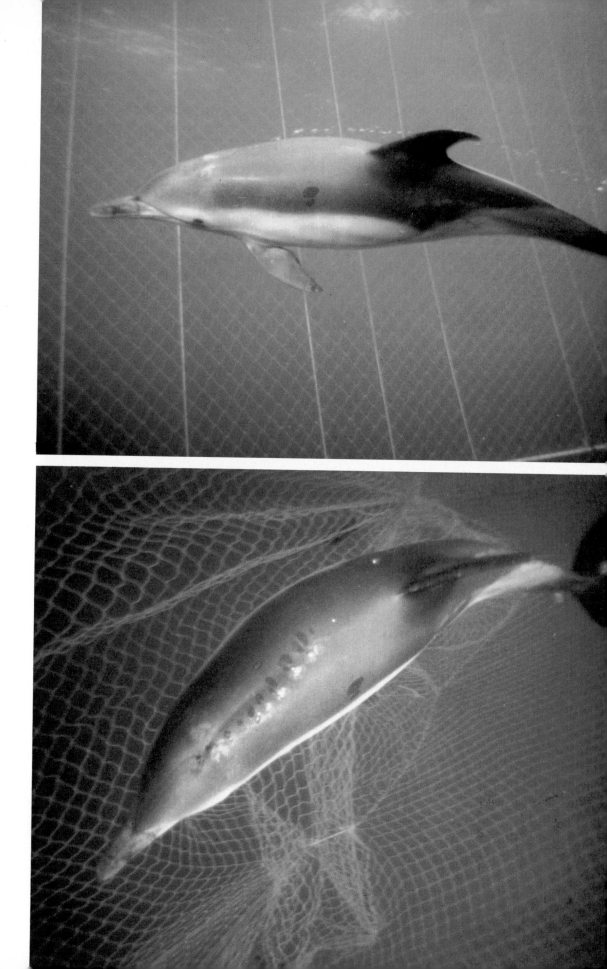

intention of turning these dolphins into performing animals. At the time, all we were interested in was using the tank's acoustical equipment to maximum advantage in order to record the sounds of dolphins living in circumstances which approximated freedom.

On one occasion, we left the female (who, by then, was quite tame) alone in the tank. *Calypso* then moved a fair distance away, for the sounds of our engines and of the propellers turning interfered with underwater sound recordings.

We hoped that the dolphin, left to herself in a tank in the sea, would call to other dolphins, and that a school would be attracted by her cries. And that is exactly what happened. As the dolphins approached, our sound engineer recorded their calls. The animals came to a halt some thirty feet from the tank — undoubtedly listening to what the female was telling them. But what was she saying? "Help me"? Or "Swim away, these creatures are dangerous"? We do not know. In any event, after a short time, the school of dolphins swam away and the female, perhaps disappointed, fell silent.

We were surprised that the female dolphin never attempted to leap over the side of the floating tank. Certainly, she would have been able to do it easily enough. In aquariums, dolphins sometimes move from one compartment in a tank to another simply by jumping over nets in one leap. But these are obviously dolphins who are accustomed to captivity. It seemed likely that our dolphin had no idea that a barrier might be passable. She was accustomed to the vastness of the sea. Anything that loomed before her, therefore, was something strange and unfamiliar. Never, during our observation of dolphins on this expedition, did a single dolphin attempt to jump out of the tank — despite the fact that an adult dolphin is capable of leaping to a height of ten feet. Sometimes, our dolphins inspected the net closely, but they always ended by swimming away from it. They seemed afraid that, if they pushed against it, they would become entangled.

Animals not yet deformed by captivity were necessary for the kind of experiments that we had in mind. We intended to place blinkers over the female dolphin's eyes so that we might observe how she would guide herself when she was sightless.

The dolphin allowed us to put the blinkers on her, but the kind of blinkers that we were using obviously were uncomfortable for her. She rubbed herself and thrashed about and was evidently unhappy. We therefore removed the blinkers.

Albin Dziedzic had another pair of blinkers, which attached by means of suction. We tried them on the dolphin, but these seemed as uncomfortable as the others. Everyone therefore set to work to make a blindfold of foam rub-

Before beginning our experiments in echolocation, the dolphin is blindfolded.

ber that would not hurt the animal. When it was finished, it was held over the dolphin's eyes by the strap from a diver's mask, which was passed under her neck. The animal showed no signs of discomfort.

Although deprived of her sight, the dolphin swam around the tank without the slightest hesitation and without touching the net. Falco was in the water with her, and he reported that there was no discernible sound as she swam. It was obvious that the sound waves, used by dolphins as "sonar," are emitted at a frequency which makes them inaudible to humans. Falco, however, felt that the dolphin's success may have been due to her knowledge of the location of the net and of the air bags.

To test Falco's theory, we installed iron bars around the tank at intervals of about two feet, then we dropped the net. The dolphin, wearing her blindfold, swam among the bars without touching them. With the net gone, there was no longer any barrier between her and freedom. Yet, she did not dare swim away. The fact that she could not see had most likely made her even more cautious than usual. Falco then led her back to the center of the tank.

The experiment was repeated several times as Jacques Renoir filmed it.

The following day, we put the same blindfold on the male dolphin and then turned him loose in the tank with the unblindfolded female. They swam side by side and were never apart for an instant, with the male swimming against the female and imitating every movement she made.

We then removed the female from the tank and returned her to her vat. The blindfolded male at first had no trouble swimming alone, but then, he grew tired. A current began to move through the tank, and it was enough to

(Left) The blindfolded dolphin is about to find his way around the pool by means of sound.

(Above and below) A dolphin equipped with an underwater camera is freed in the hope that he will rejoin his school and film their movements for us.

send the dolphin against the net and to entangle him in it. The first time this happened, the animal tried desperately to free himself, but thereafter he knew that a diver would come to free him immediately, and he simply waited, motionless, for help to arrive.

Our friend Dziedzic was delighted by the results obtained by means of the floating tank and the system of hydrophones and other recording equipment with which it was equipped.

"I was able to get some absolutely incredible recordings," he reported later, "which it took me almost a year to analyze. I was able to follow the movements of a dolphin within the tank solely on the basis of his echolocation signals and by using the hydrophones to triangulate."

Some dolphins were better subjects than others and lent themselves very well to experiments as well as to filming. Nonetheless, we never kept any dolphin, even the best subjects, for more than two days. As soon as an animal showed the least indication of fatigue or weakness, we released him immediately. Falco was responsible for deciding at what point a dolphin was ready to return to freedom in the sea.

"Falco's diagnostic ability is really astonishing," Dr. François says. "He knows dolphins so well that he was able to know intuitively when they were not well. He simply looked at them. I think that he could tell somehow from the way an animal moved, just as some specialists are able to tell if a dog is sick by the way it walks or moves its spine."

It had occurred to me, on more than one occasion, that it would be worthwhile to attach a camera to a dolphin's back. I felt certain that one or more dolphin cameramen would be able to film some extraordinary scenes of the group life of dolphins. My plan was to have the dolphins return to their school, and then we would recapture them later and remove the cameras from their backs.

For our first venture, we chose a particularly large, strong animal. The capture had been difficult precisely because he was so strong. Then we put a harness on him and attached a camera to it. This procedure required a considerable amount of time, and when we had finished our work, the school was already one or two miles away. As soon as we released the animal, he headed directly toward his friends; but he did not catch up to them, either because he was exhausted by the ordeal of his capture or because the camera slowed his speed.

Several dolphins from the school swam toward him, but they remained a safe distance away from him and ended by returning to the school alone. When one animal sees something abnormal in the appearance or behavior of another animal, there is a tendency to avoid the latter.

On April 18, we captured a 275-pound male and, following the same procedure, we attached a camera to his back. The dolphin was able to swim, but his speed was hindered by the camera. His companions in the school swam past him, without waiting for him. Soon, our dolphin cameraman was alone in the sea. We recaptured him, removed the camera and harness, and then released him.

For each of these attempts, we used a different, fresh dolphin. But at no time did any of these animals succeed in swimming at his normal speed while carrying the camera. The harness and the socle impeded him, and the camera was obviously cumbersome. None of them managed to catch up to his school or to remain with his companions. And the film that was taken by our dolphin cameramen was totally without interest.

Our experiences with the camera-carrying dolphins lead me to believe that the Americans, who were trying to train dolphins to carry explosives, may have been disappointed in the results they obtained. It should be remembered, however, that they were working with Bottlenosed Dolphins, which, at a length of eight feet and a weight of over four hundred pounds, are more powerful than the Common Dolphin of the Mediterranean.

Still, we did not give up our attempts to find out how dolphins behave among themselves when they are alone in the sea. We simply turned to other methods. One of these was to equip a dolphin with a radio transmitter, following the example of William Evans of the Naval Undersea Research Center.‡ Once again, however, we found that the harness used to attach the transmitter to the dolphin's back hindered the animal's movements and reduced his speed. Even worse, the flexible antenna of the transmitter actually acted as a brake. Obviously, we had no trouble in finding our radio dolphin after the experiment, since he never succeeded in getting very far away from us in the first place, or in catching up to his school.

We made use of a completely different approach by having a diver attach a bag of fluorescein to a dolphin. (Even a small amount of this substance will leave a long, green trail in the water.) We thought that we would thus be enabled to see where he went and what he would do.

Our divers stood by, ready to relieve one another in following the dolphin's trail, and we were just congratulating ourselves upon our ingenuity when the dolphin suddenly dived and disappeared. Of course, it was impossible for the divers to see where the dolphin had gone — because of all the fluorescein in the water.

To this day, the secrets of the free dolphins are safe.

‡See Chapter Eight.

Chapter Seven

A WORLD OF SOUND

We were in the Mediterranean, off the coast of Spain, near Almeria. The weather was splendid, and we were able to lower the floating tank and record the sounds of the dolphins at our leisure. As in our previous recording sessions, we were using three antennaed hydrophones which had been arranged at three different angles in the tank. Two underwater television cameras had also been positioned in the floating enclosure, so that we could relate the animals' sonic signals to their movements.

On this occasion, there were three dolphins in the tank, all of them captured the previous day. They were perfectly calm and seemed already to have adapted to their tank. Their movements were normal, as was their respiration. Every twenty seconds or so, they rose to the surface to breathe.

The sea was absolutely flat, and *Calypso*'s equipment was able to pick up every sound from the tank without interference. By analyzing these sounds by means of our oscilloscope, and by synchronizing them with the images being received on our television cameras, we were able to put together an audio-

(Left) A diver marks a dolphin with a fluorescent chemical so that we can follow his trail in the water.

visual record which constituted a glimpse into the sonic world of the dolphins.

It is a world very different from our own. The first reason, obviously, is that it is a world of water, and also that dolphins are capable of emitting and perceiving sound at frequencies higher than those at which humans are able to hear. Moreover, the human ear is not equipped to hear in the water.

The noises which we picked up were weak and occurred at intervals. These sounds were the well–known "clicks," as they are called; and even "attention clicks," that is, infrequent, but regular clicks which indicate that the dolphin is attentive to its environment. It is that clicking sound which, when accelerated, repeated, and intensified, makes it possible for the dolphin to perform a sonic exploration of the world around him. He perceives the echo of the sounds he makes and, from them, is able to deduce the existence and the shape of the obstacles in the area. This is the "echolocation" system of the dolphins.

Contrary to what is commonly believed, the dolphin does not make con-tinuous use of this system. When an animal is in a tank or pool, where the water is clear and where he is familiar with the location of the walls, he does not need it, or use it. The dolphin's sense of sight is acute, and a few clicks are sufficient to give him an adequate idea of the size of his tank. If, on the other hand, a dolphin is placed at night into a tank with which he is unfamiliar, a steady series of echolocation clicks will be forthcoming.

As soon as our three dolphins came near the nets which circumscribed the floating tank, the rhythm of sonic emissions accelerated noticeably. The larger openings in the nets, which were harder to locate, seemed particularly to disconcert them, and the clicks increased. These might be called "warning clicks." Then, as soon as we threw a fish into the tank, the clicks became much louder to enable the dolphins to locate their prey.

Obviously, the dolphin's echolocation system is not nearly so simple as the above description might lead one to believe. For one thing, the so-called "clicks" of the dolphin are not constant with respect either to quality or to loudness. Sometimes the signals are amplified and transformed into sounds so unexpected as to startle observers: grindings, clapping noises, squeaks, and so forth. And sometimes these same clicks are inaudible to us because they are emitted at too high a frequency.

It is noteworthy that in none of these variations does the dolphin make bubbles in the water.

A blinkered or blindfolded dolphin's sonar system is so acute that it en-ables him, at a distance of fifteen or eighteen feet, to distinguish between two fishes. This has been verified by experiment, and it shows that the dolphin's echolocation system is extremely sensitive. The ability to identify and classify an object, demonstrated by this experiment, obviously presupposes the existence of mental processes which go beyond simply locating a fish. A systematic choice between two objects presumes the ability to retain and to make use of stored data. In other words, it presupposes the existence of memory and of the ability to recognize forms by means of sonic silhouettes. We are far from being able to analyze and judge these abilities in the dolphin. But, for the moment, it may be said that "what is clearly evident, and what is most remarkable, is the dolphin's ability to adapt his sonar to the most varied situations."*

The Mysterious Organ

It is not known which of the dolphin's organs is used to emit the clicking sounds. One of the subsidiary mysteries is this: How can the dolphin make sounds without having vocal chords? There has been much discussion of this and other questions, but no positive answers have yet been produced.

For the past twenty-five years, thirty or so laboratories in various parts of the world have been engaged in breeding dolphins for study by perhaps a hundred specialists. Thus far, the only certitude we have is negative. We know that the dolphin's sonar signals do not come from its blowhole, and they are not accompanied by air bubbles — unlike the communications signals which we will discuss later.

It seems generally accepted that all of the precise data that a dolphin gathers when he is near his prey, or in the vicinity of an obstacle, can be obtained by a signal which passes through his snout.

Directional sensitivity plays a most important role in the echolocation process. In commercially produced radar and sonar systems, manufactured for the purpose of locating objects of various kinds, the finest possible sonic "brush" must be used. In the dolphin, the rostrum, or beak, assumes the function of the sonic brush when the animal is near its prey.

For long-distance acoustical perception, it is likely that the dolphin makes use of an organ common to other toothed whales: a hollow, located in the forward part of its head, which contains a fatty matter not unlike wax. Within this mass is a network of tissues which may act as an amplifier which serves to magnify sound at a higher rate than the surrounding tissue. The role of this "amplifier" (a role which is possible but over which there are disputes) would be to focus, by successive reflections, the sonic waves which occur with

*"Les systèmes sonars animaux," in Congrès de Frascati, Vol. I, p. 444. R.-G. Busnel, editor

(Above) The pool, with its electronic equipment, is left to float alone in the sea with its captured dolphin.

(Left) The pieces of iron in our floating pool are used in our echolocation experiments.

a certain incidence. (There are commercially produced directional antennae based on this principle.)

The clicks made by a dolphin for purposes of echolocation are of uncertain origin. Some say that the sound is produced by muscular action, just as the human larynx can be used to produce a clicking sound.

It is known that the dolphin's tongue plays no part in these sounds.† It should be noted, however, that the sounds are sometimes produced at the rate of 800, 1,000, or 1,200 clicks per second — faster than can be produced by any muscle, or any vibrating membrane, known in nature.

It is obvious that the dolphin's clicks, as important as they are in the animal's life, remain a mystery so far as man is concerned.

Ulysses

The range of the dolphin's clicks extends from audible low frequency to the ultrasonic range, the latter being at frequencies ten times higher than

†The bat, an aerial mammal, uses its tongue to modulate the sounds. Some bats produce the echolocation "clicks" with their tongue.

those audible to the human ear. There have been times, aboard *Calypso*, when the sounds made by the dolphins were audible only to Ulysses, our dog. If Ulysses understood what the dolphins said, he did not tell us.

The dolphin, thanks to its sonar ability, is able to find its way and to pursue its prey even in the cloudiest water. He is able to perceive sounds of 150,000 hertz. The question, however, is how, and by means of what organs, he exercises this extraordinary ability. His ears — which probably were once those of a land mammal, covered with fur — have been reduced to openings no larger than pinpoints. These open at the level of the dolphin's skin, just behind the eyes, and at the base of a small groove. The disappearance of the pavilion of the ear may be due to hydrodynamic exigencies, or it may be a consequence of diving and water pressure. At this point, we have no way of knowing the reason.

Researchers have the experimental proof that the dolphin perceives echoes and his own sonic emissions through the intermediary of his lower jaw. That jaw contains major nerve terminals connected to tissues which, in turn, are connected to the animal's complex and highly developed internal ear.

The theory of the lower jaw has been corroborated by means of an experiment. A dolphin, who was trained to find a sonic source in his tank, when blinkered, put his lower jaw against that source. To achieve this he had to lie on his side or on his back. This indicates that the lower jaw of the dolphin is highly sensitive to sound. The jaw contains a fatty, almost liquid tissue which transmits the sound to the internal ear. (The cochlea of the dolphin is about the same size as that of humans, but his acoustical nerve is much larger and contains thick contact fibers.) The dolphin is therefore especially well equipped so far as hearing is concerned, and it is not surprising that sensory life is controlled largely through its sonar. The dolphin is primarily an audial creature, while man is primarily a visual creature.

The dolphin, of course, is not the only animal who uses echolocation. Bats make use of the same system, and their sonar abilities have been studied at length.‡ Busnel and Dziedzic have demonstrated that a blindfolded Harbor Porpoise can detect and avoid metal wires measuring .2 mm. in diameter. For a blindfolded bat (*Myotis lucifugen*), the diameter of the wire detected is from .07 mm. to .12 mm.*

‡The ability of the bat to guide itself by echolocation was first observed 160 years ago by Lazzaro Spallanzani, an Italian scientist; but Spallanzani's discovery was forgotten for many years. See *Les systemes sonars animaux*, R.-G. Busnel, ed.

*The reason for the differences in performance by porpoises and bats very likely has to do with the different densities of their respective milieux.

At Narragansett Laboratory, Marie Poland Fish has recorded the underwater sounds of four hundred species of fish, twenty-five species of cetacean, and ten species of seals. Echolocation, therefore, is hardly a rarity among living beings. And the more zoology widens its field of endeavor, the longer grows the list of the animals who make use of it. There are birds and one fish as well as large mammals who live in water such as the hippopotamus. According to Dr. W. M. Longhurst, the hippopotamus can detect obstacles and prey by making use of sonar, without being obliged to emerge from the water when the visibility is less than twelve inches.

Even among humans, there are blind people who have learned to guide themselves by the echo of clicks made by their tongues or their canes — clicks which bear a strong resemblance to the clicking sounds made by the toothed whales.†

Professor Leslie Kay, of the University of Canterbury in New Zealand, basing himself on the ultrasonic guidance systems of dolphins and bats, has designed a sonar system for the blind: eyeglasses which emit ultrasonic waves, the echoes of which are perceived by the blind person. The latter is thus able to detect an object eighteen to twenty feet in front of him. The principle of this device is a "sonic image," transmitted by the eyeglasses, of the person's surroundings, which enables one to distinguish the nature of obstacles — a wall, a passerby, a street lamp, etc.

Communications Signals

As intriguing as the dolphin's echolocation system may be, we were even more interested in studying the sounds by which dolphins communicate with one another. For we know that dolphins "speak" to one another and that they send out calls and warning signals.

On *Calypso*'s television screens, we were able to observe the air bubbles which rise from the dolphin's blowhole when it sends out signals of this kind. Some of the photographs, reproduced in this book, show these bubbles trailing like strings of crystal beads behind the animals. Sometimes, a single large bubble rises above a dolphin's head. It is claimed that, when observed in

†See "Les systemes sonars animaux," in *Congres de Frascati.*

(Following page) A school of dolphins in the open water off Málaga.

aquariums, this release of one large bubble corresponds to a threat, a gesture of dissuasion, or a warning.

Dolphins sometimes also exchange whistling sounds. These sounds are communications signals quite distinct from the sonar whistles in series by means of which a dolphin locates an object or an obstacle. It is beyond doubt that dolphins communicate as do many other species (birds, insects, and fish, for example). Bees, as Von Fritsch has demonstrated, have a language which is danced rather than articulated. A bee who has discovered a particularly rich source of pollen is able to explain to other bees how far away the source is, in which direction, and how plentiful it is.

Voices in the Sea

Long ago, we learned to listen to the voices speaking in the silence of the seas. In the Far North, we have heard the extraordinary sounds of the Weddell seals, which are perhaps the noisiest of the marine mammals. Their cries reverberate under the arctic ice with a strangely pathetic, almost painful note.

In the waters off Bermuda, my son Philippe and our sound engineer, Eugène Lagorio, have spent entire nights taping the extravagant concerts of the humpback whales — the singing whales, as we call them. Sometimes, there were a hundred whales exchanging roars, bellows, and mews — words that I use reluctantly to describe the sounds of the humpback whales, for those sounds, in fact, resemble those of no other animal. They are sounds which resemble trills, and the clanking of chains, and the squeaking of doors. In my mind's eye, I can see Eugène sitting in his Zodiac, the glittering sky above him and the dark, eternal sea stretching endlessly around him . . . listening to those alien voices from the sea, voices which might have come from another universe and another time.

The fact that dolphins speak is not a recent discovery. Aristotle knew it twenty-three centuries ago. Since his time, however, the land-bound civilization of the West forgot that there were indeed voices in the sea — countless voices and sounds which, to us, are still incomprehensible.

For it is not only the dolphins who speak. All marine mammals do so, and the phenomenon is only rendered more striking by its universality.

An Unknown Source

How can the dolphin produce sounds, since it has no vocal chords? It is likely that, among most species, sounds are produced only in the water. A dolphin must be in a marineland or a laboratory, and he must have the benefit of a trainer, before he can learn (quite easily) to "speak" or "sing" in the open air.

With respect to the means of producing these whistles and squeakings, it must be admitted that we know next to nothing. The sound may originate at two or even three levels, in the laryngeal passage and in the nasal passages. The formation of sounds may be attributed especially to the epiglottis comprised of two tonguelike strips surrounded by a powerful sphincter. At the upper level, in the nasal passages, there are "nasal valves" also controlled by a large muscle. These valves are able to close off the nasal passage, and they may be responsible for originating sound by partially closing the passage, or by some controlled modification of it, so that a stream of air passes through and begins to vibrate.

The secret of this phenomenon lies between the laryngeal cavity and the blowhole. What is known for certain is that the dolphin has two separate means of making sound, for he can produce, simultaneously, clicks and sounds through his blowhole.

What is the meaning of these sounds, which we call communications signals or relational signals? Do dolphins really "speak" to one another? Do they have a language? These, obviously, are the questions that everyone is asking. And the answers given to them are far from positive.

Vocabulary

Before we can determine whether or not the dolphin's sounds mean anything, it would be helpful to distinguish them and enumerate them. Obviously, it has not been possible, up to the present, to do so with "wild" dolphins. In our aquariums and marinelands, however, where one can record and study such sounds over a period of years, it is believed that a wide range of sonic signals has been detected. Researchers have tried to analyze and assort these sounds, and they distinguish some two thousand different whistles. On that basis, one might conclude that the language of the dolphins is composed of two thousand sounds — or we might say two thousand "words." It is said that Racine wrote his tragedies with a smaller vocabulary than that. In any event, the active vocabulary of the dolphin would be somewhat greater than that of many humans.

Unfortunately for our understanding of dolphins, these signals are not always the same, even among individuals of the same species. Indeed, some

(Right) With the greatest of care, we attached a radio transmitter to the dolphin's dorsal fin.

(Facing page) Then, the dolphin was turned loose in the sea.

of them seem to mean nothing at all, and those which have a precise meaning are quite few. It seems that certain series recur insistently, but we are unable to affirm that identical signals correspond to identical situations. Animals living in captivity in aquarium tanks have a much smaller vocabulary than was originally believed. And, so far as the "cries and grindings" that dolphins have been taught to make in the air, it is likely that they have no meaning at all for the dolphins.

David and Melba Caldwell have asserted that each individual dolphin has its own signal, a personal sound, which may be perceptible and even intelligible, but which is nonetheless untranslatable and untransmittable.

So far as the dolphin's famous "distress signal" is concerned, it is difficult to identify it with certainty, since it is not always the same in every case. John C. Lilly has recorded and transcribed this signal in the form of an inverted "V"; and Professor Busnel and Dziedzic have done the same in the form of an upright "V."

Of course, it may be that, if the distress signal differs from case to case, it is because it does not always have the same meaning. A harpooned dolphin, for example, may want to communicate any number of things: "Help!" or "Escape!" or "I am in pain" or "Wait for me" — at least, if we are willing to admit that these translations from man's language may correspond to the reality of an animal's behavior.

It is possible that dolphins living in their natural environment may be capable of expressing many things which elude us. As Professor Busnel has

pointed out, "Given our present knowledge of dolphins, we must admit that we know nothing of the semantics of the sounds made by dolphins."

Even so, it seems impossible to deny that dolphins make use of communications signals. They appear to be capable even of describing complex situations, of recounting what they have seen, to other dolphins. Reliable witnesses report cases in which individual dolphins are sent ahead by a school to reconnoiter a passage or to scout for danger. It would therefore seem that there must be communication of some sort — communication which, like communication among bees, implies an elaborate range of expression.

An Unsuccessful Experiment

Professor J. Bastian, of the Scripps Institution, designed an experiment intended to demonstrate that dolphins are able to exchange information — even complex information — among themselves. He placed two dolphins in a tank: a male and a female who had known one another over a long period of time. The tank was then divided into two parts by means of a net. A light signal was installed on each side of the tank. When the signal was given, each dolphin was supposed to press on a right pedal or a left pedal according to whether the light blinked or shone continuously. When a point was reached at which the dolphins' response was 97 per cent satisfactory, the light signal on the male dolphin's side of the tank was disconnected. Yet, the male continued to respond satisfactorily by means of information provided by the female.

The two animals seemed to exchange numerous acoustical signals while in the tank, and these signals were picked up by the experimenters by means of hydrophones and then recorded on tape.

In order to ascertain whether the information passed from the female to the male was indeed communicated through these signals, Professor Bastian separated the dolphins by soundproof neoprene panels. The male's responses were then satisfactory only in 54 per cent of the cases. But as soon as an opening was made in the panels, the male's performance leaped to 86 per cent satisfactory.

Thus, it was demonstrated that dolphins are able to communicate, and that one animal can explain to the other what must be done in a particular instance.

So far so good. Yet, we must remember that, when dealing with dolphins, very little, if anything, is what it appears to be. Professor Bastian's experiment was repeated — and failed. Bastian himself no longer believes in the validity of the experiment. He now believes that some unintentional exterior signal indicated to the dolphin what he was supposed to do. And that stimulus, of course, has negated all the data of the experiment.

It is true, nonetheless, that a captive dolphin communicates to a newly arrived dolphin everything that the latter must know to live in the tank, and everything that he must expect or tolerate from his human captors. Aboard *Calypso*, we have had ample opportunity to observe this phenomenon in our floating tank.

This does not necessarily presuppose an "exchange of thoughts" between two animals. The behavior of a new dolphin in an unfamiliar situation may be explained by imitation — a process readily observed, in a highly developed form, among chimpanzees. In this instance, one dolphin would swim slowly around her tank, showing its boundaries to another dolphin who had just been placed into the tank. The latter would follow the first dolphin closely. Rather than an exchange of thoughts, therefore, there would be an exercise in social help.

Dialogue

Killer whales have an acoustical system at least as well developed as that of dolphins. T. C. Poulter, an eminent specialist, has provided us with an account of conversation between a captured specimen and a group of killer whales which remained at liberty.

In 1966, Edward I. Griffin, Director of the Seattle Aquarium, purchased a twenty-three-foot killer whale, weighing four tons, from two Canadian fishermen for the sum of $8,000.‡

The animal was located at the mouth of the Bella Coola River, near the village of Namu. In order to get him to Seattle, it was necessary to manufacture a gigantic net supported by forty-one empty oil barrels. The whale, enclosed in the net, was then towed from the mouth of the Bella Coola to Seattle. Throughout its two-week journey southward in the Pacific, this bizarre convoy was escorted by a school of killer whales. A male and two females — perhaps the family unit of the captured specimen — exchanged whistles and cries with the captive in what can only be described as a dialogue. But what kind of dialogue? We have no way of knowing. What did they say? Were the sounds calls, or complaints, or expressions of emotion? Were they sounds of encouragement and advice? In any event, the captive killer whale, though responsive and obviously sensitive to these whistles, never once attempted to escape from the net. The only indication of his nervous state consisted in movements of his dorsal fin.

Calls in the Night

During our expedition in the Mediterranean, we attempted to learn at least whether a captive animal could carry on a conversation with the school to which he belonged. We therefore captured a female dolphin and placed her in the floating tank. *Calypso* then moved away, leaving the dolphin alone in the tank. We remained at a distance of six and a half kilometers (about four miles) from the dolphin, but we were in constant contact with the tank by radar and radio.

In the middle of the night, the isolated dolphin began to make sounds. These were not ultrasonic noises. They were perfectly audible to us; and Albin Dziedzic and other experts in animal acoustics described their reception as perfect.

We were surprised by the persistence of the sounds made by our captive dolphin. And we thought that we sensed in her "voice" a certain note of emotion, of pathetic appeal. Her cries intensified and resembled those of a wounded animal. Was it a distress signal?

‡See *The Whale: Mighty Monarch of the Sea*, by Jacques-Yves Cousteau and Philippe Diolé. Doubleday & Co., Inc., New York, and Cassell, London, 1972.

Two captured dolphins swim side by side in the floating pool.

(Right) Experiments in the pool are filmed by *Calypso*'s cameramen.

The female's cries were of such a wide range that our tapes of them represent truly an embarrassment of riches. Every indication is that the dolphin was calling in the night to the school from which she had been separated. If so, her efforts were not in vain. The school came, and other cries resounded in the dark water. But, as we have often observed on such occasions, as soon as the school understood that there was nothing it could do for its captured member, it fell silent and swam away.

A Non-Language

It should be kept in mind that the school of dolphins, even though it did nothing, nonetheless came to see what had happened. Therefore, there must have been a moment during which information was exchanged between the dolphin in her tank and the dolphins in the open water. But does this exchange imply the existence of a language, in the sense in which linguists accept that term?

"No," says Professor Busnel. The dolphin's sounds were merely relational acoustical signals. They were indeed signals, but not language. They were composed of elements which cannot be broken down; and those elements cannot be assembled according to the rules proper to language, that is, into combinations forming words and phrases. For language does not consist essentially in signals, however numerous, but in the ability to put these sym-

bols together according to a system which engenders a more or less unlimited number of combinations. This is what is known as "syntax." But when two dolphins communicate, they make use of a single signal, or of successive unrelated signals. This is what specialists call a "pseudolanguage," or a "protolanguage," or a "zero-syntax language."

It is not impossible that, someday, dolphins may arrive at a true language. For the present, however, we have no proof either that dolphins speak, or that they are capable of speaking.

Moreover, language is expressive of abstract notions: the past, the present, and the future. This is what characterizes human language and also what makes it possible to extend the human vocabulary to the infinite. We have no experimental proof, at the present time, that free dolphins are capable of devising a vocabulary, or that they are able to increase their capacity for expression.

Finally, language depends in large measure upon culture, life styles, and environment. It is possible that dolphins, living at close quarters with humans, may come to acquire some sort of language. Language can be learned over a long period of time. A human infant normally does not begin to speak before the age of two or two and a half years. What is required is an intimate common life with the mother and the affectionate monologue concomitant with that life. (This, in effect, was what occurred with Jean Asbury and Dolly.) We know, for example, that children left to themselves — "wolf children," as they are called — do not speak and cannot learn to speak once they pass a certain age.

The American researcher J. C. Lilly claimed to have taught English to dolphins — a claim which was strongly contested and criticized in scientific circles, notably by a Soviet scientist, L. G. Voronine. Lilly asserted that the Bottlenosed Dolphin was capable of imitating the human voice and of learning words which designated objects. Since that time, many experiments in American laboratories have shown that dolphins are capable — as Lilly claimed — of producing aerial sounds which some authorities have assimilated to imitations of the human voice in a different acoustical register. And Dr. Lilly was probably quite right in thinking that he heard, on a tape, the sound of a dolphin imitating the laugh of Lilly's secretary. However, no one has observed a similar phenomenon since that time.

Because dolphins have no vocal chords, however, the sounds that they make resemble whistles more than words, and one must have much patience to be able to recognize a word like "ball" or "hat" in the sound emanating from the blowhole of a dolphin.

There is nothing particularly astonishing in the fact that a trained dolphin is able to "fetch" a hat, a ball, or a ring floating in its tank when the name of the object is spoken. This may merely be the result of training, of voice obedience — as it is in trained dogs. The animal would learn the sonic signals which are first of all the symbols of objects and then the symbols of actions. It has been experimentally demonstrated that, in practice, the dolphin relies more upon the trainer's gestures than upon his words.

This limited success does not necessarily imply that there is a possibility of a "dialogue" between man and animal. The actual communications among dolphins, or between men and dolphins, are programmed and limited, whereas language in its proper sense is a non-determined operation — that is, an open operation in the course of which the speaker is free to combine, in an unpredictable order, the signals at his disposal.

The crux of the problem is to determine whether or not dolphins will be able to "combine" in this way one day. We know that a chimpanzee has only recently succeeded in doing so. The young animal, raised by a human family, is able to express abstractions: the past and the short-term future. He invents gestural signs.* He is able to associate sounds in a logical manner in order to communicate a simple, but new, idea. He combines signals so as to arrive at an expression more complex than the one that he has been taught. He *creates*. This particular chimpanzee, therefore, has a language. It is, of course, an individual language and one which is operative only between the chimpanzee and the human who created the language.

Primates apparently have outdistanced dolphins on the road leading to human mental activity. There is no reason to believe that the dolphin may not catch up to the chimpanzee. Experiments with primates have been going on for much longer, and are much more advanced, than those with marine mammals. We are in an era of new knowledge with respect to the brains of primates.

Dr. Dreher, in California, has taken a different tack from that adopted by Dr. Lilly. Instead of trying to teach dolphins to speak English, he has tried to learn "dolphinese." He isolated several whistle signals, which he then reproduced in an aquarium. These signals seem to have a definite meaning. However, it has not been possible to draw any positive conclusions from this experiment.

The whistles made by dolphins are modulations in frequency. There are

---

*At the University of Oklahoma, Professor Allen Gardner and his wife have taught the deaf-mute sign language to three monkeys. The animals are able to put together simple sentences by combining nouns and verbs. Professor Rumbaugh has taught a monkey to operate a computer keyboard, and the monkey is able to put together sentences in Yerkish — a language of geometric designs. In a similar experiment, Professor Premack and his wife, using colored blocks, have succeeded to teaching a monkey an optic language.

whistled languages among human beings which make use of the same kind of modulations. Professor Busnel has made a study of whistled languages still in use in various parts of the world: at Kuskoy, in Turkey; in France's Ossau valley, at Aas; and above all on La Gomera,† one of the Canary Islands; and in Mexico. Whistled languages are used in areas where the human voice is lost in the wind, or where it does not carry because of topological barriers. At La Gomera, for example, the cliffs are so steep that the natives invented a whistled language as a means of communicating so as to avoid having to climb up and down the cliffs or walk around them. Whistlers on Gomera "speak" at distances of up to six miles. The record, it seems, is eight miles.

There is a remarkable analogy between the "sonagrams"‡ of the whistled languages and those of the underwater whistles of dolphins. The dolphins' sounds represent the same kinds of modulation, though their modalities are much more limited and are produced at a much higher frequency.

An analogy between physical structures therefore allows one to hypothesize that the whistling sounds produced by dolphins could, in theory, be used as the phonetic elements of a true language.

To the extent that the dolphin's sound-modulations are variable (modulations which, unfortunately, have not yet all been recorded), one is justified in thinking that they constitute a system of acoustical communication analogous to that found among many other animal species. Nonetheless, even if we concede the existence of a certain vocabulary — the extent of which is unknown — we still lack a vital element in deciphering that vocabulary. As Professor Busnel says, "We have no Rosetta Stone to give us the key to the dolphin's whistles." That is, even if we assume that each whistle has a particular meaning, we have no way, at present, of knowing what that meaning is.

It is known that whistled human communication may be, and is in fact, a prop for language. On La Gomera, a whistler — a *silbador* — can express formulas like the following: "Don't forget to buy a loaf of bread on your way home tonight," or, "Take the sheep to the meadow up there." Such a language, obviously, functions as well as one which makes use of words.

The point, as made by Busnel in Washington, is that if we are going to teach a language to a captive dolphin, it would be better to use a whistled language than a vocalized, articulated language. A whistled language is one

†Many other whistled languages are used around the world: in Oubangui and in the Island of Fernando Poo, in the Gulf of Guinea, where the "Bubis" use a very elaborate language by blowing in whistles.

‡The graphic transcription of frequency, time and intensity, by means of special devices, of sounds produced.

On the island of La Gomera, Jacques Renoir films the natives who make use of a whistled language.

which a dolphin would find it easier to perceive, analyze, and repeat.

It may seem an idle dream to think of communication between dolphins and human whistlers; but it may also be the beginning of a communication between the two species. For whistled languages represent a "language skeleton" which is adequate to express what one wishes to say. This mode of expression may be the vehicle of human communication with dolphins — so long as dolphins have something to say. And that is the real problem.

It is necessary, nonetheless, to translate our vocalized language into a whistled laboratory language as a means of starting the linguistic apprenticeship of dolphins. In this way, we would be able to teach them signals which would not necessitate the use of organs (vocal chords) which dolphins do not possess, and which would be contained within the dolphin's own acoustical register.

W. Batteau, an American acoustician, became interested in this idea and, with Professor Busnel's approval, built an electronic device capable of converting the sound of the human voice into a whistled voice. This machine was used in an experiment with two dolphins in Hawaii. After several months of work, it was shown conclusively that the dolphins were capable of assimilating this whistled language. It was demonstrated that they were able to learn, to memorize, and to repeat twenty-six different messages. However, the dolphins had not reached the point where they were able to associate the sonic signal with the object which it signified. At that point there was a tragedy. Dr. Batteau was drowned off Hawaii, and the experiment was abandoned.

After having placed much hope in the possibility of a dialogue with dolphins, we must recognize today that our projected dialogue was perhaps a dialogue of the deaf, or at least an illusion. At the moment, research has paused so that we may take stock of where we are. It has occurred to us that, before being able to "talk" to dolphins, it might be better to get to know dolphins better and, above all, more objectively. This, no doubt, will be the work of several years.

It is our own firm opinion that present studies of the intelligence and the sounds of dolphins are violated by the conditions in which they are carried out. Captivity represents a dramatic handicap. The shock experienced by these sensitive animals, at the trauma of capture, disturbs them profoundly. In captivity, they are given shots of antibiotics, stuffed with vitamins, and fed protein compounds. These dolphins — who are usually adults — are wholly without preparation for this kind of treatment.

Moreover, the species most often used for study is the *Tursiops truncatus*, or Bottlenosed Dolphin, because the Bottlenosed is more robust and more docile in captivity. But he is not necessarily the most intelligent of the dolphins. The ability to learn, to imitate, and to obey, which the Bottlenosed possesses in a marked degree, is surely not a definitive indication of intelligence. Indeed, this ability may complicate research rather than facilitate it.

The fundamental problem of captivity is one of space and freedom. One can only imagine the suffering of an animal enclosed, even for a short time, in a container where there is barely space for its body. It is true that captured dolphins are placed into larger tanks as soon as they arrive at the aquarium or marineland to which they are destined. But it is equally true that, in these tanks, the slightest sound the dolphin makes is echoed from the tank's walls. The animal therefore moves in water filled with incomprehensible echoes. Yet, we know that sound plays a primordial role in the life of a dolphin. We can only conclude that a dolphin in such an environment must exist in a state of total disorientation.

In our marinelands, dolphins find companions in captivity. They do tricks. They participate in shows. They have fans. But the behavior patterns which they develop in these conditions have very little to do with those which obtain when a dolphin lives at liberty in the sea.

We have succeeded in creating a personality common to captive dolphins. And it is that personality that is being studied, without taking into sufficient account that we are dealing with animals that have been spoiled and perverted by man.

It may be said that we have studied dolphins in captivity only because there was no way for us to study them in the sea. Yet, it has always been our intention, aboard *Calypso*, to do precisely that: to study marine life in its natural environment. We learned, at the very beginning of our efforts, that it was extemely difficult, but not impossible. We have succeeded on two separate occasions. Given the time and the means, this approach should at least be tried. It would certainly provide us with some unexpected information on the social life and behavior of dolphins.

The method we used during our expedition in the Mediterranean represents a compromise. It certainly is by no means an ideal solution, but it may offer the advantage of a rather good opportunity for observation.

Dolphins captured very quickly and painlessly were not made to undergo the ordeal of imprisonment in a concrete tank. Our floating tank probably reduced to a minimum the stress which is so harmful to dolphins. Our three inflated air bags supported a net which was almost forty feet deep. This space was sufficiently large for a dolphin to feel practically free. They were in their proper *milieu*, that is, in the sea. The net, with its widely spaced knots, allowed them to see the water around them, to see other dolphins, and to hear them. They were not isolated, as they would have been in an unfamiliar environment.

It is true that the dolphins were obviously somewhat alarmed at their capture. But they did not have the opportunity to adapt to captivity, or to be deformed by it, for we never kept a dolphin in the tank for more than two or three days. Often, they were detained for much shorter periods than that. Some of them were set free on the same day they were captured, or during the night, after one experiment.

We always hoped that the group remained in the area, for we had an idea of how desperate the "prisoner" could feel if its calls were not heard. We already knew that dolphins were social beings. They are extremely attached to one another. But we had particularly striking proof of the attachment, in the vicinity of Málaga and Gibraltar, during our Mediterranean expedition. It is difficult to imagine the degree of comfort that one dolphin is able to give another in captivity. As soon as two dolphins were alone in their tank, their behavior underwent a transformation. They swam side by side. They rubbed against one another. And none of these manifestations seemed to have sexual characteristics. One might say that dolphins have an intense need for affec-

Dolphins have no sense of smell and no "scent." In order to recognize one another, they must touch — as this male and this female are doing.

tion. Their emotional lives are highly developed.

Perhaps the best procedure would be to capture two dolphins simultaneously, both from the same school, so that the bond of affection between them would already have been formed in the sea rather than in a tank. The two dolphins would not necessarily have to be a couple. The emotional bond between individuals of the same sex seems stonger and more durable than that between male and female. We have observed that males in the sea do not swim with the females. The two sexes associate only during the mating season. Then, as soon as mating has taken place, they lose interest in one another. It is possible that we will find dolphins are more amenable to friendship than to love. . . .

Chapter Eight

THOUGHT IN THE SEA

It was morning. Aboard *Calypso*, everyone was absorbed in his work. The mechanics were disassembling an outboard motor under their green canvas shelter on the aft deck. The cameramen were working on their underwater camera. On the bridge, Jean-Paul Bassaget and Chauvin were bent over their charts, and, behind them, the radioman was performing the mysterious rites of his office. A typical workday.

The sea was like a pond under a sky ablaze with sunlight.

Then there was a shout: "The dolphins!"

It came from François Dorado, who was repairing the Zodiac on the aft deck. The fact that he shouted "The dolphins!" rather than a simple "Dolphins!" is significant. To us, these mammals are indeed *the* dolphins, and an encounter with them is a happy event, an event which involves its own rites and requires an immediate series of interventions on our part.

Instantly, everyone aboard *Calypso* swung into action. Prezelin, Bonnici, and Delemotte rushed to the prow, from which vantage point they could observe the dolphins more closely. Delcoutere raised the hatch leading to the observation chamber and disappeared down the stairwell so that he could watch the dolphins beneath the surface. On the bridge, Bassaget and Chau-

vin were watching them through binoculars. It was a large school — large enough, certainly, to make it worth our while to investigate. Bassaget ordered the engines cut, and *Calypso* now moved noiselessly through the water on her own momentum.

All around us there were dolphins, their dorsal fins plainly visible above the silken surface of the sea. One of them leaped from the water, and, for a moment, the graceful arch of its light gray body flashed in the sunlight. In the blue immensity of sea and sky, the point at which *Calypso* had come to a halt seemed a privileged space, a tiny enclave reserved for the meeting of dolphins and men.

I have often wondered why these encounters with dolphins have always taken on a festive appearance among us; why everyone aboard *Calypso* is suddenly so joyful and enthusiastic. It is certainly not because we are unaccustomed to contact with marine animals. We have dived with them for the past quarter century. We have played with groupers in the Red Sea, with octopuses at Seattle, with humpback whales at Bermuda. . .

The divers would say: "It's not the same thing at all. Groupers are ugly, and octopuses are alien. Whales are too big. But dolphins are beautiful, and they're just the right size — hardly bigger than humans, and much more agile."

All that is true. But I know that there is more to it than that. When we meet dolphins, it is like meeting friends, or relatives. We feel that they are beings with whom we share the secrets of the sea. *Calypso*'s divers are proud of their intimacy with the sea, and dolphins are living symbols of the unusual life that they lead. No, they are more than symbols: they are witnesses.

A Long Experience

Perhaps it will not be taken amiss if we say, in all modesty, that we know more about the behavior of free dolphins than anyone else. Other observers have confined their observations to dolphins in marinelands, aquariums, and laboratories. But, for the past twenty-five years, *Calypso's* team has encountered, followed, and observed dolphins in the sea — something that has been possible to no other team. Our advantage has been, obviously, that we have observed dolphins in their natural environment. That is, in the open sea. No aquarium, no tank in a marineland, however spacious it may be, can begin to

(Left) Even though we never keep dolphins for more than a short while in our floating pool, they quickly become accustomed to the presence of our divers.

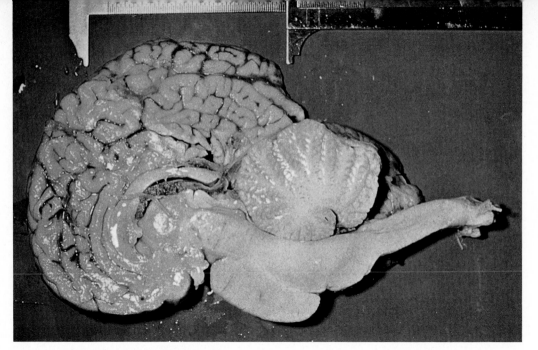

The brain of a dolphin. (Photo, Naval Undersea Center.)

duplicate the conditions of the sea. And no dolphin who inhabits one of those aquariums or one of those marinelands can be described as a "normal" dolphin. Therefore, the conclusions drawn by observing the behavior of such dolphins are often misleading when applied to dolphins as a whole.

Having said that, let us add immediately that twenty-five years of observing dolphins has not begun to reveal the secrets of these marine mammals. It is hardly likely that even another quarter century would suffice. Yet, we have learned enough to know for certain that the direct observation of animals living at liberty in the sea has a much greater value than the experiments and research undertaken with captive animals as subjects.

If there is one conclusion we can draw from our twenty-five years of experience, it is this: So far as the dolphin is concerned, the essential questions asked have been asked in the wrong terms. The result has been mass confusion, with the scientists on one side, demanding proof, and an enthusiastic public on the other side, weaving fables and anthropomorphism into a saga of science fiction.

It is our opinion, in fact, that all the efforts made to judge the behavior of the dolphin, and to measure his "intelligence" or to understand it, are exercises in futility.

In order to speak of intelligence, one must know what intelligence is. Intelligence depends upon the physiological and sensory equipment of a given species. If we base ourselves purely upon anatomy in this respect, we can say that the dolphin comes right after man on the scale of evolution. Indeed, the brain of the dolphin weighs more than that of a human — 1,700 grams for the dolphin, and about 1,450 grams for man. Only one human brain is known which weighed more than that of the average dolphin: that of Georges Cuvier, the French zoologist and palaeontologist, which weighed 1,800 grams. The size of the dolphin's body relative to that of its brain is only very slightly more than that of man.

The size of the Bottlenosed Dolphin's brain at birth is comparable to that of a human infant at birth. But the rate of growth of the dolphin's brain is considerably faster than that of the human brain.

What is most striking is the extraordinary exterior resemblance of the dolphin's brain to our own. There is a major development of the cerebellum and of the cerebral surface, a considerable size of the cerebral hemispheres, and a high cellular density. It is an extremely structured brain; and it is likely that, in comparison to other species of animal, the dolphin has at least the mental capacity of the chimpanzee — if not more.

With respect to the brain and the cerebellum — that is, the co-ordination of movements and the nerve center of the intellect — the relationship between the two is slightly better in the dolphin than in man. There are certain anatomical differences in the cortical structures of dolphins and man. For instance, the thickness of the cortex is not the same, the cortex of the dolphin being thinner than in the analogous areas of other large brains. Human intelligence depends primarily upon the cortex. The area of the cortex which has to do with sound is much larger among dolphins than among humans, while that having to do with sight is smaller. The olfactory lobe of the dolphin is atrophied.

But, as we shall see, though the dolphin may be lacking in certain sensory areas, his existing sensory equipment is capable of supplying abundant and precise information — information sometimes superior to that at man's disposal — which is necessary to life in the sea.

The physiological equipment of living beings does not absolutely or automatically imply a certain level of "intelligence." There is no direct correlation between the size and the structures of the brain.

Intelligence, in the sense that that term is generally accepted, is partly the product of a social and cultural environment. It is not merely a composite of our physiological possibilities. The intellectual potential of our brain can be activated only by a certain number of factors — the accumulation of knowledge by the communication of information, by means of one's life style, and so forth. Otherwise, it remains untapped.

The Four Conditions

Therefore, when we try to measure the "intelligence" of a monkey, or a

Jacques Renoir, in the Zodiac, films dolphins swimming around *Calypso*'s stem.

dog, or a dolphin, by basing our determinations on the weight of the animal's brain or on its neurological equipment, we are creating a problem which does not exist in reality. It may, in certain cases, be permissible to compare animals among themselves; but animals cannot be compared to man or measured by his standards. For man is the only being who preserves the four prerequisites necessary for the elaboration of a civilized society: the brain, the hand, language, and longevity.

Dolphins fulfill three of these conditions. Their brain is almost the equal of our own. And even though they may not have a language in the strictest sense of that term (although that remains to be proved), they are undoubtedly able to communicate among themselves. They live a sufficient number of years — at least twenty or thirty years, or as long as prehistoric man — to be able to acquire experience and knowledge. What they are lacking is the hand, which is the essential tool of civilization.

There are also other factors which come into play.

The offspring of humans are born helpless. They must be watched over and cared for over a period of years. That period is used by adults to educate the child and to initiate him into human language. Human children develop mentally over a span of years, and this development presupposes both the constant attention of the parents and an environment where virtually everyone speaks the same language, uses the same objects, and resolves most of the same problems by acquired formulas.

Infant dolphins, on the other hand, are already complete when they are born. Education can add little to what they are. Physiologically speaking,

A dolphin allows himself to be carried along by the wave from *Calypso*'s prow.

they are finished beings at birth.

Finally, dolphins do not live in the same element as man. Water is their home, and they cannot leave it without dying. This imposes a heavy burden on them, for it is water which turned the hand of their ancestor into a flipper.

The dolphin's struggle for survival in the sea has not had the same formative effect on him as man's struggle on land. "Cetaceans," says Alpers, "have lived in the sea, cut off from all contact with other mammals (except for man and sea lions) for sixty million years or more. During all that time, unlike monkeys, dogs, cats, elephants, and horses, they have not been compelled to share their environment with other intelligent or semi-intelligent animals. Their only companions, and their prey, have been fishes, who are their inferiors. We do not know what degree of intelligence they possessed when they first went into the water, or if that intelligence has increased or changed since the time when they changed their environment."

It is intriguing to speculate whether the potential which the dolphin possessed in one environment — on land — might not have been stunted in another environment. Is it possible that a mammal who was "off to a good start" on land has been spoiled by an easy, non-competitive life in the sea?

Sensory Equipment

The senses of the dolphin have developed unequally, and this is the reason why their relational lives are so different from our own. In certain respects, they are better endowed than we; and in others, they are inferior. Unlike ourselves, for example, and unlike most mammals, toothed whales are probably completely devoid of a sense of smell — a sense which plays such an important part in the lives of fishes.

So far as sight is concerned, dolpnins are superior to man and to fishes but approximately equal to other mammals. The fields of vision of the two eyes overlap considerably in a forward and downward direction, which makes possible the dolphin's stereoscopic vision. The eyes are extremely mobile and can turn upward, forward, downward, and even backward, along the dolphin's side. Even more remarkable, the dolphin's vision is as good in the open air as it is in the water. Trained dolphins can leap fifteen or eighteen feet into the air and seize a fish held in the mouth of their trainer. This trick presumes that the dolphin can go from subaquatic vision to aerial vision with exceptional rapidity and assurance. In fact, a captive dolphin's tricks in and out of the water, with balls and rings and fish, attest to his great visual acuity. Pilot whales and killer whales are capable of the same sort of performance and have the same exceptional vision. Man, on the other hand, is not well equipped to see in the water.

There are, however, blind dolphins: dolphins who live in fresh water, or in estuaries in India and in South America where the water is very cloudy, and whose eyes have atrophied. These dolphins depend on their echolocation system in order to locate and seize their prey.

The dolphin's acoustical equipment, as we have mentioned, is especially well developed. The dolphin's life is based upon constant acoustical exploration. He listens and watches constantly in the sea. Obviously, therefore, sight and hearing are the two senses which are most important to him. The auditory nerve (the eighth cranial nerve) is highly developed and is the largest of the cranial nerves. In the cortex, the auditory center is exceptionally large. And the dolphin's ear is modified for use in the water.

The sensory cells, which allow the dolphin to perceive the highest frequency sounds, are of large size, and each one has its own nerve fiber. (In man, several cells are in connection with one fiber.) The same nerves are equally developed in other animals, such as mice and bats, who depend largely on hearing.

According to Dr. Winthrop Kellogg, formerly Professor of Experimental Psychology at the University of Florida, the acoustical system of the dolphin "has undergone a remarkable adaptation in the course of geological time, and this marvelously sensitive organ is specially equipped to perceive vibrations in the water."

Experiments have shown that dolphins hear frequencies of 150 kilohertz, i.e., 150,000 vibrations per second. The limit of human hearing is 14 to 16 kilohertz, which corresponds to the sound of a strident whistle. The limit of monkeys is 33 kilohertz; that of cats, 50 kilohertz; and that of mice, 80 kilohertz. Only bats, at frequencies of 175 kilohertz, have keener hearing than dolphins.

Hearing undoubtedly plays a more important part than sight in the search for food, in the finding of directions, in the perception of depth, and in communication among dolphins. A blindfolded dolphin is able to skirt around a line stretched ten or twelve feet above the surface, simply by relying on his echolocation system.

The dolphin's sense of taste, which has been little studied, has not atrophied like his sense of smell. At the base of his tongue, the dolphin has numerous papillae containing taste buds similar to those found in man and in herbivorous animals. It is not known precisely what role taste plays in the sensory life of dolphins, but it is possible that the gustatory terminals which cover a part of their palate and tongue enable them to follow their schools and to detect the presence of certain fishes. As Bébert Falco has observed in our floating tank, dolphins open their mouths frequently. It may be for the purpose of obtaining certain information through their sense of taste.

A Marvelous Skin

No one who has ever touched the skin of a dolphin is likely to forget the silken, elastic, soft feel of it. The fact that the dolphin's skin is sensitive and delicate has a great influence on the animal's behavior, both because the dolphin is very cautious of any action that may damage its skin, and because, once a dolphin trusts a human, he enjoys being petted. All dolphin trainers and keepers are aware that the contact of the human hand, once a dolphin has come to permit such contact, is a decisive factor in training an animal.

In mating, or merely in their social lives, dolphins rub against one another, caress one another with their flippers, or even rub themselves against a brush in the tank or against the shell of a tortoise.

The dolphin's skin undoubtedly has much to do with the animal's "stunts" in the water, since it allows him to attain greater speed. The body is

(Following page) Although the dolphin was swimming at full speed, our Zodiac managed not to lose sight of him.

absolutely smooth. The ears are no more than minuscule holes. There is no scrotum. The dolphin's hydrodynamic lines, in other words, are perfect. Even at high speeds, their movement through the water causes little turbulence which would act as a brake. In the United States and in the U.S.S.R., studies have been undertaken to determine why the dolphin is able to move through the water with a minimum of resistance.

The skin's tegument and its fatty layer surely have something to do with this ability. Even more important are the longitudinal folds which are formed on the surface of the skin, while the dolphin is swimming. These folds help increase speed by eliminating turbulence. "These marvelous swimming machines," Professor Budker has remarked, "move as though by magic and are capable of producing ten times more power per pound of muscle than any other mammal." Indeed, experimentation with a Bottlenosed Dolphin has revealed that the power developed by a swimming dolphin was only about two horsepower. As early as 1936, Sir James Gray, of Cambridge University, pointed out the great disproportion between the power developed by the dolphin and the speed which was attained. Since then, this phenomenon has been known as "Gray's Paradox." Sir James observed that "the form given by Nature to the dolphin is more effective than that of any submarine or torpedo conceived by man."

Researchers have generally assumed that the secret of the dolphin's speed in the water has something to do with the animal's shape. In 1955, Max O. Kramer, a German engineer who was a refugee in the United States, asserted that it lay instead in a peculiarity of the dolphin's skin. He noted that the animal's exterior tegument, far from being impervious to the water, was permeable and that under it was a harder layer of interior fat about 1.5 mm. in thickness. This fatty layer covered a multitude of small vertical grooves filled with a spongelike substance which is absorbent in water and which can squeeze out four fifths of the water it absorbs. Kramer theorized that this "second skin," which is sensitive to pressure, was able constantly to absorb the oscillations which appear on the surface when a wave, or turbulence of any kind, is caused by water resistance.

Respiration

The respiratory rhythm of dolphins, and other toothed whales, varies according to the conditions in which the animals find themselves at any given time. It should be noted, however, that observations on this subject were made almost exclusively in laboratories.

When the dolphin is not disturbed, and is swimming in a normal manner near the surface, he breathes once or twice per minute. But when he is disturbed, excited, or frightened, the rhythm increases considerably and reaches a rate of five or six times per minute.

Before a deep dive, which may last seven minutes and probably longer, the dolphin hyperventilates his lungs by a series of deep, rapid breaths. This procedure increases the oxygen content of the lungs and facilitates the elimination of carbon dioxide.

Unlike man, a dolphin empties and then refills his lungs almost totally with each breath, even when swimming normally.

The depth to which dolphins can dive varies greatly according to species and even according to individuals who may be more or less trained. The Bottlenosed Dolphin normally swims at a depth of between 100 and 150 feet; but the celebrated Tuffy, who participated in Project Sealab, was accustomed to diving to a depth of 1,000 feet. And there is some evidence that dolphins descend to depths of perhaps 2,000 feet.

The tractability of dolphins has made it possible to use them in experiments which may contribute to an increased knowledge of the physiology of diving. One dolphin was trained to exhale the residual air in its lungs after his deep dives, while he was still under water. The air was exhaled into a funnel connected to a tank. It was therefore possible to study and analyze the composition of this air, which had been modified by deep diving.

To Sleep — Perchance to Dream

A dolphin cannot sleep for more than five or six minutes at a stretch without the threat of drowning. It appears that the animal, in its state of half-sleep, sinks slowly downward in the water, and then rises again without ever really losing consciousness. His breathing, unlike our own, is not automatic and unconscious. But, since dolphins are not subject to the effects of weight, it is likely that they need less sleep than humans do.

A sick or injured dolphin, if he is greatly weakened or loses consciousness, sinks and drowns. In such circumstances, dolphins help each other. An incapacitated dolphin is sometimes supported at the surface for hours, or even days, by one or two other dolphins.

When a school of dolphins begins to doze, it is quite likely that one or two individuals remain awake to act as guards. This is also the case among certain groups of land mammals.

I have witnessed the awakening of a school of sleeping dolphins off the coast of Africa. The school was spread over a fairly wide area, with the indi-

A Zodiac and one of our other small craft approach a school of dolphins.

vidual animals a good distance from each other. When *Calypso* drew near, one dolphin roused all the others by crying. The entire school was suddenly awake in the sea around us, and the water churned with their movements.

Mutual Assistance

The social sense of dolphins and their often remarkable behavior have sometimes given the impression that they help one another, and even that this mutual assistance is one of the laws of the school.

We have often witnessed scenes which attest to the social solidarity of which marine mammals are capable. Aboard *Calypso*, in the open sea, we have noticed that when a dolphin was injured, two or three other dolphins of the school approached to help him and support him. Meanwhile, the entire group came to a halt a short distance away, as though waiting to see what

Two free dolphins photographed while diving.

would happen. If, at the end of a certain time, the "relatives" or "friends" were not successful in getting the injured dolphin to rejoin the school, the school simply continued on its way. Those who had gone back to assist the unfortunate animal were obliged to swim after the school, for a dolphin cannot survive alone in the sea, away from others of his own kind.

If mutual assistance is a law among dolphins, it must be recognized that it is not an absolute law and that there are exceptions.

Here are two distinct instances, the first of the law and the second of the exception:

In 1962, during one of *Calypso*'s expeditions, with Busnel and Dziedzic, we tried to capture some pilot whales — animals particularly cautious and difficult to approach in the water. We were following them in the sea, trying to get near enough to use a light harpoon. Finally, we succeeded in placing the harpoon in one of the whales, but the Zodiac, in its haste to reach the animal, became entangled in the harpoon's line and was unable to move. The pilot whale then began to cry as loudly as he could. Almost immediately, two other whales arrived and positioned themselves one on each side of the wounded whale. They moved their bodies against his and, thus supported, the whale was able to free himself to swim away.

In 1965, Albin Dziedzic also tried, with a vessel of his own, to capture a pilot whale. He encountered a large school of them near Alicante and managed to harpoon a young male in the midst of the school. The whale dived immediately, but the harpoon line held firmly and the animal was unable to escape. He therefore began to cry very loudly. Although he was literally surrounded by innumerable pilot whales, not one of the other members of the school came to his aid. After a few minutes, several of the school dived, then returned to the surface, and the entire school swam away, leaving their wounded companion alone.

It should be obvious how dangerous it is to generalize about the behavior of toothed whales, and how that behavior can differ from instance to instance. It may be that the social hierarchy plays a role indicating the conduct of the group so that assistance is given to a leader, or to a female in danger, but not to immature young whales. This is obviously a hypothesis, since we are just beginning to learn about the social structures of pilot whales and about the impact of such structures on the lives of individuals in the school. We know only that such structures exist and that they are very likely of great importance.

Games

There is one activity of dolphins which, while not confined to them, never ceases to astonish us. I am referring to their games and to their love of play. Many other species of animal love to play — cats are a notable example — but dolphins, by the powers of observation they display and by the ingenuity they show, lead us to attribute to them a behavior not unlike our own. Perhaps it is because they show signs of a sense of humor while playing.

In the Florida Marineland, for example, a dolphin amused himself by making a surprise attack on some pelicans and pulling out their tail feathers, but without harming or biting the birds. And a female dolphin chose a sea tortoise as her toy, pushing it with her snout around the tank.

All trained dolphins seem to take pleasure in performing their stunts, but they also love to play among themselves. They sometimes spend hours throwing a fish, or a piece of cloth, or a ring.

One dolphin discovered that if he placed a feather near the water-outlet valve of his tank, the feather moved rapidly away, then stopped. He therefore repeatedly placed the feather in the proper place to watch it move away. Another dolphin saw what the first dolphin was doing and immediately took up the game.

We know that such behavior is not inspired by the boredom of captivity, and that it does not result from training, for dolphins also play when they are at liberty in the sea. They push any floating object before them — a piece of wood, or, like Opo, an empty bottle.

Dolphins also love to surf, and they allow themselves to be carried on the crests of waves, just as human surfers do. (In Florida, on at least one occasion, dolphins actually joined human surfers.) And, like humans, they wait for a particularly big wave.

This spontaneous behavior, which resembles playfulness and presupposes the existence of a well-developed spirit of invention, is sometimes considered as evidence of a highly evolved form of intelligence. And here, of course, we are once more face to face with a problem of our own creation.

Outside the Animal Kingdom

Much that has been written and said about dolphins tends to set them apart from other animals, to locate them somewhere outside the animal kingdom. The public looks on them as less than human, but as nonetheless in the process of becoming our equals.

Such an attitude has serious consequences with respect to our treatment of dolphins. In view of the intelligence of dolphins, we would have particular obligations to them. Beings so close to man would merit special consideration, particularly in the form of that respect due to brothers who are not our inferiors. To the physiological and psychological problems presented by dolphins, therefore, would be added a new problem, one of the moral order.

We should point out, first of all, that the reasoning in the above paragraph is specious. We have obligations not only to dolphins, but to all animals, and to all men. Man today is ready to believe in and to respect a moral animal, whether it is a horse, a dog, a cat, or a dolphin.

Physiologists, acousticians, biologists, and experts on cetacean life — all except Dr. Lilly — are of the opinion that dolphins are not essentially different from other mammals; that there is no natural difference between a dolphin and, say, a monkey or a dog.

This is an opinion which many people will find unsympathetic. We are inclined to attribute a kind of superiority to an animal whose brain weighs more than the human brain. At the same time, the social mores of the dolphins, comparable to those of man and of monkeys, seem to indicate the existence of a bond between us and them. It also inspires us with an affection and a curiosity which we do not feel for other animals. Indeed, it must be admitted that the relationship between man and dolphins is, above all, an emotional one.

The Affective Aspect

If our scientists can be blamed for any fault, it is that in their concern with objectivity, they have failed to give adequate consideration to those things which cannot be measured and analyzed. I mean, to the affection and devotion which dolphins seem to offer to man.*

The answer to that statement has been made already, and it will no doubt be repeated. "This aspect of sentimentality," say Professor Busnel and Albin Dziedzic, "was created by man out of his romantic illusions. Dolphins feel no more affection or emotion with respect to man than a dog does. Probably even less."

It would be possible to retort, or course, that the dog has been man's friend and companion for the past 60,000 or 100,000 years. The dog was created and formed by man. It is a product of human civilization. Whereas the dolphin, marooned in his aquatic world, isolated from us, was unable to experience a common life with man until very recently.†

It is only today, by reason of man's new curiosity about life in the sea, that we have taken an interest in the dolphin and have noticed that the dolphin has probably been interested in us for a long time. He mingles with swimmers, he rides children on his back, and he saves drowning humans.

Ten or twelve thousand years ago, dogs circled around neolithic campfires, seeking the company of man, warning him of the presence of wild animals, and trying to help him in the hunt. Today, the dolphin protects swim-

---

*Some of these emotional states are able to be measured. For species of so-called laboratory animals, there are tests which yield quantitative values. So far as the dolphins are concerned, however, since the number of subjects available for experiments is so limited, such problems have hardly begun to be studied.

†The exception may have occurred in the course of the Minoan civilization (2500 – 1300 B.C.), as we shall see in a subsequent chapter.

Two dolphins swimming side by side.

mers against sharks and helps fishermen find a catch of mullet. Who can tell what the dolphins will be to us in eight or ten thousand years? Will our remote descendants look back in wonder at the twentieth century, when dolphins were regarded as "mysterious" animals with strange ways and an even stranger "language"? Will our great-grandchildren perhaps wonder how we ever managed to survive in the sea without the aid of the dolphin?

Captain Cousteau and Professor Busnel in conference before *Calypso*'s closed-circuit television screen.

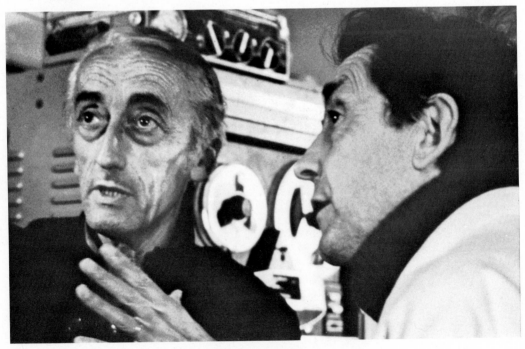

Chapter Nine

THE EDUCATION OF DOLPHINS

The docile nature of dolphins, and the fact that they have never bitten any-one, inclines many people to regard them as part of the human adventure and to make domestic animals of them. Thus, one or more species of cetaceans would become the marine equivalent of the horse or dog on land. For *Tursiops* is not the only marine mammal to have been revealed as a potential auxiliary of man. The pilot whale, as well as the killer whale, has also given evidence of qualities equal, if not superior, to those of *Tursiops.*

For over twenty years, toothed whales have been subjected to experimentation in numerous laboratories and in the thirty or so marine circuses. The first free dolphins to accomplish missions in the sea, assigned to them by man, were released in 1964.

It is clear that this vast effort has not yet allowed us to learn which of these animals is more suitable for collaboration with humans, any more than it has enabled us to reach a consensus on exactly what to expect of the marine mammals.

At the present time, the Bottlenosed Dolphin is highly favored for exhibition in the marinelands and aquariums of the United States. They are captured off the Florida coast and near the mouth of the Mississippi. The

preference for the Bottlenosed is based upon the ease with which they may be trained. However, other species, such as the Spotted Dolphin (*Stenella*), make equally good students. Since 1970, a number of American establishements, particularly on the West Coast, have killer whales living in capitivity, and these mammals have given evidence of exceptional qualities. Caldwell cites the case of a "false killer whale" who, having seen a performance by dolphins, performed the same tricks as the latter without benefit of having been taught them.

The fact is that it is still too early to be able to know which of the marine mammals is most suitable for collaboration with man. They have simply not been tested sufficiently as yet. We should remember that it required ten thousand years or so for the animal breeders of the prehistoric and historic periods to create the domestic animals we have today. These helpmates are the end product of a very long process of selective breeding and crossbreeding. We have not yet even begun this process with marine animals. It is a task which presupposes a knowledge of all the available forms of toothed whales, whereas, in the Delphinidae family alone, we are aware of the existence of some forty-eight species. And there are approximately ninety species of "small cetaceans," including Delphinidae.

The Capture

A number of Americans have learned to specialize in the capture of dolphins in the sea and even in training these animals before selling them to aquariums and marinelands. One of the best known of these entrepreneurs was the late A. V. Santini. Santini pursued a dolphin in a speedboat, threw a net over it, then dived into the water to complete the capture by hand. It is said that Santini was able to calm and immobilize a dolphin simply by placing his hands on him. It is worth noting, in this respect, that some marine mammals cease struggling as soon as they sense that there is no hope of escape.

One trainer at Key Largo, Florida, sold fifty dolphins in an eight-month period. The price of a trained dolphin depends on the kind of performance he is capable of giving, but even an untrained dolphin in 1970 was priced at $400.

It often happens in dolphin hunts that animals are injured. Moreover, no

(Left) The dolphin show at the Palos Verdes Marineland.

more than one or two of every five captured are actually kept. Those one or two are the dolphins who will consent to eat, or those who are young enough to be amenable to training. The others are turned loose in the sea in more or less good condition.

It is impossible to determine beforehand whether or not a particular dolphin will be able to adapt to captivity. Professor Busnel reports that, in his laboratory in Denmark, dolphins captured in the Baltic were literally eating out of his hand ten minutes after they were taken, while there were others who would accept no food at all.

The capture of dolphins for commercial purposes is now forbidden in the United States, and the law prohibiting such capture is enforced with great vigor. In France also, a decree was issued in November, 1970, at the request of professors Busnel and Budker, which reads: "Considering the contribution of Delphinidae to the ecological equilibrium of the seas and their value in the area of technical and scientific research, it is forbidden to destroy, pursue, or capture, by any means whatever, even without the intention of killing such animals, all marine mammals of the Delphinidae family [dolphins and porpoises]. These restrictions do not apply to operations undertaken solely for purposes of scientific research."

Captivity

The behavior of dolphins in captivity varies from one individual to another, as we have already mentioned, and cannot be foreseen. Such behavior probably depends on factors of which we are not yet aware. When a dolphin is being captured, it is impossible to know whether he is a young male who is dominant or dominated. We cannot determine his social status, or even his age. This is the basis of the varying behavioral patterns which seem so incomprehensible to us. The same holds true of primates, some of whom adapt to captivity while others never resign themselves to it.

Falco's experiences, in trying to feed dolphins at the beginning of their captivity, are common in all American aquariums. A keeper at the Florida Marineland, exasperated at his inability to feed a newly arrived dolphin, began to bombard the unhappy animal with fish and even to strike him with them. The dolphin opened its mouth and, inadvertently, swallowed one of the fish. Whereupon he began eating the others voluntarily.

There are now several foods commercially available for marine animals, just as there are for cats and dogs. These have a protein-compound base. Captive dolphins eventually lose the habit of eating live fish. Caldwell gives an account of a dolphin who was fed a live mullet. When the dolphin felt the fish squirm in his mouth, he was so overcome with terror that he dropped the fish and fled to the far end of the tank. The dolphin refused to eat for the next twenty-four hours. The Harbor Porpoises raised by Professor Busnel and his team were so accustomed to being fed by hand that they simply ignored the live fishes in their tank.

Animals like these, who wait for man to provide food for them and who give up hunting, are not very far from domestication.

Generally, the process of adapting to captivity takes place rapidly, within one or two weeks. It is unusual for a dolphin to try to escape, and he ordinarily becomes sufficiently accustomed to the presence of man that, at the end of several days, he will allow himself to be petted. Indeed, a captive dolphin often appears to seek out such contact.

Affection

It is extremely difficult to determine the exact nature of the bond between the animal and his trainer. Does a dolphin become attached to his master? Indeed, does a dolphin have a "master," in the sense that a dog has one?

All trainers maintain that they know their dolphins and that their dolphins know them. We do not really know whether training would be possible, at least from the standpoint of the trainer, unless there were an affective link between man and animal. Teachers all have their favorite pupils. Trainers likewise learn to know the most intelligent animal, the one who learns fastest and who occasionally shows signs of surprising intuition and imagination.

According to Professor Busnel, the affection of a dolphin for his trainer exists only in the imagination of the trainer. It is an illusion and a myth. Busnel has run a series of experiments demonstrating that a trained dolphin will obey his trainer even if the latter is dressed as a woman. He will also obey a woman — and he will even obey a piece of wood so long as the dolphin perceives the signal to which he has been conditioned. A Beluga whale, taught to kiss its trainer, kissed him even when the man was wearing a gas mask. The conclusion drawn by Professor Busnel is that there is not a great deal of difference between the animal's behavior toward his trainer or toward another person who takes the place of the trainer.

The same phenomenon may be observed among other species. Some animal trainers teach tricks to lions and then pass the animals on to a "lion tamer" — any lion tamer — who is able to make the lion repeat the tricks

At the Marineland of Antibes, the dolphins make prodigious leaps. (Photo, Jose Dupont, Marineland d'Antibes.)

before an audience. This does not mean that the lion has no affection or aversion for the trainer or for the tamer. It means simply that a lion, upon receiving a signal to which he has been accustomed, will perform the trick corresponding to that signal.

I am not altogether certain that Professor Busnel's experiments demonstrate that dolphins are incapable of recognizing their keeper, or that they do not feel a particular affection for him. Indeed, Caldwell points out that some dolphins work better with their first trainer than with any successors; and

One of the dolphins at Antibes is able to catch a child's ball. (Photo, Jose Dupont, Marineland d'Antibes.)

some will not work at all for anyone but the first trainer. This seems to indicate that dolphins do recognize the trainer, and even that they appreciate him.

Certainly, scientists are quite right in arguing for objectivity in dealing with dolphins. But, even if we refuse to admit that the dolphin is "an animal endowed with reason," we must recognize that the dolphin is not trained as other animals are, and that he succeeds better than others in performing difficult stunts.

It is useless to attempt to constrain a dolphin, and if we strike him or punish him, we run the risk of never being able to train him at all. On the other hand, the dolphin does willingly what we ask him to do. He does so simply for the pleasure of playing, or "to please us." It is not necessary even to reward a dolphin every time he obeys. However, it does happen occasionally that a dolphin will be distracted, or will refuse to perform as requested. In such cases, the dolphin may be ill, or afraid.

Every marineland has a champion dolphin capable of giving an exceptional performance. Some of these animals execute a triple somersault. One dolphin, named Pedro, who weighs eight hundred pounds, high jumps over a bar twenty feet above the water. Others specialize in playing with balls. There is a team of two Bottlenosed Dolphins who perform a series of simultaneous leaps. Their movements are perfectly synchronized and indicate a total mastery of their bodies both in the air and in the water, as well as the perfect coordination of born acrobats.

The most extraordinary trick, perhaps, is that of the dolphin who, upon his trainer's command, will climb out of the water and lie on the edge of his tank. This act is absolutely contrary to the dolphin's nature and can be explained only by the animal's desire to please his trainer.

Happiness and Unhappiness

There is a vexing question which is often asked: Are the captive animals that one sees performing in aquariums really unhappy?

There is no certain answer to that question. Surely, dolphins performing tricks in an aquarium are better situated than the animals condemned to inactivity in a zoo. We might even say that the presence of the public, the applause, the atmosphere of admiration — all these things are agreeable to dolphins. A few minutes before show time in the Miami Seaquarium, the dolphins can be seen swimming nervously at the bottom of their tank, like jittery actors before stepping onto the stage.

It sometimes happens that dolphins will go through their whole repertoire of tricks for their own amusement and without having been ordered to do so.

We should not be misled by such signs of spontaneity. Captivity is always a terrible ordeal for an animal. Yet, there is one argument to which we cannot close our minds: the dolphins, pilot whales, and killer whales used in marine zoos and in training centers never try to escape. (The same holds true for most land animals that have adapted to captivity.) There is a common anecdote told to illustrate this phenomenon — a story which, in my opinion, is more touching than it is convincing. It seems that while A. V. Santini was supervisor of the Porpoise School of Florida, the "school" and everything in it was demolished by Hurricane Betty. Tanks, boats, and nets were all washed out to sea, along with Mr. Santini's twelve captive dolphins. All twelve of the dolphins returned to the school. Some came the day after the storm; some, a week later; and others, a month later. The returnees watched the workers rebuilding the school and splashed and sprinkled them as though they were eager for the work to be completed on the new tanks so that they could return to their homes.

Deformation

The public often imagines that because dolphins in captivity seem so friendly, they are easy to study and make perfect subjects for experiments in behavior.

It is true that dolphins have been used in experiments of all kinds. It is also true that, living together in their tanks, in contact with the public, dolphins form habits and invent or imitate certain forms of conduct so as to please their trainer. Thus, new "cultures" are being formed; cultures which are more or less capable of being passed on; cultures which are peculiar to each marineland and which conform to its characteristics, its program, and its life style. In this respect, a group of captive dolphins is comparable to a human group.

Experiments performed in marine zoos may be interesting and instructive so long as we do not forget that the subjects used in these experiments have been conditioned and deformed, and that they bear little resemblance to dolphins living in freedom in the seas. It is especially important to bear this in mind when dealing with the psychological aspects of beings as complex as marine mammals. It is certain that the study of human psychology, if it were undertaken exclusively in prisons, would also lead to misinterpretations and absurd generalizations.

The dolphins that one sees in aquariums today are often representatives of the third generation of dolphins in captivity. These grandchildren of free dolphins have never seen the sea. And, among the surviving grandparents, it is understandable that the memory of liberty has faded somewhat. Some of these older dolphins have been in prison for fifteen years. It is hard to believe that, in that period, their behavior has not been modified drastically.

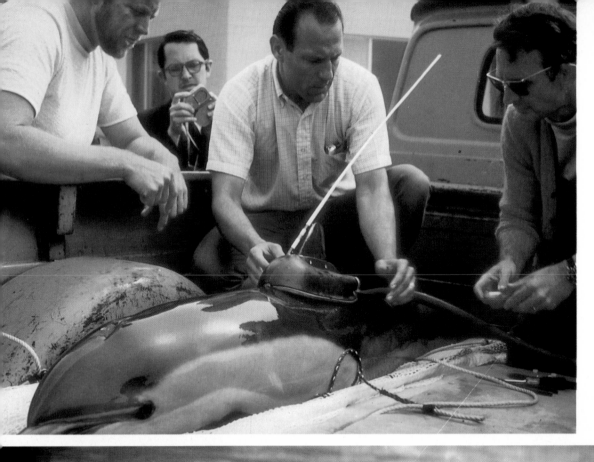

(Above) At the Marineland of Florida, a dolphin was photographed while giving birth. Notice that the baby dolphin emerges tailfirst. (Photo, Marineland of Florida.)

(Upper left) William E. Evans' team, at the Naval Undersea Center at San Diego, attaches a transmitter to a dolphin's dorsal fin. (Photo, Naval Undersea Center.)

(Lower left) A submerged dolphin equipped with a radio transmitter. (Photo, Naval Undersea Center.)

Regarding the life span of the dolphin, we have some fairly accurate data. The age of a dolphin can be determined by an examination of his teeth; and, on that basis, it appears that a dolphin lives for twenty to twenty-five years, and perhaps longer. (The pilot whale lives for twenty-six years — but senility sets in at the age of eighteen.)

It happens frequently that dolphins become ill. They seem especially prey to human disease caught from visitors. They are subject to epidemics of influenza and to hepatitis. When a dolphin is ill, he no longer eats or plays. Then, his temperature is taken, he is given injections, and sometimes he is even X-rayed.

Since breathing is a conscious function among dolphins, the use of anaesthesia has always proved fatal to them. Now, however, progress has been made in this area, and it has become possible to undertake surgical procedures.

Naval Training

The U. S. Navy has undertaken to train dolphins and other marine mammals, such as killer whales and sea lions. The dolphins used in these experiments were trained for use in studying the physiology of diving, as messengers and carriers of tools and as scouts assigned to detect and recover submerged objects. Caldwell affirms, however, that these dolphins were not used to carry explosives, or to attach explosives to the hulls of ships, as is generally believed.

The two main training centers for dolphins are the Naval Undersea Research and Development Center, at San Diego, and the Oceanographic Institute of Hawaii, at Honolulu. At the Mote Marine Laboratory, in Sarasota, Florida, Dr. Perry Gilbert is studying methods of training dolphins to combat sharks.

Training begins in a tank which can be opened to communicate with various enclosures. The dolphin is first taught to press a button which rings a bell, then to go down a passage after having received a signal. Next, he learns to carry a ball or ring to a swimmer or diver. All these things are designed to persuade the dolphin of the necessity of learning. Or, as the trainers say, the dolphin must be taught to learn.

Once a dolphin has been taught to learn, he is transferred outdoors to a complex of floating enclosures. It appears that this transfer necessitates a new education, for the transferred dolphin seems to have forgotten, at least for the first few days, everything he had learned up to that point.

In this new training area, the dolphin is taught to return to its trainer on command, since this is indispensable if a dolphin is to be regarded as dependable. This training is not very difficult. The greatest obstacle is to teach a dolphin to overcome its fear of swimming from one enclosure to another and, strangely enough, of swimming down the passage which leads into the open sea. Dolphins seem to feel not the slightest urge to escape. Sometimes they return to their tanks from the sea even before they are called.

The specific signals or commands for the numerous exercises must be as different as possible, so as to avoid confusing the animal. And each signal must correspond to a well-defined activity.

Next, the dolphin is trained to work with a boat. At first, the boat remains motionless on the water. Then it moves, and gradually it increases its speed. The dolphin becomes accustomed to leaping above the surface and to diving deeper and deeper. This phase of the dolphin's training occupies at least two weeks and takes place in the bay next to the Hawaii Research Center. Finally, the training area moves into the ocean and remains there for several weeks, some two hundred yards offshore.

Impressionable Recruits

Obviously, it is not nearly so easy to train a dolphin as might appear from the above paragraphs. The training process depends upon many factors,

The mother dolphin turns on her side to facilitate nursing. The mother's breasts are situated on either side of her genital orifice. (Photo, Marineland of Florida.)

Dolphins like to tease the sea turtles with which they share their tank (Photo, courtesy of Marineland of Florida.)

not the least of which is the character and the physical and psychological state of each animal. One finds the same types among marine mammals as among army recruits. Some are goldbricks, some are lazy, some are stubborn, and some — perhaps the minority — are "good soldiers."

One major factor in training dolphins is the impressionable nature of these animals. They are easily frightened and confused. A new situation, or an unfamiliar object, is sufficient to disturb their behavior patterns. Training must therefore progress by stages. Change should be as slight as possible so as to allow the dolphins to pass from one stage to another almost without being aware of it.

Despite all the precautions that one may choose to take, success is never certain in training dolphins. No matter how conscientious and experienced the trainers are, even dolphins who have completed their training are known to stage incidents. They may refuse to work, for example, or even to enter their enclosures. At that point, a new course of training must begin. It may also happen that dolphins training in the open sea are distracted by the fish swimming around them. That is natural and understandable, but it nonetheless upsets the training schedule.

Even in such cases, escapes are very rare. At **Point** Mugu, the first such training center established by the American Navy,* over a period of five years, which included 1,600 work sessions with dolphins and 600 sessions with sea lions, the center lost only one dolphin and one sea lion permanently. The other animals who escaped all allowed themselves to be recaptured or returned to the center on their own, sometimes after having been away for two weeks.†

The primary purpose of all these centers is to train dolphins who will eventually be turned loose in the sea to accomplish certain assignments. At the San Diego Center, there are several dolphins, as well as a killer whale and several sea lions, who live in the ocean near the center and respond to the calls of their keepers.

To achieve this result, it is necessary to be as familar as possible with the life style of marine animals living at liberty in the sea, regardless of the good will and the learning ability of the animals involved. Persuasion and affection are of much more importance than constraint. Training, in this instance, does not follow the usual pattern of alternating rewards and punishments. A dolphin usually obeys willingly and does whatever he is told to do, out of curiosity or out of playfulness. But any attempt to use force, or any kind of rough treatment, reduces the animal to helplessness or makes him ill.

A Dolphin Researcher

Dr. W. E. Evans, a biologist at the Naval Undersea Research Center, has specialized in the study of dolphins at liberty. In the pursuit of his specialty, Dr. Evans makes use of a catamaran designed as an observation craft by the center. Between the two hulls of the catamaran, there is a plastic underwater observation chamber from which two observers, with cameras, may follow the movements of the dolphins and sharks which, in the autumn, are especially numerous off the California coast. This device makes it possible to

*The Point Mugu center was closed in 1970 and its functions divided between the facilities at San Diego and in Hawaii.

†This information was provided through the courtesy of Mr. Blair Irvine, of the Naval Undersea Research and Development Center.

record the cries of dolphins in their natural environment and to gather data on the social conduct of dolphins in the sea, on their sexuality, on the compositions of schools of dolphins, and on the hierarchy which prevails in those schools.

Dr. Evans also makes use of other means of investigation. He was the first one to use a dolphin as a research agent among his own kind. But, instead of strapping a camera to the animal's back, as we did, he has attached a radio transmitter to a dolphin's dorsal fin. This transmitter sends out various data on the duration and depth of a dive, on the route followed, on "territory," on the relationship between the depth of a dive and the depth at which plankton are located, etc. The transmitter begins to operate as soon as the animal returns to the surface to breathe.

When using the transmitter, Dr. Evans avoids interference from boat engines and propellers by making use of a sailboat, the *Saluda*. Philippe Cousteau and Jacques Renoir were Dr. Evans' guests aboard the *Saluda* for a week while he conducted his experiments. It was proved once more that it was possible to attach recording devices to marine mammals and perhaps even to train them to play a part in gathering data on the life of dolphins in their natural environment. But it was also demonstrated that a dolphin carrying a radio transmitter is slowed in his movements — just as our camera-bearing dolphin was in the Mediterranean. Or even more so, since Evans' transmitter contained an antenna which seemed especially to hinder the dolphin's movements. Nonetheless, Dr. Evans was able to follow the movements of a dolphin for seventy-two hours, and it was possible for him to establish that the transmitter-bearing dolphin, despite the fact that his form had been modified, was accepted by his school.

By using a goniometer, Dr. Evans was able to locate the dolphin with the transmitter whenever it surfaced to breathe. But, hampered as the dolphin was by the radio, he tired rather quickly. The clamps by means of which the transmitter is attached to the dorsal fin loosens when the magnesium solder which holds them in place begins to dissolve in the water. It would seem that it would perhaps be better to study the possibility of using miniaturized devices.‡

‡We once attached an underwater camera to a gray whale named Gigi, and she seemed not at all inconvenienced by the camera's presence. However, the relation between the strength of the whale and the weight of the camera was quite different from that of Dr. Evans' dolphin and radio transmitter.

(Right) One of the Marineland's dolphins has dragged his ball down to the bottom of the tank. (Photo, Marineland of Florida.)

From his underwater observation sphere, Bill Evans observes the behavior of sharks and dolphins. (Photo, Naval Undersea Center.)

The information sought by Dr. Evans had to do with swimming speed of free dolphins and the number of times and the depths to which they dived. A special device was supposed to provide such data.

A dolphin swimming toward a distant destination moves at a speed of eight or nine knots. During this moderate effort, he dives but not very deeply, and he normally remains without breathing for five-minute periods. There are instances of dolphins remaining in a dive for fifteen minutes. It is known that they dive to a depth of three hundred feet and that they may attain a depth of one thousand feet. From our minisub, we have never seen dolphins at great depths.

Tuffy: Liaison Agent

Tuffy, a male Bottlenosed Dolphin weighing three hundred pounds and measuring over six feet in length, was trained at the U. S. Naval Center at

An assembly of sharks around Bill Evans' sphere. (Photo, Naval Undersea Center.)

Point Mugu, California. Subsequently, he was used by the Navy in two experiments in undersea living: Sealab II and Sealab III.

Tuffy's assignment was to act as liaison agent between the undersea houses and the surface. He carried messages back and forth, and, occasionally, tools. Dolphins have an enormous advantage over divers in this kind of work. Since they are not subject to decompression accidents, it is not necessary for them to observe the various stages of ascent. Tuffy would dive to a depth of more than three hundred feet, and then, upon command, he would shoot to the surface like an arrow.

Tuffy had another very important assignment, which was to guide lost divers back to the undersea house. Since the men occupying the house had nitrogen in large quantities in their blood, when they became lost on the bottom it was essential that they find their way back to the house without delay. They could not rise to the surface without making long stops for decompression, or without being placed in a decompression chamber. Therefore, each diver had been supplied with an electric bell for use in summoning Tuffy. The bell was audible to Tuffy at a distance of 1,500 feet. As soon as he heard it, he seized the end of a nylon line, which was wound on a spool and attached to the entrance to Sealab, and carried it to the diver.

Experiments conducted at Point Mugu have shown that dolphins are able to tow three times their own weight. A four-hundred-pound dolphin has no difficulty at all in towing a half-ton load.

One of the greatest problems in training a dolphin for a particular task is to find out at what point the conditioning to which the animal has been subjected makes it possible to rely on him. When can a dolphin be "turned loose"? What will he retain of his training when he is once more alone with the instinctive impulses which have guided his species for millions of years? One is certain of success only when a liberated animal returns to his home port after having accomplished his mission.

Training of this kind is unprecedented. Therefore, those who undertake it are obliged to rely upon their intuition and to improvise training methods.

It is a well-established fact that dolphins spontaneously come to the aid of man in the sea. We have already mentioned several anecdotes, some of them going as far back as the time of Pliny the Elder, which attest to this behavior.

During World War II, a dolphin pushed a raft, containing six American airmen shot down by the Japanese, to a small island.* The U. S. Air Force, perhaps encouraged by this example, has studied the possibility of supplying its pilots with a small transmitter which would reproduce the distress signal of dolphins. The purpose of this transmitter would be to summon dolphins to the rescue of airmen adrift in the sea. The problem, as we have already pointed out, is that the dolphin's distress signals vary greatly. And we have described the controversial nature of the problem of the dolphin's sonic signals.

One area in which the dolphin's reputation is well deserved is that of fighting sharks. Dolphins do battle with sharks and usually emerge victorious from such encounters. Their superiority lies in the fact that they attack as a group and are able to devise tactics, whereas the shark fights alone. Moreover, dolphins are able to charge an enemy with incredible force and ram into its most sensitive region (the ventral area) with their tough snouts. A stroke to

*Airmen Against the Sea, by George Llano.

(Right) A pilot whale, or blackfish, performs with the dolphins at the Marineland of Palos Verdes.

the shark's liver — which is the dolphin's customary tactic — is usually enough to put the shark out of commission. (The abdominal cavity of dolphins is very large, and their highly developed livers make them invulnerable to such attacks themselves.) It does not appear that, in these battles, the dolphin makes use of his teeth to bite his enemies.

Dolphins do not attack sharks on sight. In captivity, the two animals sometimes live peaceably together — as sharks and dolphins do in the Miami Seaquarium. Sometimes the shark will take the initiative and attack a young or ill dolphin. Then, the entire group of dolphins will unite to attack the predator. It is certain that there is no love lost between dolphins and sharks.

The hostility of dolphins toward sharks has been useful in training dolphins to protect swimmers against attack by sharks. In South Africa, Professor Taylor has taught two dolphins, Dimple and Haig, to chase away sharks from swimmers' beaches.

In Sarasota, Florida, Dr. Perry Gilbert is making a systematic study of the reciprocal behavior of dolphins and sharks. He places specimens of both species into a single tank and observes their reactions according to each species and according to the respective size of the animals. The encounter is filmed, and the sounds of the animals are recorded on tape. The experimenters are particularly interested in discovering whether the dolphin's acoustical signals have the effect of terrorizing the shark or keeping it at a distance.

The progressive training method consists first in placing the dolphin into a tank with a motionless, dead shark. Later, the dead shark is pulled through the tank on a line. And, finally, the dolphin is confronted by live sharks of different sizes.

Of the four dolphins subjected to this course of training, only one was recognized as a champion shark fighter, and he was released to stand guard before a Florida beach.

It has not yet been determined precisely what kind of assistance we can expect from dolphins in the sea; but it seems that, with a minimum of training, they are capable of assuming the role of protectors and guards.

The training program undertaken by S. Fitzgerald is not designed to teach dolphins to attack sharks on sight, but to train them for a more complex function: patrolling and giving the alarm when sharks are sighted. In so doing, dolphins would truly become man's helpers in the sea.

Chapter Ten

THE FISHERMAN'S FRIEND

Oppian, a Greek poet of the second century and the author of poems on fishing, states that dolphins were in the habit of pushing fishes into the nets of fishermen. But Pliny the Elder was even more explicit than Oppian. This Roman writer lived in Gaul, and around 70 A.D., he was procurator of the Province of Narbonne. He was a man of insatiable curiosity, and he was constantly assembling material for his *Natural History*, a massive work in thirty-seven books. There is a passage in Book IX which seems based on Pliny's own observations:

"There is, in the Province of Narbonne, in the territory of Nimes, a pond named Latera, where dolphins fish with humans. On a certain day, a boundless school of mullets leave the pond and head for the open sea through a narrow channel which connects the two bodies of water. This channel is too narrow to allow the use of nets; and no net would be strong enough to support the weight of such a mass of fish. These mullets know the time of the flood tide, and then they make straight for deep water, hastening through the only place where it would be possible to block their passage. As soon as the fishermen become aware of this movement, a great crowd of people assemble at that spot, eager to see whatever may be seen. Everyone calls out in a loud

voice: 'Simon!' [Apparently the popular name for dolphins at that time.] Then the dolphins come, arranged in ranks as for battle. They block the way into deep water and push the frantic mullets back toward the shallows where the fishermen encircle the fishes with their nets, which they hold by means of forked sticks. Nonetheless, the mullets try to jump over the nets, but they are caught by the dolphins who, for the moment, are content to kill them and to defer their meal until the victory has been won. When the battle is at its height, the dolphins take pleasure in allowing themselves to be encircled by the nets so as to press agains the mullets; and, so that this pursuit does not cause their enemies to flee, they slip softly among the boats and the nets and the swimmers so that there is no opening left for escape. And, although they leap in the water, none of the dolphins tries to escape from within the nets, except when the nets are lowered before them. When the fishing is over, the dolphins divide the mullets they have killed; but, as though conscious of having deserved more than the recompense for a single day, they wait until the following day, and they eat not only the fish, but also bread dipped in wine.

"That which Mucian relates concerning the same method of fishing in the Gulf of Iasos differs from the present instance in that here the dolphins come without being called to receive their share from the hands of the fishermen. Each boat takes one of the dolphins as a partner, even though this all takes place at night, by torchlight."

Since the period of Antiquity, Pliny's story has been regarded as a popular fable, and it has often been cited as an indication of the author's credulity. No doubt, Pliny was credulous to a point, but in the present instance, at least, he seems not to have been victimized by the imagination of the Gauls of the South. The name of the pond, Latera, is preserved in that of the village of Lattès, in the South of France; and the channel "too narrow to allow the use of nets" still exists at Palavas-les-flots, where the waters of the ponds of Méjean, Le Grec, and Pérols empty into the sea. There is no doubt, therefore, that Pliny was scrupulously accurate, at least so far as the setting of his story was concerned.

And how about the dolphins today? Fishermen in the area still cast their nets for mullets, but the dolphins no longer come to their assistance. Somewhere between the time of Pliny and our own, contact seems to have been lost with the friends of the fishermen.

Still, Pliny's story is not as improbable as it may sound. In Mauritania, a long distance from the South of France, and at a spot along the Atlantic,

(Left) Imragen fishermen on the beach at Nouamghar, in Mauritania.

fishermen still count on the help of dolphins, as they have for thousands of years, to catch mullets weighing from seven to nine pounds. Members of the Imragen tribe claim to have recourse to the help of the dolphins to push mullets into their nets as the mullets pass along the coast during their migrations.

Archaeological discoveries lead us to believe that, during the neolithic age, and perhaps even before, fishing was practiced along this stretch of the African coast. It is probable, in any case, that men have fished there uninterruptedly, in the same spot, since prehistoric times. The Imragen are a very ancient tribe who are neither Arabs nor Berbers. They have always been tributaries of more warlike peoples and of the Marabouts who were their oppressors.* They turned toward the sea for their food, while the Moors remained attached to their deserts and occupied themselves with pillaging, slave trading, and camel racing.

Even today, on this coast of arid dunes, where the desert touches the Atlantic, there is a human island, a tiny group of people who, having turned their back to the Sahara, place all their hopes in the sea. These people are divided among four or five miserable clusters of huts. But they are not a sedentary people. They roam the desolate coast of Mauritania, where only a few shrubs grow and where salty ponds and mudholes alternate with dunes and banks of bare, hard sand.

This is the domain of the marine birds: the pelicans, cormorants, pink flamingoes, and white spoonbills. It is also the home of clouds of buzzing flies.

It was here, in 1816, that a sailing ship ran aground — a ship the wreckage of which is famous: the *Medusa.*

It is one of the most desolate, sinister, and sun-baked areas on the face of the earth.

The Imragen, who number no more than three hundred today, move along the coast to follow the movement of the fish. Whenever they halt, they erect their *tikitt* — miserable shacks of straw — or their tattered tents.

The Water and the Fish

Some of the Imragen fish almost the whole year, while others fish for only two or six months. In the spring, they gather around the rare water holes, where a brackish, muddy liquid oozes through holes in the sand. For the main preoccupation in this arid country is to locate water. For food, the people have only fish. And during the summer, when there is no more fish, they join

*Raphaelle Anthonioz, "Les Imragen, pecheurs nomades de Mauritanie," in *Bulletin de l'IFAN*, t.XXX.

the Moors in the desert and drink camel's milk.

The abundance of fish along this coast is incredible. The stretch of water between Cape Blanc and Cape Timiris — a distance of about eighty miles — is reputed to be one of the richest in the world in marine life. From September to the end of February, vast schools of mullets follow each other in their migration southward. These schools cover areas hundreds of yards long, from twenty or thirty yards wide, and one to two feet in depth.

The mullets are so abundant that the Imragen, it is said, sometimes make a catch, according to their traditional methods, of six to eight thousand pounds. They then place the fish in the sun to dry.

It is not known precisely who the Imragen are. The word *Imragen* is of Berber origin and appeared in comparatively recent times. It means "those who hunt" or "those who cultivate the land." We know only that the Imragen are not of Moorish stock — though some of them may well be of mixed Moorish and black antecedents. In any event, they were an enslaved and captive people who paid tribute to the more powerful Moorish chieftains until they were liberated by the French colonial administration. Even under the French, however, the Imragen continued to pay tribute, in kind, to their Moorish overlords.

The Imragen have no ethnic cohesion, in the sense that they are united neither by blood nor by religious belief. Their only bond is their common and exclusive activity: fishing. In pursuit of that activity, they have remained on the shore of the Atlantic since time immemorial, while, inland, their oppressors and captors changed with the ebb and flow of historic tides: Sanhadja Berbers, Hassanic Arabs, Moors.

It is not beyond belief that the Imragen were fishing from these same beaches in neolithic times. At Ganeb el Hafeira, in the southwestern Sahara, small balls, marked with a groove, have been found in a prehistoric site. It is interesting to note that the present-day Imragen weight their nets with terracotta balls almost identical in shape to those found at Ganeb el Hafeira. (The Imragen call them *idan*.) Moreover, numerous prehistoric fishing implements have been found along the coast frequented by the Imragen.

According to a tradition, the origins of which are lost in the mists of antiquity, the Imragen, from the earliest times, were aided by dolphins in their mullet fishing. They still consider the dolphin as a benevolent and prestigious animal, and it is forbidden to kill any dolphin. In exchange, it is expected that the dolphins, like those mentioned by Pliny, will push mullets into the nets of the Imragen.

We were greatly intrigued by this "legend" of the Imragen, and we resolved to see what was true and what was false in it. We therefore sent a team

(Above) The Imragen, sitting beside their nets, watch the first dolphins arrive.

(Right) The first mullets are taken in the nets of the Imragen fishermen.

to Mauritania, under the supervision of Jacques Renoir. This team was assured of the co-operation of Professor Busnel and of the support of General du Bouchet.

We had chosen the period at which fishing was best, that is, the period from December to February. Our team of divers and cameramen departed in December, from Nouakchott, to journey to the land of the Imragen tribe at one of their preferred fishing spots — Nouamghar, three miles from Cape Timiris, on the Bay of El Merdja.

Our men found not a village but a grouping of several families surrounded by screaming children and swarming flies. There were fewer than ten *tikitt*; windowless, and even smaller and more ill-smelling than one would think possible.

There were a few odoriferous fish drying in the sun, and the nets had already been cast. But we had chosen badly. Fishing was not at all good, and the mullets were late in arriving that year. Thus far, no one had spotted a single dolphin, even though watches had been posted at the summit of the

dunes to scan the surface of the sea.

Our expedition had required a considerable amount of equipment. From jeeps and station wagons we unloaded an air compressor to fill our air tanks, tanks of compressed air, cameras, diving gear, floodlights, jerrycans of fuel, and a Zodiac with two motors. All this was piled on the beach and on the dunes, where it had been unloaded, while our men busied themselves with raising their tent.

The Imragen women had hidden themselves in their huts, while the menfolk sat on the sand and watched the new arrivals without a flicker of sympathy. The fishermen, as we learned later, were upset by the absence of the dolphins. The mullets are their only source of food, and without dolphins, they could not catch the fish. This was good reason indeed to worry. For selling salted fish provided them with the small amounts of money the Imragen needed to buy the other necessities of life: sugar, salt, and tea.

When darkness fell, campfires began to appear among the huts, and the divers approached warily, offering cigarettes and attempting to engage the Imragen in conversation. The women — the older women first — began to appear in the doorways of the *tikitt*. These women, it was learned, were most hostile to the divers. They were afraid that the presence of our team would prevent the dolphins from approaching the beach to help the fishermen. Apparently, they had understood that our friends intended to swim in the sea and to go near the dolphins. For centuries, the Imragen had regarded the dolphins as their special friends, and as the friends of no one else. No doubt, they felt that the dolphins would not like these Frenchmen who breathed in the water. We meant absolutely no harm, of course; and if we believed for a moment that our presence would have deprived these poverty-ridden people of the help of the dolphins, we would have decamped immediately. By then, however, we had had sufficient experience with dolphins to know that these mammals do not restrict their benevolence to any particular segment of mankind.

It was not easy to persuade these women of the truth. They shook their black-veiled heads obstinately. What was diving to them? Or cameras and film? They were concerned about their familes and their children. If the Imragen have not experienced famine for centuries, it is because of the mullets and the dolphins, who come from the sea. Therefore, anything that comes from the interior could only be hostile. For that was where the warlike Moors came from. . . .

Fishing plays such an important role in the activities of the Imragen that it is at the very center of their mental lives. It is surrounded by superstitions and religious observances. Our divers were not unsympathetic to the anxiety of these poverty-stricken tribesmen. Eventually, the conversation grew more candid, and the chief of the fishermen asked Renoir and Falco not to go into the water and risk preventing the arrival of the dolphins.

The divers did not know quite what to do. Their equipment was piled on the beach. Was it to go unused? Would their work and hopes all be in vain because of the superstitions of these poor people who alternately pleaded and threatened in their frantic attempts to dissuade them from diving? Finally, a compromise was reached. Falco and Renoir agreed not to go into the water so long as the dolphins had not yet made their appearance.

The following morning, a long period of waiting began. Imragen and the divers sat next to each other on the beach, their elbows on their knees, looking at the sea as it sparkled in the sun. Occasionally, one of the watchmen on a dune shouted: a school of mullets was approaching. Immediately, a fisherman began striking the surface of the water with pieces of wood. This was the signal intended to attract the dolphins. But no dolphins appeared. The school of mullets passed along the beach, but not even the smallest dolphin intervened to push the fish toward the beach where everyone and everything was ready. The fishermen were sitting two by two, each holding the extremity of a net which ended in a stick. Yves Omer and Bébert Falco were in the diving suits, the camera on the sand next to them, trying to be as inconspicuous as possible. They were faithful to their agreement. They would go into the water only if and when the dolphins made their appearance.

A Marabout, kneeling in the sand and surrounded by moaning women, muttered incantations.

The Killer Whales

Suddenly, far out in the water, a fin appeared, followed by others. They were not the fins of dolphins, but of killer whales. The presence of the school was probably what kept the dolphins at a distance. Dolphins are frightened of killer whales, and they flee at the first sight of the latter's huge triangular dorsal fins or at the first sound of their shrill whistles. The divers understood at once why the dolphins had not appeared on schedule; and they knew that they would not come so long as the whales were in the area. Obviously, something would have to be done. Otherwise, the Imragen would be convinced that we water-breathing Frenchmen had deliberately deprived them

After the dolphins have herded the mullets toward shore, the fishermen use sticks to push the mullets into their nets.

of their catch and, therefore, of their livelihood. Even worse, these poor fishermen along with their wives and children, would face a year of virtual starvation.

Falco and Omer jumped into the Zodiac and sped out toward the killer whales. In the small craft, they charged each of the mammals in turn, forcing them out to sea. The *corrida* lasted for more than an hour. Finally, the killer whales, deafened by the din of the outboard motors, and confused by the maneuvers of the Zodiac, decided to withdraw.

Falco and Omer had barely returned to the beach when the sea began to churn and boil. The dolphins had finally come, and they were pushing the

mullets before them.

Immediately, Jacques Renoir and Michel Deloire grabbed their camera equipment and ran into the water.

Fishing

The mullets, rolling one on top of the other, were already nearing the beach. They churned frantically in the water as the dolphins encircled them, forcing them into a compact mass and then throwing them into the air in a brilliant explosion of shining scales. The dolphins themselves seemed to be in the grip of a frenzy. They seized fishes in their mouths, turning them to swallow them headfirst, and then threw themselves back into the middle of the school.

Meanwhile, the Imragen, who had removed all of their clothing except a leather loincloth, were raising the nets by placing the pieces of wood at the ends of the nets on their shoulders. Then they ran toward the water and, swimming vigorously, spread the nets and, with a wide, turning motion, herded the mullets toward the beach. A second net was thrown farther out, and then another still farther.

Dolphins and men mingled in the water. The mammals swam among the fishermen, their mouths gaping open as mullets leaped around them.

A dog moved along the beach, half running and half swimming, in pursuit of mullets. The dog belonged to a blind man who was in the water with his net. There were so many mullets that even he caught his share, and he gathered them with an eagerness that was touching to witness.

On the beach, the women were shrieking with joy, while their naked children jumped and shouted.

The first enthusiasm had created much disorder in the water, but in order to take advantage of the wealth which was literally pushed up to the feet of the Imragen by the dolphins, a bit of discipline was necessary.

The fishing of the tribe is regulated by very strict customs. The fishermen, divided into teams of two men each, do not all go into the water at once. The elders of the village decide, by drawing lots, who will be the first to fish. Then they send out the other teams, one after the other. There are mullets enough for everyone.

Despite their poverty and their privations, the Imragen revealed themselves to be real athletes. Under their bronzed skin, strong, well-defined muscles were clearly visible. Their way of fishing must keep them in shape.

With a net measuring sixty to ninety feet in length, each team caught from 250 to 300 pounds of fish at once and returned to the beach carrying a wriggling, struggling, shining yellowish mass of mullets whose scales glittered in the sun with the fire of diamonds. As each team returned, they were met by women who loaded the fishes into other nets which they placed upon their heads. They then set off at a slow trot, bent under the weight of their loads, their bare feet sinking into the sand. Occasionally, our men saw a mullet work free of the net and fall to the sand, where it twisted and turned under the blazing sun.

Visibility Zero

Jacques Renoir and Michel Deloire, in the midst of fishermen, mullets, and dolphins, rolled in the water. The other divers joined them. Occasionally, one of them succeeded in touching a passing dolphin. Sometimes, everything disappeared into a mass of foam.

The cameras were aimed, but it was necessary to record the movements of the dolphins and the details of their intervention. The cameramen therefore left the center of the struggle and moved away. But they could no longer see anything. The water was cloudy. It is truly clear and calm only when the wind is from the east or northwest — which should be the prevailing wind at that time of year.

It is certain that, without the dolphins, the fishing would not have been nearly so good. They are excellent fish beaters. A dolphin does not need clear water to seize, with astonishing precision, a jumping mullet. His echolocation system enables him to locate his prey and seize it in one effective gesture.

Yves Omer, despite the lack of visibility, filmed the scene as best he could. He could hear distinctly the clicking of the dolphins' sonar as they pursued the mullets at full speed.

Finally, the number of mullets lessened. The dolphins went back to the open sea. And the fishermen returned to the beach to estimate the results of their first fishing of the season. They were smiling broadly. They knew that our team, by chasing away the killer whales, had enabled the dolphins to return. The atmosphere was noticeably warm and friendly.

The Man-Dolphin

Our cameramen and divers returned to the beach wondering whether they had gotten any usable footage in the cloudy water. They stood on the sand, discussing the film as they removed their diving gear. Jean-Clair Riant pulled off his hood, and his mass of blond hair tumbled around his ears.

No Imragen had ever seen a blond before. And Riant, to confuse matters, also had a blond beard. The women of the tribe swarmed around Jean-Clair, asking one another if this was not a man-dolphin. The men remarked that our vinyl diving suits indeed resembled the soft, supple skin of the dolphins.

On the Mauritanian coast, everyone knows that the dolphin's reproduc-

The mullets are initially piled up on the beach. Later, they are taken to drying huts.

The mullets leap from the water in an attempt to escape the dolphins.

tive organs are located within his abdominal cavity. This arrangement accounts for the animal's perfect hydrodynamism. Was it the same for Jean-Clair Riant? Jean-Clair was obliged to remove his diving suit to show that he was a man like other men. It was a moment of universal hilarity.

An hour later, there was an alert. The watchers signaled the arrival of another school of mullets. The children began beating the water with their sticks, and the dolphins obediently appeared, their dorsal fins erect, their backs humped, pushing mullets before them to the beach.

For the Imragen, fishing is a matter of life and death. For the dolphins, it seems to provide the opportunity for an orgy. But so far as the mullet itself is concerned, does the combination of man and dolphin pose a threat to its survival as a species? The general opinion of experts is that it does not. The fishing of the Imragen, as spectacular as it may be, is actually less murderous than it appears. It has been calculated that 90 per cent of the mullets herded by the dolphins and the Imragen manage to escape.

A Difficult Chore

After the fishing is over, there are still difficult chores to accomplish. The fish must be prepared and dried. This is the work of the women and children,

but, if the fish have been plentiful, the men also help in this task. First, the head of the fish must be cut off. Then the fish is split in two and its bones and entrails are removed, along with its eggs. It is then washed in the sea.

Some fish are simply set out to dry, while others are salted. The eggs of the fish are placed between two planks to be flattened, then they are salted and dried for seven days. Poutargue, a dish made from these eggs and from the salted fish, has a ready market along the Mediterranean coast.

On this occasion, fishing had been exceptionally good. The Imragen were no longer hostile toward us, and they no longer felt that our presence was unlucky. After all, we had driven away the killer whales, the enemies of the dolphins. Women, children, and fishermen, everyone sang our praises. We were invited to participate in the celebration that would be held that night to honor the return of the dolphins and the abundance of fish.

In the dim light of carbide lamps and of campfires fueled by the bones of the mullets, we watched the Imragen express their joy in singing and dancing to the sound of drums. These songs and dances distinguish the Imragen from the Arabs and the Berbers; for dancing is held in contempt by the Moors, while it is widely practiced among the Imragen, who dance to express their joy in happy circumstances. Until late that night, we listened to the sounds of that modest celebration in honor of the dolphins and of the sea which, since prehistoric times, has fed the men of the desert around the edge of this bay. For the Imragen may be miserable indeed. They may have no trees or lands or flocks, but at least they have never gone hungry — thanks to the dolphins.

A Problem In Identification

Professor Busnel was astonished to see the dolphins hunting mullets so near the shore, sometimes in very shallow water only a few yards from the beach. The dolphins were from seven to ten feet in length, and they were difficult to identify. We were certain that they were not always the same dolphins, for there were differences in length. Moreover, judging from the shape of the dorsal fin, they seemed to belong to two different species. They were black, or very dark maroon. We found a skull on the beach and sent it to the British Museum for identification. It is now "the largest specimen that we have in all the collections of the British Museum," wrote F. C. Fraser, the celebrated cetologist.

We wondered whether the dolphin in question was the *Tursiops* — perhaps a species other than *truncatus*. The *Tursiops*, or Bottlenosed, is vaguely defined. The Mediterranean *Tursiops* does not resemble that of Japan or of Florida; and the *Tursiops* of Mauritania may be different from the others, at least in size. We still do not know the answer to those questions.

Professor Busnel identified one dolphin which is considered to be rare. In the course of two fishing sessions, in a group of from ten to fifteen large dolphins, Busnel noticed a specimen with the humped dorsal fin characteristic of the *Sousa teuszi*, which was identified in 1892 when one of the species washed ashore near Duala. Professor Busnel is the first specialist to see a live specimen.

It is possible that the gratitude of the Imragen toward the dolphin is not entirely justified. It seems unlikely that the dolphins intentionally "collaborate" with man by helping him to fish. They push the mullet school toward the beach so that they themselves can capture them more readily. Yet, it would be very difficult to convince the Imragen that the dolphins, as sacred animals, do not show a special benevolence in driving the fish into their nets.

One may suppose that the fishing, which has been practiced for millennia in this favorable spot, exercises some attraction for the dolphins, just as it does for the humans who live in the midst of the hostile desert. One dare not say that man and dolphin eventually became accustomed to one another's presence here. In any event, it appears that there is greater attachment on man's part to the dolphin than on that of the dolphin to man.

There are other instances of similar collaboration in other parts of the world. In Florida, many local fishermen are convinced that dolphins maneuver in such a way as to drive the fish into their nets.

Less unlikely are examples of association between men and dolphins in fresh water. In Burma, for instance, each village has its dolphin (*Orcella fluminalis*), which answers to its name and participates in the village's fishing. In 1954, F. B. Lamb* witnessed the activity of another fresh-water dolphin (*Inia geoffrensis*) in South America on the Tepegos River. A fisherman began by tapping his boat with his oar. Then he whistled in a particular manner. The dolphin appeared. As the boat advanced, frightening the fishes and sending them toward the bottom, the dolphin pursued them and forced them to rise within the reach of the fisherman.

It may be that, one day, the dolphin will truly become man's helper in the sea; that he will consciously and ingeniously send schools of fishes into our nets. But we have not yet reached that stage.

---

*Professor R.-G. Busnel, *Symbiotic relationship between man and dolphins*, Proceedings of the New York Academy of Sciences, 1973.

Imragen fishermen always work in pairs, and these two-man teams enter the water one after the other.

Nets are laid out all along the beach at Nouamghar. To the left, one can see dolphins herding mullets toward the nets.

Chapter Eleven

THE RIGHT TO RESPECT

For a long period of time, at least during the whole of Antiquity, man honored and respected dolphins. There was a true alliance between dolphins on the one hand, and fishermen and seamen on the other. Poets hymned the virtues of dolphins; and it was forbidden to kill these animals both because they rendered such estimable service to mankind and because of the superstitious fears that a dolphin's death awakened in man.

Much later, during the modern era, when sensitivities had been blunted, respect for marine mammals gave way to organized massacre, carried out with murderous weapons. European fishermen began using larger and larger boats, and, in the the course of the twentieth century, they observed that their catch had diminished alarmingly. The fault, they complained, was that of the dolphins, Beluga whales, and seals, and they succeeded in persuading their governments of this libel. The results were predictable. In France, for example, the Naval Registry required that fishing boats carry a firearm aboard, and there was a bounty paid for every dolphin's tail that a fisherman brought back with him.

The regulations, and the bounty, no longer exist. But the belief somehow lingers that dolphins are the enemies of fishermen.

Once, such beliefs may not have seemed important. There were many dolphins in the sea, and it was difficult to believe that they might one day be in danger of extinction. But today, when dolphins are being hunted and killed by the hundreds of thousands for commercial purposes, the danger has become very real. Whales, finally, are protected by law. But dolphins are not. Everywhere in the world, they are being slaughtered to provide canned food for dogs and cats, since the price of meat has made it expensive to use beef or pork for such purposes.

Tuna Fishing

An even more imminent danger to dolphins is represented by modern tuna-fishing methods, as they have been practiced commercially for the past twenty years, especially in the Pacific.

Fishermen are aware that schools of dolphins and schools of tuna move together in the sea. The dolphins swim at the surface, and the tuna swim beneath the dolphins, at the same speed. The dolphins are therefore visible from the surface, and the fisherman who spots a school of dolphins knows that there may be a school of tuna underneath.

For many years, a hook and line, with live bait, was used in catching tuna. In the 1940s, however, fishermen began using a net of cotton fibers, a material which tears easily. Sharks attacked the nets, and this, combined with the cotton fiber's tendency to rip, resulted in the escape of great numbers of tuna. Nonetheless, the use of these nets quickly became common.

Between 1956 and 1961, the American tuna fleet was completely modernized. Now, nylon nets were being used, along with new fishing techniques, and the catch of tuna increased considerably. By 1966, 62 per cent of the tuna caught with nets in the American tropics of the Pacific were found under schools of dolphins. One can imagine what the consequences were to the dolphins.

In the course of our encounters with dolphins, and while we were diving with them, we frequently observed that they were accompanied by schools of tuna.

Little is known about the reasons for this association between species. At first, it was believed that dolphins and tunas were in search of the same food, but recent observations have failed to confirm that hypothesis.

Another explanation was offered: the tunas sought out the company of dolphins in order to protect themselves against attack by sharks. If so, the security thus obtained is precarious indeed, for sharks have often been seen swimming through schools of dolphins without being attacked or even hindered.

A third hypothesis is that tunas tend to group near objects floating in the sea.

The California Fisheries Bureau, after numerous experimental studies, arrived at the conclusion that tunas seek out the company of dolphins in order to take advantage of the latter's directional ability. For dolphins, as we have mentioned, have a perfect directional sense and are able to orient themselves even on the surface.

In the Trap

In the midst of the confusion concerning the reasons for the association of dolphins and tunas, one fact remains: tunas seem to follow dolphins very closely. The present technique of tuna fishing is based upon the supposition that this is so, at least as tuna fishing is practiced off the California coast and also, to a lesser extent, in the waters of Brazil, Peru, and Canada, by boats of 1,000 to 1,500 tons, equipped with refrigerated compartments.

When a school of dolphins is sighted, the ship comes to a stop and small boats are lowered. The latter engage in a "round-up" of the dolphins, herding them together while a powerful speedboat deploys a heavy net in an attempt to encircle the dolphins.

The purpose of this maneuver is to confine the dolphins in a tight circle or, if this proves impossible, to keep them in close ranks in the direction of the wind. Meanwhile, deeper down in the water, the tunas presumably are following the movements of the dolphins. If the dolphins swim against the wind, the tunas precede them and then are more difficult to catch.

The net is then closed, capturing the dolphins and the tunas together. When this technique was first employed, the fishermen did not know quite how to go about getting rid of the dolphins. They hauled them aboard, separated them from the tunas, and then threw them back into the sea, dead or injured. Obviously, this took a great deal of time, and required much extra work. To move a 300- or 400-pound dolphin, whether it is dead or alive, is not an easy task. The American Government has notified the Pacific fishing fleets that they will no longer be allowed to operate unless they develop a method which allows dolphins to escape unharmed from their nets.

In the past few years, fishing fleets have begun to adopt a more efficient and less cruel method of disposing of the dolphins. This technique is known as "backing down." Half the net is hoisted aboard. Then, the tunas are at the forward end of the net, and the dolphins at the rear end, as far as possible from the ship. Upon an order of the captain, who is positioned in a crow's-nest, the ship's engines are reversed. This maneuver causes the far end of the net to sink, and the dolphins are able to escape.

This technique is not as simple as it sounds. The tunas can also escape from the net by following the dolphins. The captain must therefore, at the proper moment, give the order for the boat to resume its forward movement so that the net is raised again and the tunas are trapped.

These are dangerous maneuvers so far as the dolphins are concerned. Some of them become entangled in the net's openings and drown. There are always fatalities among the dolphins during a catch. Some of the fishermen try to free the dolphins caught in the net and, in so doing, run serious risks.

Among the dolphins who play an important role in the fishing for tunas in tropical waters, specialists have distinguished three species. One of them has not yet been identified. The other two are the *Stenella graffmani*, and the *Stenella longirostris*. Fishermen call the former the Spotted Dolphin — obviously because of its spots. The latter is known to them as the Spinner Dolphin, from its habit of leaping and spinning in the air. It is not known whether this peculiar gymnastic is simply a sign of exuberance, or an amorous demonstration, or a distress signal. Trainers have taught the Bottlenosed Dolphin to perform the same maneuver, but in this case it is a matter of special training. No free dolphin, except the Spinner Dolphin, performs this kind of acrobatic spontaneously.

Protection

Off the West Coast of the United States, modern fishing vessels catch 45,000 tons of tuna every year. At the same time, it was estimated that tuna fishing, in 1971, cost the lives of 250,000 dolphins. In other words, the American tuna-fishing fleet alone was responsible for the deaths of a quarter of a million dolphins — and there is no reason to think that the fleets of the other tuna-fishing nations are any more concerned about dolphins than the Americans are. The total number of dolphins killed every year by tuna-fishing must therefore be enormous.

On October 21, 1972, the Congress enacted a bill entitled "The Marine Mammal Protection Act," the provisions of which were entrusted to the National Fishery Service for enforcement.

In January 1973, the Pacific fishing fleet sailed from San Diego carrying

Louis Prezelin, one of Calypso's divers, presents a fish to Aida, a killer whale at the Vancouver Aquarium.

three representatives of the Service. The assignment of these representatives was to compute the number of dolphins killed and to study the means suitable for eliminating, or at least for reducing, that massacre.

At the same time, an aerial survey was undertaken in an attempt to determine the present dolphin population. Thus, far, this laudable project has not led to any conclusive results.

Various proposals have been submitted describing ways to reduce the number of dolphin deaths during tuna fishing. The most notable of these suggests the use of a net designed to allow the dolphins to escape more easily.

Dr. Fish is conducting experiments in California with a view toward installing underwater transmitters aboard fishing boats. These transmitters are intended to reproduce the cries of killer whales — the dolphins' most feared enemies. It is possible that the killer whale's war cry, broadcast at the proper moment, might inspire the dolphins to escape more rapidly from the net.

The Misfortunes of the Beluga Whale

In Europe, in the years following World War I, there was a veritable campaign, as absurd as it was groundless, waged against the Beluga whale, which was accused of stealing the catch and destroying the equipment of fishermen. The uproar smacked of mass hysteria based upon a misuse of terms, for the true Beluga is very rarely found in European waters. At the mouth of the Loire, for example, there is only one instance of a Beluga ever having been washed ashore. The word "Beluga," in fact, was used as a popular catch-all to designate any marine animal suspected of interfering with the fishing industry; and the French Navy had standing orders, for several years, to use their cannon against any such animals.

The real Beluga whale inhabits the polar regions and only rarely leaves the waters of the Arctic. "In one hundred and forty years," Professor Budker says, "only twelve Belugas were washed up on British shores, and these were mostly in the North."

The word "Beluga" means "white" in Russian. The Beluga is a toothed whale and is often called the "white whale." Adults reach a length of fifteen to seventeen feet. The Beluga has no dorsal fin, but it is one of the rare Delphinidae which has the semblance of a neck. It feeds on fish, mollusks, and crustaceans. It is hunted along the Canadian coast and in Alaskan waters — in the White Sea and the Sea of Okhotsk — for its oil and meat. Its hide is highly prized, for it is one of the very few cetaceans to yield a usable leather. A young white whale is dark gray and becomes lighter as it matures.

Beluga hunting has been sufficiently widespread for the Canadian government to pass legislation designed to protect the species from extinction.

A Marineland Boarder

The pilot whale is also a dolphin, but one of more than usual size since it attains a length of nineteen to twenty-two feet, while the more usual size for dolphins is six to eight feet.

The pilot whale, or *Globicephala melaena,* is black — whence its popular name of Blackfish. It is also known as the Ca'ing Whale. On its underside, it has a large white marking. Its head, different in shape from that of the dolphin, is round and has no snout or beak. And, compared to the face of the dolphin, it has no "expression."

The pilot whale has a talent for adaptation and understanding which makes it a desirable boarder in marinelands, especially since, in addition to those advantages, it is of much more impressive size than the dolphin. It seems to bear up well in captivity, and the many pilot whales in American institutions are able to perform the same tricks and stunts as dolphins — that is, they are able to catch balls, ring bells, answer to their names, etc. This ability comes as something of a surprise, for the pilot whale's blank face seems somehow less alert than that of the dolphin.

The taming and training of the pilot whale is due largely to the efforts of the Marineland of the Pacific, in California. The results already obtained show great promise for the future and lead one to hope that the pilot whale may be destined for something better than life as a circus performer. It is already being used by the U. S. Navy to recover practice torpedoes.

Free pilot whales live in schools which comprise as many as several hundred individuals. The movements of the school seem to be controlled by a leader who swims at the head of the school.

Several times during *Calypso*'s expeditions we encountered pilot whales, but they proved to be even more difficult to approach than dolphins.

In 1948, we accompanied Professor Piccard aboard the *Elie Monnier* when he dived in his bathyscaphe, the FNRS II. I have told the story elsewhere of how we succeeded in getting the bathyscaphe down to a depth of 5,500 feet. As it turned out, the bathyscaphe's only defect was that it was not seaworthy — for it was damaged, not in the great depths of the sea, but on the surface, by the swell. Nonetheless, we demonstrated that the FNRS II could go down and then rise again under its own power. That demonstration made possible the use of all the other bathyscaphes which have been built since that

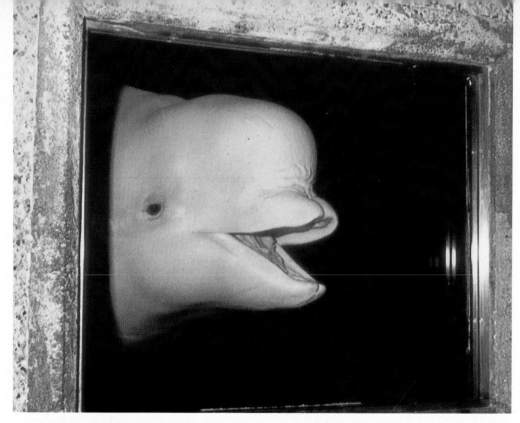

(Above) A beluga whale at the Vancouver Aquarium inspects his visitors through a porthole. (Photo, Vancouver Aquarium.)

(Right) This killer whale was photographed by Louis Prezelin.

time.

On the return trip, we were passing through the Gibraltar straits when we sighted a school of pilot whales. The weather was exceptionally good, and I did not want to miss the opportunity to film these mammals. Therefore,

Philippe Cousteau encountered a pilot whale off Catalina Island. The whale was willing to be photographed.

Frédéric Dumas and I set out in a small boat, with a sailor manning the oars. Whenever we attempted to get close to the pilot whales, however, they dived and disappeared, only to reappear a few minutes later at a greater distance. The game of hide-and-seek continued for several hours. We tried to foresee where the animals would come to the surface again, but we were always wrong. Finally, we managed to guess correctly, and we were on the spot when the school surfaced. Our guess was a bit too accurate, perhaps, for it turned out that we were in the middle of the school. One of the whales surfaced alongside the boat, and he was so frightened by what he saw that, with a flip of his tail, he sent everything flying into the air: the boat, the sailor, Dumas, myself, and the camera. We waited there in the water, while the school sped away, until the *Elie Monnier* came to fish us out.

Cuttlefish Eaters

Shortly before that incident, during the same expedition in 1948, we had another interesting experience with pilot whales. We were off the Cape Verde Islands, taking soundings in deep water. The bottom was some 12,000 feet below us, and, for the first time, we were getting echo readings from the D.S.L. — the deep scattering layer. The layer was especially thick at about 850 feet, and it was of that characteristic black which might lead one to believe that it was the bottom of the sea rather than a layer of animals. The only indication that it was indeed the latter was that, in certain places, the layer was very thick, and at others it was thin.

While we were busy with our soundings, we noticed a group of pilot whales near our vessel. There were about twenty of them, and they seemed to be swimming at an unusually slow pace. They did not appear to be going anywhere in particular. Instead, they swam around in the same area, occasionally disappearing in a dive.

Remember that this was in 1948. We still had much to learn, not only about life in the sea but also about ourselves. Without feeling a single twinge of conscience, we harpooned one of the animals to try to find out the reason for this strange behavior. We hauled the whale aboard and proceeded to dissect him. In his stomach we found the remains of several hundred cuttlefish. This was an interesting discovery from two viewpoints. It proved that

(Right) Two beluga whales in their tank at the Vancouver Aquarium.

pilot whales hunted for food at a depth of 1,200 feet, in the D.S.L composed of cephalopods. It also demonstrated that cuttlefish do not live solely in coastal waters, but that they are pelagic animals which are found in great numbers in deep water. Pilot whales also feed on squids.

We were astonished at the enormous quantity of undigested cuttlefish beaks in the whale's stomach. He and his companions obviously had stuffed themselves and were allowing their food to digest, which explained why they were moving so slowly. For once, they did not seem particularly eager to get away from us.

One occasionally hears reference to the "suicide" of pilot whales. This "suicide" refers to the fact that these mammals are sometimes beached in great numbers along the coast of northern England. It has been said that some of these accidents are intentionally provoked by fishermen from the Faeroe and the Shetland islands. The fishermen herd one or two individuals of the school toward land, and the rest of the school follows. Other instances of beached pilot whales have occurred on the coasts of France.

In 1973, thirty or so pilot whales were washed up near Charleston, South Carolina. The entire group was immediately hauled out to sea again, but only a few of them remained there. The rest returned to the beach. Once more they were towed out into the open water. And once more they all returned to the beach. A strange phenomenon, for which there is no adequate explanation.

Representatives of the Smithsonian Institution visited the site and re-moved the organs of the pilot whales, thinking that there might be a physio-logical reason for this mass suicide — an epidemic of some kind, for example. An examination, however, revealed that the animals were in normal health.

It is interesting to note that these beachings always occur in the same areas. One explanation offered is that the topological configuration in such areas interferes with the pilot whales' echolocation signals. But if this were so, it seems unlikely that, when stranded animals are towed far out into the open, they would immediately return to the beach.

There are instances, as we know, of captive dolphins allowing themselves to die, or even of causing their own deaths. But there is no obvious reason why pilot whales, living at liberty in the sea, should engage in mass suicide.

Researchers at the Smithsonian Institution have made an interesting discovery at one of the areas where pilot whales regularly allow themselves to be beached. They have excavated a large number of fossilized pilot-whale bones which appear to be several millions of years old. The mass suicide of

(Right) At the Vancouver Aquarium, a killer whale shows his teeth. The killer whale, unlike the dolphin, has no built-in "smile."

pilot whales, therefore, is not a recent phenomenon. Indeed, it antedates man on the earth. Thus, it can be explained neither as a consequence of commercial fishing nor as that of pollution.

Pilot whales, like dolphins, are creatures of sentiment. There is no instance we know of where a pilot whale became attached to humans, as Dolly and Nina did. But there is at least one case of a whale being passionately fond of a dolphin. The two mammals lived in the same tank in an aquarium. They played together and remained constantly side by side. After several years, the dolphin died of an infection. For several days, the pilot whale kept the corpse of his friend afloat at the surface, and allowed no one to take it away from him. Finally, he was tricked into surrendering it. Then the pilot whale refused to eat. He began to lose weight and was obviously wasting away. The management of the aquarium decided to release the pilot whale in the sea, hoping that this would save the animal's life. Even then, it was difficult to cope with the animal. He remained next to the boat, looking at the men with that expression of puzzled despair sometimes observed on the faces of animals who suffer without understanding what is happening to them. It was a mute, pathetic appeal from the injustice of life and death.

Of all the toothed whales, perhaps the narwhal is the most bizarre. It has a "tusk," which is actually a disproportionately long tooth on the left side of the upper jaw. The narwhal sometimes reaches a length of twelve or thirteen feet, but the average length is about nine feet. The tusk may reach a length of eight to nine feet. It is spirally twisted from right to left. It happens occasionally that a specimen may have a second tusk on the right side.

Only the males have the tusk, the function of which is obscure. It seems not be be used in hunting for food, for the female narwhal, who has no tusk, feeds herself without difficulty. Nor is it a weapon, since the narwhal is not an aggressive animal. Certain specialists hypothesize that the tusk is, in fact, a secondary sexual attribute.

Narwhals live in arctic waters in groups of approximately ten individuals. They are hunted by the Eskimos for the sake of their tusks, which fetch a good price in the ivory market.

These, in brief, are the members of the Delphinidae group. All members of the group have attractive characteristics, or exceptional abilities, or some rare attribute like the spiral "horn" of the narwhal. We can only hope that the public sympathy, which is slowly developing toward this family, may awaken in us the respect due to the intelligence and the innocuous character of its members. Then, perhaps the absurd massacres of the past will never again be repeated.

Chapter Twelve

AN ANCIENT FRIENDSHIP

The bond between dolphins and humans is very old, perhaps as old as that between the dog and man. It goes back, in any event, to the prehistoric period, even though it is difficult to assign an exact date to its beginning. One indication of this fact is the recent discovery, in South Africa, of prehistoric engraved images of dolphins. One can discern the figure of a man swimming among the dolphins.*

The artists of the Aegean civilization have left us handsomer and more precise representations of dolphins. In the palace at Knossos, the bathroom of the queen was decorated with a frieze of dolphins.

It seems certain that the people of ancient Crete were familiar with marine animals to an extent that would be forgotten until the twentieth century. The innumerable vases decorated with images of the octopus, also bear witness to the sympathy of the Aegeans for an animal often despised and feared among other peoples, and that we have tried to rehabilitate.

So far as the dolphin is concerned, an interesting question has been raised. Were dolphins more than mere images and mere subjects for artistic works? Some historians believe that the Cretans had tamed dolphins. Today,

*David K. Caldwell and Melba C. Caldwell, *World of the Bottle-Nosed Dolphin.* Philadelphia, 1972.

we know that it is possible to do so. The ships of Crete, says Gustave Glotz, "which would not have ventured onto the sea without having a fish tied to its prow, could not have found a better pilot than the dolphin."†

And it was the Cretans who, having learned that, to the South of Parnassus, on the heights dominating the Gulf of Corinth, there was an ancient sanctuary, established there a new sanctuary to which they gave the name of the dolphin: Delphi. They had been guided to that spot by their dolphin-god.

Delphi is the most famous sanctuary of Greece. It was thought to be the center of the world. It was there that the famous oracle spoke. And it was there that Apollo, the god of light, had his sanctuary. For, according to a legend older than that of the Minoans, the place had been given the name Delphi because the god had first appeared there in the form of a dolphin. This was the reason why the dolphins of pre-Hellenic Crete were honored as gods.

Dolphins apparently were more numerous in the Mediterranean in the second millennium before Christ than they are now, and they always showed signs of that willingness to fraternize with man which we see today. The Minoans and the Mycenaeans, being seafaring peoples, no doubt responded to these advances, and a friendship was born. That friendship would blossom and die, not to be recalled until the twentieth century when man and dolphin renewed their ancient contact.

Theseus the Diver

The maritime heirs of the Aegeans were the Phoenicians and the Greeks. The heritage they received included both the Aegeans' secrets of navigation and naval architecture and their respect for the dolphin and their belief in his role as protector. For centuries, the peoples of the Mediterranean believed that a dolphin's presence in the vicinity of a ship was a good omen, and that the animal's disappearance announced a forthcoming storm. When a ship was lost, the way to safety lay in following the course of a dolphin. Everyone knew that the animal would lead them safely home.

If it happened that fishermen accidentally caught a dolphin in their nets, the animal was released immediately.

†G. Glotz, *La Civilization égéenne.*

(Left) A picture of Snoopy, one of the dolphins at the Marineland of Antibes. (Photo, Jose Dupont, Marineland d'Antibes.)

The image of the dolphin is found everywhere on Greek ceramics. Theseus is depicted as surrounded by them, and sometimes they are represented as mounts for warriors. On the famous Euphronius cup, dating from the fifth century B.C. (now in the Museum of the Louvre) there is an image of Theseus at the bottom of the sea, surrounded by dolphins, receiving a golden crown from the hands of Amphitrite, goddess of the sea. The crown was the prize won by the first diver.

The Etruscans, a race of excellent seamen from Lydia, often depicted dolphins in their funeral frescoes. One famous example is found in a Tarquinian tomb of the sixth century B.C., where the dolphins are shown leaping out of the water around a fishing boat.

The dolphin appears, above all, on the coins of the ancients — coins being the essential tool of maritime commerce. On silver pieces of Syracuse, for instance, the nymph Arethusa is shown surrounded by dolphins.

The famous Taranto dolphin, which serves as the mount for the hero Taras (who gave the city of Taranto its name), in addition to its religious, commercial, and maritime significance, also serves to record a legend which may or may not be true: Taras, son of the sea-god Neptune, is supposed to have founded Taranto on the spot to which he was carried by a dolphin.

Some forty Greek cities used the image of the dolphin on their coins. The animal's form, more or less stylized, is also found on anchors, and it was used as the trademark of various prominent Greek and Roman shipowners. Following a model which probably goes back to the ninth, or eighth, century B.C., the Phoenicians showed the dolphin's body twisted around an anchor or a trident. This emblem was chosen by the celebrated Venetian printing house of Aldo Manuzio, in the sixteenth century, for their sumptuous editions of the Greek and Latin authors.

The anchor and the trident are also attributes of the god Poseidon and are used to indicate that the dolphin is the lord of navigation, by virtue of his power and speed as a swimmer, and also of his wisdom and prudence.

The Romans too showed the dolphins in their works of art. On a mosaic in Ostia, we can see dolphins swimming among the ships of a commercial fleet, looking very benevolent and vaguely amused. Their presence indicates that the Roman fleet was actually animated by Greek beliefs and traditions. From the port of Knossos to Ostia, port of Rome, dolphins have survived the ships which once honored them.

It would be wrong for us to think that the Aegeans, Etruscans, Greeks, and Romans used the dolphin to decorate their walls, shields, vases, cups, and coins simply because the dolphin's shape lends itself to ornamental use. Such an approach to art may be characteristic of the twentieth century, but it was

A silver coin of ancient Syracuse, depicting the goddess Arethusa surrounded by four dolphins.

(Above) A dolphin fresco in the Queen's chamber at the Palace of Knossos. The fresco dates from *c*. 1600 B.C. (Musee Archeologique d'Heraklion. Candie.)

(Left) A Greek dolphin ceramic from the fourth century B.C. (Louvre Museum.)

(Right) Fishermen accompanied by a dolphin. Note that the fishermen's boat is itself in the shape of a dolphin, as depicted in this Etruscan representation of the sixth century B.C. (Photo, Giraudon.)

alien to the people of the ancient world. These images have a meaning, and perhaps several meanings. They are symbolic of something else — but of what, we can only guess. Lacking any precise text or inscription, we sense a funereal meaning in these images, but we do not know for certain. Many ancient symbols having to do with the sea and with water had such a meaning. One indication of the significance of the dolphin symbol is found on a mosaic in the Museum of Antioch. This mosaic shows dolphins carrying the souls of the departed to the Isle of the Blessed. The concept may have been part of the Aegean heritage, for the people of Crete assigned that same role to dolphins.

The symbolism of the dolphin, as it existed in the Mediterranean basin for some four thousand years, is not explained by the Greek and Latin texts that we possess. The only information we have comes to us almost solely from anecdotes and testimonials which illustrate the good will of dolphins toward man.

According to the Greeks, this good will was explained by the fact that dolphins were actually men who had been transformed into marine mammals, in the following circumstances: "Dionysos, having borrowed a ship to go to Naxos, saw that the sailors were heading toward Asia, no doubt with the intention of selling him into slavery. Therefore he turned their oars into serpents, filled the ship with ivy, and commanded invisible flutes to play. The ship was held motionless in the twisting vines, and the sailors, driven mad by what they had seen, threw themselves into the sea, where they were transformed into dolphins."‡ Dolphins, therefore, are friendly to man because they are repentant pirates.

From the time of Homer, classical literature abounded with stories of this kind, which have generally been regarded as fables or myths. Today, since we know more about the behavior of marine mammals, we may choose to judge them otherwise.

Several of these legends, in fact, in the light of modern knowledge, take on a certain element of truth. For example, Telemachus, the son of Ulysses, when still a child, fell into the water and was rescued by a dolphin. For that reason, Ulysses always wore a ring engraved with the image of a dolphin. Today, we know that dolphins do rescue drowning humans, and that they seem particularly fond of children.

In the fourth century B.C., Aristotle gave an accurate description of the anatomy and the behavior of dolphins. He noted that the dolphin was a mammal and could not be classified among the fishes.

‡Grimal, *Dictionnaire de la mythologie grecque et romaine.* Paris, 1963.

A *skyphos* representing six warriors mounted on dolphins. (Photo, Museum of Fine Arts, Boston.)

In Pliny's *Natural History*, we find the following: "They [dolphins] are solicitous for each other's well-being. A dolphin was captured by a king of Caria and leashed to the port. The other dolphins assembled in a crowd, attempting, by showing their sorrow, to excite the king's mercy. Finally, the king ordered the captive to be released. Moreover, young dolphins are always accompanied by an older dolphin, who serves as a guardian. And witnesses have seen a dolphin carried by his companions so that he would not fall prey to the monsters of the sea."

Many readers in past centuries have simply shrugged their shoulders, when perusing Pliny's writings, and accused the old Roman of naiveté. Yet, there is little that Pliny says that cannot be verified by our own experience. "The dolphin," Pliny states, "is friendly to man and is charmed by music, by harmonious instruments, and particularly by the sound of the hydraulic or-

(Above) An Italian cup from the fourth century B.C., representing Apollo in his chariot. To the left is a dolphin — the animal sacred to Apollo. (Louvre Museum.)

(Left) A pair of dolphins in the open sea.

gan. He does not regard man as a hostile being, but swims forward of ships, leaps playfully around them, runs races with them, and, no matter how full the sails, always outdistances them."

We know that dolphins are sensitive to music. Aboard *Calypso*, our two guitar players, Louis Prezelin and Dr. Millet, on several occasions attracted dolphins by music.

It is also Pliny who tells us the story of a dolphin who lived in Lake Lucrino. A boy, the son of a poor man who lived in a town near Naples, came every day to feed the dolphin. The boy and the dolphin became friends, and every morning the dolphin carried the child on his back across the lake to

A Greek plate depicting Thetis and the dolphins. (Museum of Fine Arts, Boston.)

school. In the afternoon, he would meet the child and carry him back so that the boy would not have to walk around the lake. One day, the child did not come. He had died during the night. The dolphin waited. When he realized that his friend would come no more, he died of sorrow.

Pliny's nephew, known as Pliny the Younger, in a letter to Caninium Rufus, relates the story of a young boy at Hippo who had been saved from drowning by a dolphin. The two became fast friends, and the boy rode on the dolphin's back, played and jumped and dived with him as the whole city crowded on the beach to watch this spectacle. The dolphin allowed other children, and even adults, to pet him.

This, of course, is exactly what happened with Nina at La Corogna, and with Opo in New Zealand, almost two thousand years later.

The dolphin, after having been a symbol among the Cretans, Etruscans,

A Greek ceramic cup decorated with the figures of three dolphins. (Louvre Museum.)

Greeks, and Romans, was assimilated into the Christian bestiary and into the heraldic art of the West. He became the symbol of rebirth. He was the intercessor who guided and supported man in the sea and allowed him to return to land cleansed of his sins. He was the guide who saved the shipwrecked man and carried him to port, that is, to salvation.

It should come as no surprise, therefore, that Christ the Saviour, like Apollo, was often represented in the form of a dolphin. There are several

(Following page left) The dolphin, when swimming, moves alternately beneath and above the surface.

(Following page right) Falco capturing a dolphin at *Calypso*'s stem.

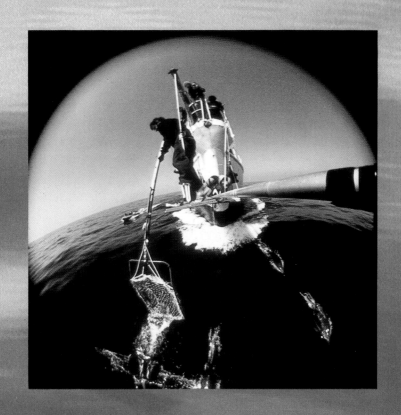

animals with which man has had an intimate association since the dawn of history. The bond between man and some of these animals — the dog, for instance, and the horse — is reasonably well defined. In the case of other animals (and I am speaking particularly of the dolphin), it is nebulous and precarious. Surely there was a good reason why the peoples of the ancient world chose to surround themselves with images and representations of dolphins. Certainly, the general belief that dolphins were man's helpers and protectors in the sea was not without some foundation in fact. Yet, beyond the few stories contained in the works of Pliny and other ancient writers, we know very little about how the dolphin came to play such a notable role in the artistic and religious life of the ancient Mediterranean world. Is it possible that now, in the mid-twentieth century, we are just beginning to unveil a "secret" that was no secret at all to our ancestors? Can it be that the dolphin is not a new friend in the sea, but a very old friend whom chance — or destiny — has once more led us to recognize?

For centuries, reports of humans being carried on the backs of dolphins were treated as legends. The photograph above, however, shows a dolphin at the Marineland of Antibes carrying a young girl on his back. (Photo, Gilbert Pressenda.) Below, a Greek vase of the fifth century B.C. shows a Nereid mounted on a dolphin. (Louvre Museum.)

Chapter Thirteen

THE PROMISE OF THE FUTURE

What does the future hold for dolphins?

In twenty years, or in fifty years, if the good will and curiosity now shown them continues, there is little doubt that they will be living in increasingly close contact with man.

At that time, diving will constitute a considerable part of man's scientific, industrial, and social activities. There will be increased contact between divers and marine mammals. And, since the dolphin is a well-equipped animal from a physiological standpoint, these encounters will have an effect upon him and will influence him, educate him, and change his behavioral patterns.

Rats and other animals living in cities change their behavior in accordance with man's routine. Rats know at what time one's garbage is put outside, for example. And, in England, tits have learned to use their beaks to pierce the cardboard or metal covers on the milk bottles left outside one's door. We can only speculate what effect man's intervention in the sea will have on dol-

(Left) These two dolphins are "talking" to one another. Notice the bubbles rising from the blowhole of one of the dolphins.

phins, killer whales, Belugas, and sea lions. How will these animals profit from that intervention? And how will they use what they learn?

The number of animals trained for missions in the sea will no doubt be much larger than it is now. They will serve as guides and as liaison agents with their fellow dolphins still roaming the sea in schools.

Finally, one must think of what is happening, and of what will happen, in our aquariums and marinelands. Surely, the number of these establishments will be greatly increased. More animals will be held captive. And it is in captivity that animals are modified and changed. Domestic animals, after all, are wild animals which have been first confined and then bred by man. They are new animals, transformed animals, only in the sense that such animals do not exist in nature. Thus, in Mesopotamia, in the Indus valley, and in Egypt, five or six thousand years ago, man created hogs, goats, and cattle totally different from wild animals. So far as the dog is concerned, it took sixty thousand years to make him what he is.

Experimental Biology

The origin of the dog combines in the mists of time with that of man. The dog seems linked to man. He is man's perennial companion. What makes this possible is the dog's extreme polymorphism, his versatility which renders him susceptible to any metamorphosis. The dog's size, shape, color, and behavior have been changed by accident, by mutations, and by breeding.

Are cetaceans as amenable to change as dogs? It is still too early to tell. In any event, there has been an important event to which too little attention has been paid. Two species of dolphin — a Bottlenosed Dolphin and a Steno — have interbred in captivity. Hybridization is an essential tool of breeders. By crossbreeding, the breeder is able to develop certain qualities and to eliminate certain defects. It is the means by which man changes life and attains mastery over the other animals — a mastery which constitutes the most important chapter in human history and which has been called "a vast undertaking in experimental biology."

Will this work be undertaken in systematic fashion by zoologists? If so, where will it lead? Will we be given a companion and helper to take our place in the water and to work with us in the sea? Very probably. We are almost at

(Right)Yves Omer and Falco attach an underwater camera to a dolphin's dorsal fin.

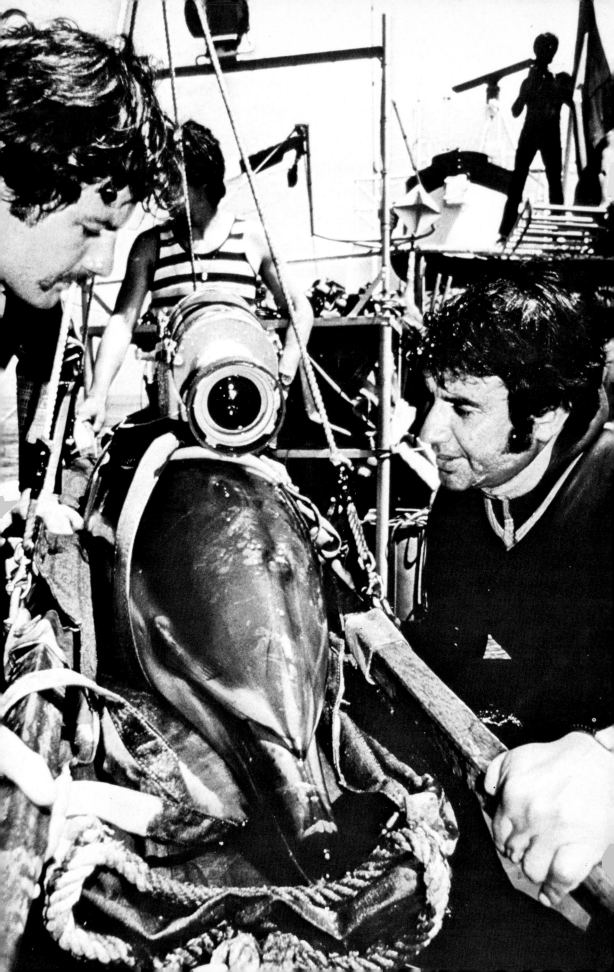

that stage now. We do not have the ability to locate objects in cloudy water, or to find the source of a sound. Our senses do not function well under water, while those of the dolphin are miracles of effective performance. The use of those senses on our behalf may render us invaluable service. The dolphin may become our great helpmate in the sea, the equivalent of the horse on land as it was almost four thousand years ago.

The Ultimate Step

The brain of the dolphin — its development and its structures — presents a major problem. What will become of that organ after fifty or a hundred years of close association between dolphins and men? The dolphin's brain is capable of memory, of associating ideas. It may, someday, be capable of language, like that of the primates.

Throughout this book, we have been especially careful to avoid exaggerating the mental potential of the dolphin even at the risk of disappointing the reader. When necessary, we have gone out of our way to demythologize dolphins and to strip away elements which, however appealing they may be, are redolent more of folklore than of fact. Even so, we must remember that what is not true today may be true tomorrow. Today, the dolphin is an animal. Tomorrow, human contact may make the dolphin something more than an animal. What promise the future holds for us — and what responsibility!

A mosaic decorating a basin of the fourth century A.D. found at Utica, in North Africa.

Acknowledgments

We acknowledge a debt of gratitude to a number of scientists who have given us the benefit of their advice in the preparation of this work. Our special thanks go to the following:

Professor Paul Budker, Director, Laboratory of Cetacean Biology, École Pratique des Hautes Études

Professor René-Guy Busnel, Director, Laboratory of Acoustical Physiology, CNRS, Jouy-en-Josas;

Mr. Charles Roux, Assoicate Director, Laboratory of Reptiles and Fishes, National Museum of Natural History;

Mr. Albin Dziedzic, Laboratory of Acoustical Physiology, CNRS, Jouy-en-Josas.

Photo Credits

The photographs appearing in this book were taken by Henri Alliet, Ron Church, Jan and Philippe Cousteau, François Dorado, Marie-Noëlle Favier, Ivan Giacoletto, Andrée Laban, Edmond Laffont, Jean-Jacques Languepin, Yves Omer, Louis Prezelin, André Ragiot, Jacques Renoir, and Jean-Clair Riant.

Several of the photographs taken at the surface were chosen from the private collections of *Calypso*'s team.

The line drawings appearing in the appendices and glossary were executed by Jean-Charles Roux.

Iconography: Marie-Noëlle Favier.

APPENDICES

From top to bottom: *Delphinus delphis*; *Tursiops truncatus*; *Phocoena cephalorhynchus*.

APPENDIX I

The Delphinidae Family

Throughout this book, we have sometimes referred to dolphins in general terms; and sometimes we have mentioned the names of some species which are rather less known to the public than the *Tursiops truncatus*, or Bottlenosed Dolphin. This practice, however necessary it may have been, may have caused some confusion in the reader's mind — not a surprising development, certainly, even when dealing with animals so distinct from each other in shape and size. It may be helpful, therefore, for us to supply some clarifications.

When dealing with dolphins — or with cetaceans generally — the first problem we encounter is one of nomenclature. "For English-language authors," Professor Paul Budker has observed, "any Odontocete [toothed whale] less than fifteen feet in length is a dolphin if it has a beak; and if it has a rounded snout, it is called a porpoise." It does not simplify matters that, in the United States, the popular name for the most famous species of dolphins, the Bottlenosed, is "porpoise," while the British reserve that term exclusively for the Harbor Porpoise (*Phocaena phocaena*).

It would be easy to multiply examples of such confusions. For our purposes, suffice it to say that the Delphinidae are the most numerous family of cetaceans, comprising some forty-eight species. "There is no such thing as a dolphin," Professor Budker says. "There are only dolphins."

The largest member of the Delphinidae clan is the Killer Whale, which attains a length of twenty-five to twenty-eight feet and weighs about a ton. This dolphin has a rounded head, a very large dorsal fin, and white markings. It is the mortal enemy of other dolphins, and even of baleen whales. However, its proverbial ferocity is held in abeyance so far as man is concerned. Killer Whales are easily trained and are star performers in aquariums and marinelands. Their "intelligence" is remarkable — undoubtedly superior to that of Bottlenosed Dolphins.

The Bottlenosed Dolphin grows to a length of nine to twelve feet. It is very common in the Atlantic, and, so far as the general public is concerned, it is the prototypal dolphin, immediately recognizable by its beak and the rictus which gives the dolphin the appearance of wearing a perpetual smile.

The Common Dolphin (*Delphinus delphis*) is slightly smaller than the Bottlenosed. It is found in all warm and temperate seas, such as in the Mediterranean and in the Black Sea. The Common Dolphin was the species with which the ancients were most familiar and which they depicted in their artifacts.

The coloration of dolphins varies according to species. *Stenella* is spotted (its popular name is Spotted Dolphin), while the *Lagenorhynchus acutus* has white flanks and *Lagenorhynchus albirostris* has a white snout. The genus *Cephalorhynchus* is of small size, with a non-prominent beak. Its body is black and white. It is found mostly in southern waters, where it feeds on jellyfish and shrimp.

River dolphins (Platanistidae), or fresh-water dolphins, have long, narrow snouts. The Stenodelphia is found in South American waters, but a member of the Delphinidae family is found in the Mekong: the *Orcaella*. Many of these fresh-water dolphins are blind. (See Appendix III.)

The porpoise, properly speaking, is not a dolphin at all, but belongs to another genus: Phocaena. It is a cetacean of relatively small size, with a slightly developed dorsal fin and a short snout. The Common Porpoise (*Phocaena phocaena*), which attains a length of four to six feet, is found in almost all parts of the world.

Beluga Whales and Narwhals are not members of the Delphinidae family. They belong to the Monodontidae. The Beluga (*Delphinapterus leucas*) inhabits cold waters and is from ten to twelve feet in length. It is white, with a comparatively prominent neck. It is known as the White Whale, and sometimes as the White Porpoise. The Narwhal (*Monodon monoceros*) attains a length of from twelve to eighteen feet. It feeds on starfish, cuttlefish, and fishes. In the male Narwhal, a single tooth, located on the left side of the lower jaw, grows disproportionately long and sometimes reaches a length of six feet.

The *Hyperoodon rostratus*, or Northern Bottlenosed Whale, belongs to the family Ziphiidae or "beaked whales." It is being trained, with some success, in several aquariums. It is said to be the most capable diver of all the cetaceans. The giant of the family is the *Berardius*, some specimens of which reach a length of thirty-six feet.

The Pilot Whale (*Globicephala scammonii*), (family Delphinidae), also called the Blackfish and the Ca'ing Whale, may be from eighteen to twenty-two feet in length. They are found in all the oceans. They travel in groups of several hundred individuals, all closely following the leader of the group. They are black, with a white marking on their underside. Pilot Whales adapt to captivity, and several specimens have been trained successfully.

The Sub-Committee on Small Cetaceans of the International Whaling Commission, at a meeting held in Montreal on April 1–10, 1974, decided that it was necessary to review the number of Delphinidae species recognized as such. A certain number of these species are no longer to be considered as geographic variants.

From top to bottom: Bottlenosed Whale; Killer Whale; Beluga Whale.

APPENDIX II

The Cetaceans*

Cetaceans are marine mammals. They are warm-blooded creatures, and, as Aristotle noted more than two thousand years ago, they breathe by means of lungs. Fertilization and gestation are internal, and female whales nurse their offspring.

The relationship of cetaceans to land mammals is obvious, although there are anatomical differences among cetaceans which have allowed them to adapt perfectly to marine life. The fossil remains of the land ancestors of the cetaceans have not been discovered, but small bones enclosed within the muscles of some cetaceans are vestiges of a pelvic structure and sometimes represent a rudimentary femur or a tibia.

The dorsal fin, which is characteristic of all cetaceans except the sperm whale, seems to have developed within comparatively recent times, and it has no connection with the skeleton.

All cetaceans are equipped with tails that spread horizontally rather than, as in the case of fish, vertically. Also they have a blowhole or vent, at the

*This appendix is based upon the works of Kenneth S. Norris, Dr. Harrison Matthews, Dr. F. C. Fraser, David K. and Melba C. Caldwell, Ernest P. Walker, and upon the classification of the International Whaling Commission.

top of their heads, through which they breathe. The position and shape of the blowhole varies according to the species.

The order of cetaceans includes approximately one hundred species and is divided into two suborders: the Mystacoceti, which are the baleen or whalebone cetaceans; and the Odontoceti, or toothed cetaceans.

The Odontoceti

The number of teeth varies. The Goosebeak Whale has two, some species of dolphin have 260. All species are carnivorous. (Formerly, it was thought that the fresh-water dolphins of American waters fed on aquatic plants.) There are five families of Odontoceti, which include the majority of the species of cetaceans:

(1) The Delphinidae, which contains nineteen genera: *Delphinus* with *Delphinus delphis* or Common Dolphin, *Tursiops, Grampus, Lagenorhynchus, Feresa, Cephalorhynchus, Orcaella, Lissodelphis, Lagenodelphis, Steno, Sousa, Sotalia, Stenella, Phocaena* (porpoise), *Phocaenoides* (Pacific porpoise), *Neomeris* (the Southeast Asian porpoise), *Pseudorca, Orcinus* (Killer Whale), and *Globicephala* (Pilot Whale).

Gestation lasts about twelve months among *Tursiops* and Killer Whales; eleven months for the Common Dolphin; and thirteen to sixteen months for the Pilot Whale.

(2) The Platanistidae are fresh-water dolphins, living exclusively or partially in fresh water, often in the estuaries of large rivers. They are divided into *Platanista* (Ganges Dolphin), *Inia* (Amazon Dolphin), *Lipotes* (found in China), and *Stenodelphis*, the La Plata River Dolphin.

(3) The Monodontidae, comprising two genera: *Delphinapterus*, the Beluga Whale found especially in the arctic seas around North America, whose period of gestation is about one year; and *Monodon*, the Narwhal.

(4) The Ziphiidae, which are characterized by a beak-shaped snout, include five genera: *Mesoplodon, Ziphius, Tasmacetus, Berardius, Hyperoodon*. Gestation lasts ten months only for the big *Berardius*.

(5) The Physeteridae are the sperm whales, divided into two genera: the

The Narwhal (above) and the Pilot Whale (below).

Kogia, or Pygmy Sperm Whale, and the *Physeter*, or Sperm Whale (Cachalot).

Of all the Odontoceti, the sperm whale is instantly recognizable because of its oblique spout. It has two blowholes, but the left opening is the only working one. The sperm whale is characterized especially by its massive head and squared snout. The head accounts for one third of the cachalot's body length. Only the lower jaw has teeth — but each tooth is ten inches long and weighs over two pounds.

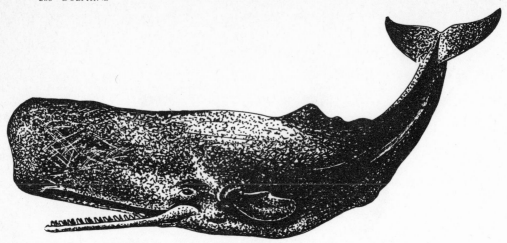

The Cachalot, or Sperm Whale, has no dorsal fin. Note, however, the bony ridge or "crest" on its back.

The sperm whale has no dorsal fin, but it does have a sort of "crest."

It is usually dark in color, with spots that lighten as it grows older.

The largest cachalots — always males — reach a maximum length of sixty feet. They weigh between thirty-five and fifty tons and feed principally on giant squid, which they seek out in the great depths of the sea.

Gestation lasts sixteen months, and the calf nurses for twelve months. A single calf is born every three years. Sperm whales live in family groups, or harems, of twenty to fifty individual whales.

The Mystacoceti

The Mystacoceti, or baleen whales, are characterized by the presence in the upper jaw of plates of whalebone (baleen), the fringed edges of which act as a sieve through which water is strained to remove the small animals on which the whale feeds. The spacing of the fringe depends upon the size of the animals on which a particular species normally preys. There are three families of Mystacoceti:

(1) The Balaenidae, which, in turn, comprises three genera:
(a) *Balaena*, of which the species *Balaena mysticetus*, or the right whale, is best known.

The right whale grows to a length of fifty to sixty feet and has black skin, except for the throat and chin which are cream-colored. One third of its body length is taken up by the enormous mouth. It has no dorsal fin and no ventral

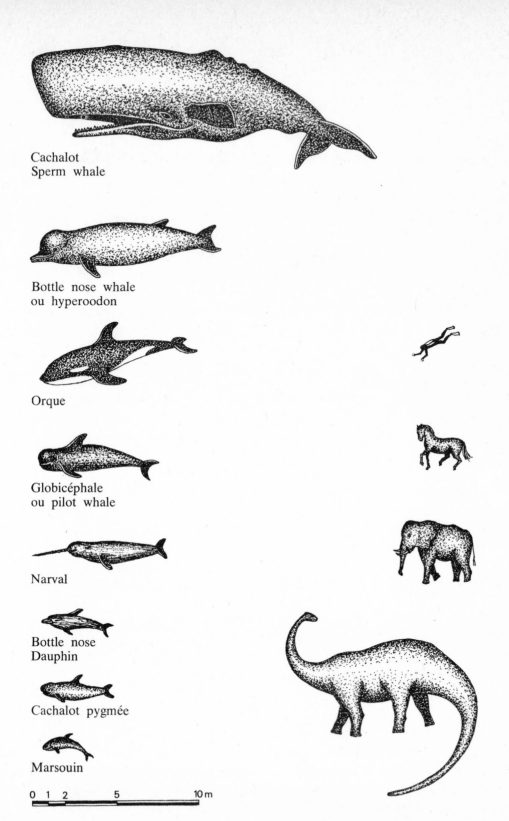

Cachalot
Sperm whale

Bottle nose whale
ou hyperoodon

Orque

Globicéphale
ou pilot whale

Narval

Bottle nose
Dauphin

Cachalot pygmée

Marsouin

0 1 2   5   10 m

The baleen whales: (from top to bottom) Blue Whale, Finback Whale, Right Whale, Sei
Whale, Humpback Whale, Gray Whale, Dwarf Right Whale, small Finback Whale.

furrows. The right whale is able to suspend breathing for from ten to thirty minutes. Its gestation period is nine or ten months, and its principal food is krill.

Right whales were still abundant in arctic waters at the beginning of the nineteenth century. By the twentieth century, however, the species was almost extinct. They are now protected by international agreement.

(b) *Eubalaena*, whose external characteristics are the same as those of the right whale except for the mouth, which is smaller and accounts only for one quarter of the total body length. *Eubalaena* includes the following species: *Eubalaena glacialis*, which frequents the North Atlantic and which, because of its modest size (forty to fifty-five feet) was hunted by the Basques as early as the ninth century. Specimens are extremely rare, and the species has been protected for the past thirty-five years. *Eubalaena australis*, which lives in the waters of the Antarctic. Fifty years ago, this species counted its members in the hundreds of thousands. Whalers almost destroyed the species, however, and, at the present time, after thirty-five years of absolute protection, there are once again a few schools in the South Atlantic, in the neighborhood of the Cape of Good Hope, and off South Georgia (an island of Antarctica).

(c) *Caperea*, to which only one species belongs: *Caperea marginata*, or the pygmy right whale, which has a dorsal fin.

(2) The Eschrichtiidae, which includes only the *Eschrichtius gibbosus* — the California gray whale, which is found near the American and Korean coasts. The gray whale has no dorsal fin. It reaches a length of between thirty-five and forty-five feet and weighs between twenty-four and thirty-seven tons. Its color is black, or slate, and its skin is mottled with grayish patches of barnacles. (The grayish cast of its skin is the result of wounds inflicted by parasites.) Sexual maturity is attained at four and one half years, and gestation lasts from eleven to twelve months. A single calf is born every two years.

(3) The Balaenopteridae, of which there are two genera:

(a) Balaenoptera, comprising the following species:

   Balaenoptera borealis, or Sei Whale;

   Balaenoptera acutorostrata, or lesser rorqual;

   Balaenoptera edeni, or Bryde's whale; and

   Balaenoptera physalus, or finback whale (also known as the common rorqual). The finback whale measures sixty to seventy-five feet in length and weighs some fifty tons. Its back is grayish. There is a clearly distinguishable dorsal fin, rather high and triangular in shape. The finback whale travels in schools of twenty to one hundred individuals. It feeds on plankton, crustaceans, and small fishes. This species mates during the winter, and the period of gestation lasts between ten and twelve months. The male attains sexual maturity at five years; and the female, between three and eight years. Physical maturity, however, is not reached until the age of fifteen. Full-grown specimens may remain without breathing for from twenty to fifty minutes. The finback whale has been one of the principal victims of whalers, and it is estimated that 90 per cent of the species has been destroyed. In 1955, there were still approximately 110,000 specimens in the Atlantic. Today, there are probably no more than 30,000.

(b) *Balaenoptera musculus*, or blue whale (also known as the sulphur-bottomed whale), is the largest of the cetaceans and the largest animal that has ever existed on earth. It reaches lengths of between eighty and one hundred feet, and the largest specimen known weighed 120 tons.

The blue whale winters in tropical waters and spends its summers in polar seas. The skin is slate blue. Blue whales travel singly rather than in schools, and they are able to remain underwater for periods of from ten to twenty minutes. Their basic food is krill.

They mate during May and June, and gestation lasts eleven months. One calf is born every two years. Sexual maturity is reached at the age of four and one half years.

The blue whale was the most avidly hunted of the great cetaceans because it yielded the greatest quantity of oil. In 1930, it was estimated that there were between 30,000 and 40,000 blue whales in the Antarctic. Today, the most optimistic estimate sets the number at 2,000 — and perhaps fewer. The blue whale is now a totally protected species.

(c) *Megaptera*, of which there is a single species: *Megaptera novaeangliae*, the humpback whale. The humpback whale, along with the gray whale, is the only species to live in coastal waters.

The humpback's average length is forty feet; its average weight, thirty tons. The upper part of the body is black, and the throat and chest are white. It is recognizable by its large white flippers, which measure a third of the length of the body. Crustaceans form its normal diet.

Gestation lasts ten months. Sexual maturity is attained at the age of three, but full physical growth is not reached until the tenth year. A calf is born every two years.

During the 1930s, the Antarctic's humpback population was estimated at 22,000. Now, there are probably not more than 3,000 specimens in the Antarctic. In the northern Pacific, however, there are an additional 5,000 specimens. Today, the species is totally protected.

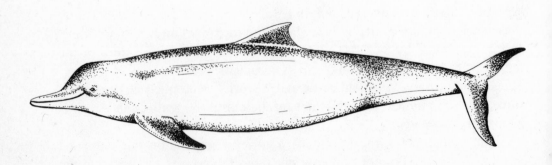

From top to bottom: *Inia geoffrensis*, Gagentic dolphin; *Sotalia fluviatilis*.

APPENDIX III

Fresh-water Dolphins

Certain species of dolphin live exclusively or partially in fresh water. These are the Platanistidae and three genera of Delphinidae (*Sousa, Sotalia,* and *Orcaella* of the Mekong, which is found both in rivers and in coastal waters).

Platanista, which inhabits the waters of the Ganges, the Brahmaputra, and the Indus, is notable for its long beak lined with many teeth and for its clearly distinguishable neck. It eats shrimp and bottom-living fishes which it digs out of the bottom. It does not venture beyond the limits of fresh water.

It is sightless. The eyes have no crystallin and no pigmented epithelium. The optical nerve is greatly reduced. Yet, by means of its acoustical equipment, it can easily locate its prey in the water and in the mud of the bottom, and it is very difficult to capture with nets.

These dolphins sometimes hunt for food in no more than eight inches of water, where they move by swimming on their side. Sometimes, small groups of Platanista live near human installations.

Among the Platanistidae, *Inia geoffrensis* or bouto dolphin of the Amazon and the Orinoco is remarkable for its small eyes, pink skin, long beak, and humped back. David and Melba Caldwell have designated it "the ugly dolphin." Occasionally, when the water is high, the bouto leaves the riverbed and ventures into the flooded forests. Unlike most fresh-water dolphins, this species lives in schools of twelve to twenty individuals, and they show signs of great social solidarity.

One species of Delphinidae, *Sotelia fluviatilis*, is a near relative of *Tursiops*. It is a small dolphin, not longer than five or six feet, and inhabits the Amazon and Orinoco basins from Brazil to Venezuela. Certain local tribes regard it as a sacred animal.

The dolphin of the Rio de La Plata, *Stenodelphis*, leaves fresh water in winter and moves into coastal waters. It feeds on shrimp, squid, and on fishes. It is also a small animal, and its skin is gray. Because of the latter trait, it is known in Uruguay as "Franciscana" — the Franciscan.

The *Sousa* dolphin is found in southern Asia, along the eastern and western coasts of Africa, at Senegal, in the Cameroons, and at Zanzibar.

The Chinese dolphin, *Lipotes* or pei ch'i, inhabits Lake Tung-t'ing. Its eyes are atrophied, and it seems almost totally without sight. It feeds on eel-shaped herbs buried in the bottom of the lake. Practically nothing is known of this species.

APPENDIX IV

Protective Legislation

In the United States:

A law for the protection of marine mammals was enacted by Congress on October 21, 1972, to become effective on December 21 of the same year. The Department of Commerce and the Department of the Interior are responsible for the enforcement of this legislation.

This new law forbids the capturing or importing of marine mammals into the United States. It also prohibits the importing of products made from any part of marine mammals.

A special permit is mandatory for the use of marine mammals in scientific experimentation or in public displays.

An exception to the law is the furred seals of the Pribiloff Islands which, since they are the victims of systematic commercial exploitation, are not protected.

Also, Eskimos and Indians who hunt cetaceans for their livelihood are specifically permitted to continue to do so.

Congress has also authorized a research program to study ways and means of reducing the numbers of dolphins killed during tuna-fishing expeditions. A separate research program is under way to determine the number of individuals belonging to the sixty-two species of marine mammals which are of vital interest to the United States.

In France:

The following is the text of the law prohibiting the capture or killing of dolphins:

"In view of the law of January 9, 1852, on maritime fishing, and particularly of Article 3 of said law;

"In view of the ordinance of June 3, 1944, regarding the reorganization of maritime fishing, especially Article 4 of said Ordinance;

"And taking into account the contribution of the Delphinidae to the ecological equilibrium of the seas and their utilization in the domain of scientific and technological research:

"Article One. It is forbidden to kill, to pursue or to capture, by any means whatever, even without the intention of harming, any marine mammals of the Delphinidae family (dolphins and porpoises).

"Article Two. The above dispositions do not apply to operations undertaken solely for purposes of scientific research.

"Article Three. The directors of maritime affairs at Le Havre, Saint-Servan, Nantes, Bordeaux, and Marseilles are responsible, each of his own territorial jurisdiction, for the execution of the present decree, which shall be published in the official Journal of the French Republic and made part of the official Bulletin of the Merchant Marine.

"Paris, October 20, 1970."

Appendix V

DOLPHINS IN THE CIRCUS AND IN THE LABORATORY

Among the institutions and establishments which breed, train, or study dolphins in captivity, we have listed those which are commercial in nature and which organize exhibitions or shows of trained animals, as well as centers for scientific research. Some marinelands, however, engage in both activities, and, in such cases, they have been listed in both categories.

MARINELANDS AND AQUARIUMS

United States.

Steinhart Aquarium, San Francisco, California
ABC Marine World, Redwood City, California
Marineland of the Pacific, California
Sea World, San Diego, California
Marineland of Florida, Florida
Ocean World, Fort Lauderdale, Florida
Miami Seaquarium, Miami, Florida
Aquarium of St. Petersburg Beach, Florida

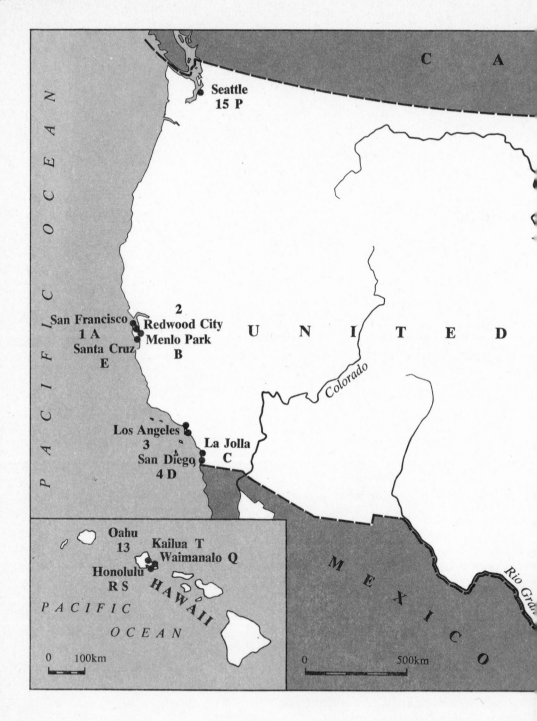

Marinelands are designated by numbers, and the various laboratories and dolphin research centers, by letters

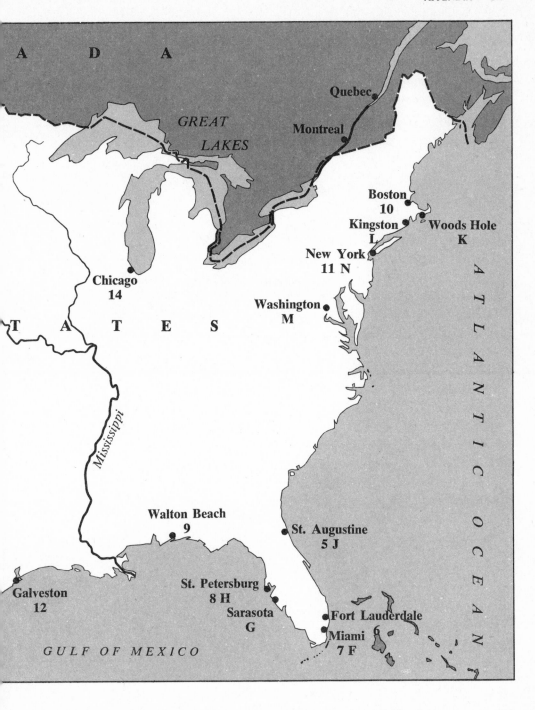

Florida's Gulfarium, Walton Beach, Florida
New England Aquarium, Boston, Massachusetts
New York Aquarium, Coney Island, New York
Sea-Arama Marineworld, Galveston, Texas
Sea Life Park, Oahu, Hawaii
Sea World, Chicago, Illinois
Seattle Marine Aquarium and Namu Inc., Seattle, Washington

Other Countries

Australia: Coolangatta, Queensland
Belgium:Anvers Zoological Garden
Canada: Niagra Falls • Vancouver Public Aquarium, British Columbia
France: Marineland d'Antibes
Germany: Duisburg Zoological Garden
Great Britain: Flamingo Park, Malton, Yorkshire • Whipsnade Zoological
    Gardens, Bedfordshire
Holland: Harderwijk
Japan: Enoshima Marineland • Ito Aquarium, Ito • Mitor Aquarium,
    Numazu • Toba Aquarium, Toba • Iruka Jima Yvenchi, Toba • Shimonse
    Aquarium, Shimonoseki • Numazu Aquarium, Numazu
New Zealand: Marineland of New Zealand, Napier.
South Africa: Durban Aquarium • The Oceanarium, Port Elizabeth
Spain: Barcelona Zoological Garden
Switzerland: Berne Zoological Garden
Canada: Niagara Falls • Vancouver Public Aquarium,
    British Columbia

Laboratories and Centers for Experimental Research

United States

Steinhart Aquarium, California Academy of Sciences, San Francisco, Cali-
    fornia.
Stanford Research Institute, Menlo Park, California.
Scripps Institution of Oceanography, La Jolla, California.
Naval Undersea Research and Development Center, San Diego, California.
University of California, Santa Cruz, California.

School of Marine and Atmospheric Sciences, University of Miami, Florida.

Mote Marine Laboratory, Sarasota, Florida.

Marine Research Laboratory, Florida Dept. of Natural Resources, St. Petersburg, Florida.

Marineland Research Laboratory, St. Augustine, Florida.

Woods Hole Oceanographic Institution, Woods Hole, Massachusetts.

Narragansett Marine Laboratory, University of Rhode Island, Kingston, Rhode Island.

Smithsonian Institution, Washington, D.C. (Marine Mammals Study Center.)

Rockefeller Institute, New York, New York

Makapuu Oceanic Center, Waimanalo, Hawaii.

U. S. Navy Marine Biosystem Division, Honolulu, Hawaii.

Dept. of Psychology, University of Hawaii, Honolulu.

Naval Undersea Research and Development Center, Hawaii Laboratory, Kailva, Hawaii.

Other Countries

Australia: Arthur Rylah Institute for Environmental Research, Heidelberg, Victoria. · School of Biological Sciences, University of Sydney

Canada: Arctic Biological Station, Fisheries Research Board of Canada, St. Anne de Bellevue, Quebec. · Marine Ecology Laboratory, Fisheries Research Board of Canada, Bedfort Institute, Dartmouth, Nova Scotia · Department of Zoology, University of Guelph, Guelph, Ontario.

France: Centre d'Etudes des Cetaces, Museum d'Histoire Naturelle, La Rochelle. · Laboratoire de Physiologie Acoustique, INRA, ERA CNRS, Jouy-en-Josas 78.

Great Britain: Department of Mammalogy, British Museum (Natural History), London. Whale Research Unit, Institute of Oceanographic Science's c/o British Museum (Natural History), London.

Holland: Museum of Natural History, Leyden. · Zoological Museum, Institute of Taxonomic Zoology, Amsterdam.

Japan: Ocean Research Institute, Tokyo University. · Whaling Research Institute, Tokyo. · Faculty of Fisheries, Nagasaki University, Nagasaki-Ken.

New Zealand: Department of Zoology, Victoria University of Wellington.

Switzerland: Brain Research Institute, Berne.

U.S.S.R.: Institute of Morphology of the Academy of Sciences, Moscow. • Institute for the Study of Nervous Activity, University of Moscow. • Faculty of Biology, University of Moscow. • Institute of Developmental Biology, Academy of Sciences, Moscow.

Illustrated Glossary

Adjutage

An apparatus designed to fit the opening of a water or gas main and used to control the flow of the gas or liquid.

Apnea

The more or less prolonged suspension of breathing.

Aqua-Lung®

The Aqua-Lung®, or diving gear, was designed in 1943 by Jacques-Yves Cousteau and Emile Gagnan, an engineer.

The principal characteristic of this apparatus is that it is an "open-circuit" device. That is, the used air is expelled directly into the water, and fresh air is provided, not in continuous fashion but whenever the diver inhales.

The air itself is stored in one or more air tanks (or "bottles" or "cylinders") which are strapped to the diver's back. Its flow is controlled by a regulator, which delivers air when the diver inhales and which assures that the pressure of the air is the same as that of the water surrounding the diver. When the diver exhales, the used air is fed into the water by means of an exhaust located under the hood of the regulator. Two flexible tubes run from a mouthpiece to the regulator. One of these is for inhalation; the other, for exhalation.

This simple and safe apparatus, entirely automatic and easily mastered, has, in effect, opened the sea to man and made it possible for a large segment of the public to experience the thrill of diving. The invention of the Aqua-Lung®, therefore, was a decisive step forward in man's conquest of the sea, and even in the history of human progress.

The Cousteau-Gagnan independent diving unit was a revolutionary departure from the old "hard-hat" diving rig which most of us recall from the movies of the thirties. The hard-hat rig — so-called because of the heavy copper helmet that it included — was complicated to use, uncomfortable, and dangerous. It required a longer period of training, and it limited the diver's field of action to a small area of the bottom. If, in the past two decades, man has truly been able to go down into the sea, it is because of the independent diving gear — and its accessory equipment, such as the "fins" invented by Commandant de Corlieu, the mask, and the weight belt — which has proved its value as a means of exploration and scientific research even more than as a piece of sporting equipment.

Yet even though man has now learned to operate autonomously in the sea, he is still susceptible to two of the dangers with which hard-hat divers had always to contend: rapture of the deep and decompression accidents.

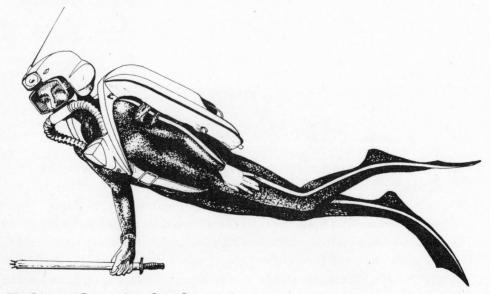

The Cousteau-Gagnon Aqua-Lung®.

Artiodactyls

A suborder of ungulate mammals the soles of whose paws bear an even number of digits. Ruminants and the pig family are artiodactyls.

Azimuth

The azimuth of a ship at sea is the angle formed by its bearing with respect to North.

Bathyscaphe

The first bathyscaphe was designed and perfected by Auguste Piccard. The bathyscaphe's first real dive took place on October 31, 1948, along the African coast off Dakar. On that occasion, the bathyscaphe, carrying no passengers, descended to a depth of 4,600 feet.

In October, 1950, an agreement between the French Navy and the Belgian National Research Foundation (Fonds National de la Recherche Scientifique) resulted in the construction of a new cable buoy and a new hull around the steel bell of the old *FNRS II*. This new design, called the FNRS III, was tested on February 15, 1954, off Dakar. With Commandant Nicolas-Maurice Houot and an engineer of the French Navy named Pierre-Henri Willm as passengers, the *FNRS III* attained a depth of 13,500 feet. In 1954 and 1958, it was used for deep dives in the Mediterranean, in the Atlantic, and in Japanese waters. After its ninety-fourth dive, the FNRS III was retired from active service.

Auguste and Jacques Piccard designed and built another bathyscaphe, the *Trieste*, which was tested in September, 1953, and which reached a depth of 10,000 feet. The *Trieste* was later acquired by the U. S. Navy and on January 23, 1960, it was used to reach the deepest known point in the sea: 36,380 feet, off the island of Guam.

Meanwhile, the French Navy, with the co-operation of the National Center for Scientific Research and the Belgian National Research Foundation, had undertaken the construction of an improved bathyscaphe. This new vehicle, christened the *Archimède*, was launched at the Toulon shipyard on July 28, 1961. In July 1962, in a series of six dives off the Kurile Islands in the North Pacific, the *Archimède* reached a depth of 30,000 feet. Since then, it has been used for deep-water research at various locations, from Puerto Rico to Madeira.

Blowhole

The blowhole is a valve located at the top of a cetacean's head. The two nostrils are situated within the blowhole. The sperm whale has two blowholes, but only one of them is functional. This organ has no connection with the alimentary canals of cetaceans, and it constitutes a major anatomical enigma.

Within the blowhole, the opening of which is controlled by a powerful muscle, there are inflatable air pockets on either side of the aperture. Two internal "lips" control exhalation and may contribute to the modulation of sound. In addition, a fleshy lamella, shaped like a tongue, serves as a cork, allowing the whale to close the blowhole more or less hermetically.

Bogue

The common name of a fish of the Sparidae family found in great abundance in the Mediterranean. Its flesh is not generally regarded as edible.

Calypso

Calypso is a former mine sweeper built in the United States in 1942 for the British Navy. She is a vessel of 350 tons, with a double hull of wood and two engines which give her a maximum speed of ten knots.

Calypso was found by Captain Cousteau in a naval-surplus yard on Malta, shortly after the close of World War II. The old mine sweeper was acquired through the generosity of a British patron, Mr. Loël Guinness.

She is remarkably easy to handle, and her shallow draft enables her to maneuver in and out of treacherous coral reefs with a minimum of trouble.

Extensive alterations were necessary before the ship could become a floating oceanographic laboratory. An underwater observation chamber was added: a well which descends to eight feet below the waterline and which is equipped with five portholes. This chamber is sometimes referred to as *Calypso*'s "false nose." Among the other changes and modifications was the addition of a double mast of light metal which was installed as far forward as possible on the deck. This mast serves as a radar antenna mount, as a sort of upper bridge from which to observe and direct a difficult passage, and as a crow's-nest from which to observe the larger marine animals in the water.

Catamaran

A sailing vessel characterized by the presence of two connected hulls.

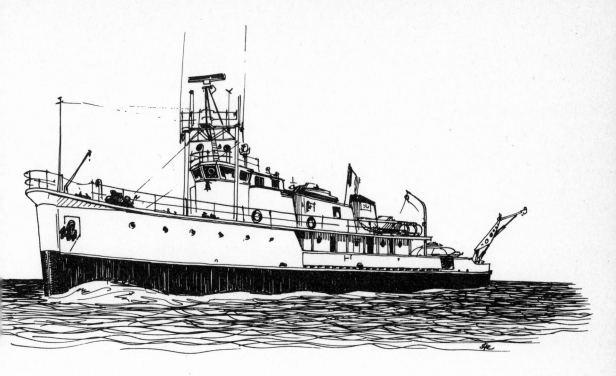

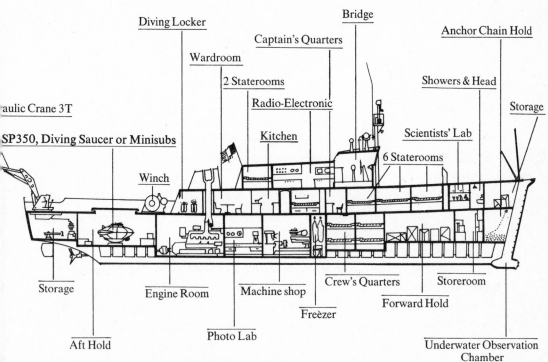

Diving Locker

Bridge

Captain's Quarters

Anchor Chain Hold

Wardroom

Showers & Head

2 Staterooms

Storage

Radio-Electronic

aulic Crane 3T

Scientists' Lab

SP350, Diving Saucer or Minisubs

Kitchen

6 Staterooms

Winch

Storage

Crew's Quarters

Storeroom

Engine Room

Machine shop

Forward Hold

Freèzer

Photo Lab

Aft Hold

Underwater Observation
Chamber

Calypso. She is 140 feet long and has a draught of seven and a half feet. She is equipped with two 500 hp engines and has a cruising speed of 10 knots. Displacement: 800 tons. She normally carries a team of twenty-nine men.

Cerebral Cortex

The uppermost layer of the cerebral hemispheres. The word "cortex" is derived from the Latin word for "bark" (of a tree).

Cochlea

A spiral canal which is part of the inner ear.

Crete

An island of the eastern Mediterranean, about 3,500 square miles in area. The civilization of Crete was the forerunner of all later major civilizations of the Mediterranean basin. It disappeared, quite suddenly and mysteriously, in the second millennium before Christ. Most scholars now believe that foreign invasion was responsible for this cataclysm.

Curare

A poison derived from various American flora of the Strychnos genus. Curare induces death by destroying all motor nerves.

Cuttlefish

The cuttlefish belongs to the family Sepiidae, order Sepioidea, subclass Coleoidea. It lives in coastal waters among vegetation and on sandy bottoms, where it finds the shrimps which are its usual diet. There are approximately eighty species of cuttlefish, most of which are found in the tropical and sub-tropical waters of the Indo-Pacific. There are only a few Atlantic species; however, cuttlefish are abundant in the western Pacific and in the Indian Ocean. There are none in American waters.

The body of the cuttlefish is oval in shape. At the edge of the mantle, there is a ribbonlike fin running the length of the body. Around the head, there are eight arms and two tentacles, which are used to capture prey. Ordinarily, the two tentacles are retracted into two cavities under the cuttlefish's eyes.

The body of the cuttlefish is reinforced by an internal shell, the "cuttlefish bone," which contains chambers filled with gas and which serves as the cuttlefish's hydrostatic equipment in swimming and floating.

The best-known species is the common cuttlefish, *Sepia officinalis*. This species was observed and commented upon by Aristotle some twenty-three centuries ago. It is found in the coastal waters of the Mediterranean, and all authorities agree that it is a strictly coastal species which is rarely found in water deeper than 450 feet.

Only a part of the cuttlefish population reaches the age of three or even four years. Its ordinary life span appears to be between two and two and one-half years.

The length of the cuttlefish's mantle is rarely more than sixteen to twenty inches. The smallest cuttlefish is the *Hemisepius typicus*, which is about 2-3/4 inches long. The largest species is *Sepia latimanus*, which reaches a length of five and one-half feet.

The mating season is in spring and summer.

Deep Scattering Layer, or D.S.L.

Deep Scattering Layer, which was so named during World War II, is a mysterious layer detected by the echo from sonar equipment at various depths and in various regions in the sea.

It has been observed that these layers rise toward the surface during the hours of darkness and then sink again during daylight. Professor H. E. Edgerton, of the Massachusetts Institute of Technology, working from *Calypso*, has succeeded in photographing these layers by using an electronic flash which he designed.

The constitutive elements of these layers are principally copepods, jellyfish, siphonophores, and eggs and larvae.

False Nose

Calypso's "*false nose*" is her underwater observation chamber. This chamber is one of the modifications which was necessary before the World War II mine sweeper could be used for oceanographic purposes. It is a metal well which goes down eight feet below the waterline and which is equipped with five portholes. The portholes are used for observing and filming marine life, even while *Calypso* is in motion.

Flippers

The flippers, or pectoral limbs, of cetaceans serve to remind us of the land origins of these marine mammals. An X ray of a flipper reveals the bones of five "fingers" (except in the case of the rorqual, or finback whale), of a "wrist," and of an "arm."

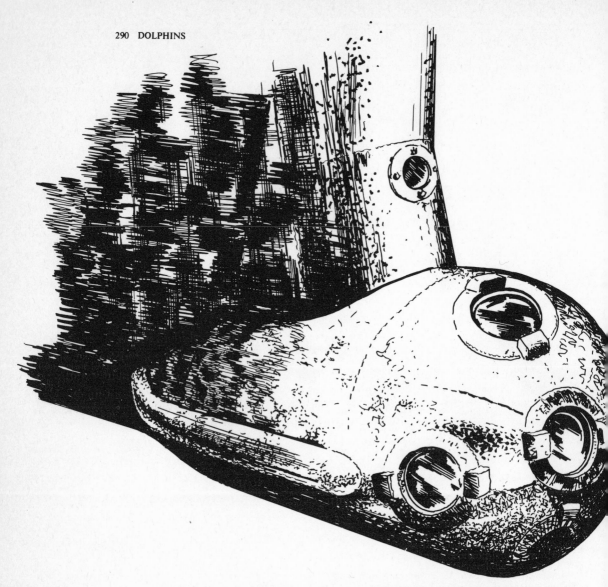

Calypso's "false nose" is a metallic well which leads to an observation chamber located eight feet beneath the waterline. This chamber has five portholes, which are useful not only in observing marine life, but also in photographing and filming it.

Flourescein

Fluorescein is a phthalein-based coloring agent. In solution, it is fluorescent.

Grouper

Groupers are sedentary fish that live in grottos and coral indentations, preferably on sandy bottoms, in water of various depths. They are adept hunters and attack their victims with great speed.

Groupers were once very numerous along the coasts of the Mediterranean, where they were hunted to excess because of their value as food. They are still abundant in African waters and also off the shores of both North and South America.

There are many species of groupers of various colors in tropical waters. In its proper meaning, the term "grouper" designates only members of the family Serranidae — which includes many fishes: *Ephinephelus, Cephalopholis*, etc. — but especially those belonging to the genera *Sterolepis* and *Promicrops*. The latter, which may reach an adult size of ten feet, is found along the coasts of Africa and also in American waters, where it is known as the Pacific jewfish or the giant sea bass.

Harpoon

The harpoon has been used since the dawn of history for fishing and hunting. In primitive times, it was made of wood or bone, with either one or two rows of barbs.

The *harpé*, as the Greeks called it (the word was derived from the Semitic *hereb*), is depicted on monuments dating from the third millennium before Christ. In the language of the Basques, those intrepid hunters of whales, the word *arpoi* (taken from the Greek root) means to "capture alive."

The present form of the harpoon is described in a text dating from 1474.

An important modern improvement was the addition of a pivoted crosspiece to the head, which prevents a harpooned animal from shaking the weapon loose.

Hawser

A line composed of several strands which is used for docking a ship or boat.

Hydrophone

A microphone designed for use in recording sounds in a liquid milieu.

Keeling

To keel a vessel is to turn up its keel, in dry dock, so as to scrape algae and barnacles from its hull, to inspect its condition, to paint it, or to effect repairs. Depending upon the work to be undertaken, keeling is classified either as major or minor.

La Méduse

On June 17, 1816, a French frigate named *La Méduse* left the Island of Aix, with three other vessels, bound for the colony of Senegal in West Africa. On July 2, *La Méduse* ran aground along the Arguin Bank. The crew tried for five days to get the ship afloat again. Then they constructed a raft, sixty feet in length and twenty feet in width, and 149 of the survivors were loaded aboard. The rest of the crew was distributed among five lifeboats secured to the raft by lines. Seventeen men, too drunk to take part in the evacuation of the ship, were left aboard *La Méduse*, which sank shortly thereafter.

The survivors drifted for twelve days without food or water. At the end of that time, they were rescued; but, by then, only fifteen of them were alive. The others had been devoured by sharks, or by the other occupants of the raft.

The Raft of La Méduse, a celebrated painting by Géricault, first exhibited in 1819, hangs today in the Louvre Museum.

Lamparo

Lamparo is a Provençal word meaning "lamp." It is used (especially by Mediterranean fishermen) to designate a fishing session in which a light is used to attract the fish.

Level Reef

A level reef is a coral plateau, more or less long and unbroken, which extends along a shoreline or on top of another reef that is completely surrounded by water. Level reefs are found in tropical shallows.

Minisub

There are several types of minisubs, or diving saucers, designed by Captain Cousteau and developed by the Center of Higher Marine Studies at Marseilles:

The *SP-350*, a two-passenger vehicle, is equipped with a cinematographic camera, a still camera, a hydraulically operated pincer and lift, and a storage basket. It has been used in over 600 dives. One *SP-350* can be parked in the rear hold of the *Calypso*.

The *SP-1000*, or sea flea, carries only one man but is designed to be used in conjunction with a second *SP-1000*. It has two exterior cameras (16mm. and 35mm.), both controlled from within, and tape recorders for recording underwater sounds. It has been used in over 100 dives. Two *SP-1000s* can be taken aboard the *Calypso*.

The *SP-4000*, or Deepstar, is capable of diving to 4,000 feet. It was built for Westinghouse and was launched in 1966. Since then, it has participated in over 500 dives. It is a two-man vehicle, with a speed of three knots.

The *SP-3000* was built for CNEXO. It attains a speed of three knots and carries three passengers.

Minoan Period

The Minoan is a period of Cretan history running from the third millennium B.C. to 1100 B.C. It is divided into the Upper Minoan (2400–2000B.C.), the Middle Minoan (1900–1600), and the Lower, or Recent, Minoan (1550–1100).

Mullet

The mullet is a member of the Mugilidae family and is classified as a bony fish. It is a coastal fish and is very common in temperate seas. It grows to two feet in length and reaches a weight of about twelve pounds. Its lateral line is not clearly visible, and its belly is white and soft. Mullets have flat, wide heads. They have very small teeth, or no teeth at all. Their scales are large, shiny, and well defined.

Mullets live in schools.

Mycenaean

The adjective Mycenaean is used to designate the ancient city of Mycenae in Argolis, or the civilization typified by the people of that city. The Mycenaean civilization followed that of the Minoans and dominated a large part of Greece, spreading into the islands of the Aegean and into Asia Minor. The Mycenaeans controlled the western Mediterranean, and their ships ventured into the North Sea and the Baltic to trade for amber and tin.

The empire of the Mycenaeans attained its peak *c.* 1400 B.C., then disappeared quite suddenly *c.* 1100 B.C. It was at the latter point in time that the Mycenaean citadel was completely destroyed.

Neurone

A nerve cell together with its processes.

Octopus

The octopus is a cephalopod mollusk having eight arms of equal length. The arms are equipped with sucker discs. Although it is a mollusk, the "shell" of the octopus is vestigial, or altogether absent.

There are numerous species of octopus — all generally sedentary animals — found in every sea. The largest specimens attain a size of between six and seven feet. In some species, the salivary glands secrete a strong poison; and the bite of one species, native to Australian waters, is fatal to humans.

The third arm of the male octopus contains a channel or groove along its length. The animal's spermatophores pass down this groove. The arm is called the hectocotylus, and it is used to fertilize the female by introducing the spermatozoids into her pallial cavity.

Pelvis

An anatomical term for the usually basinlike bones to which the hind limbs are attached. In man and other land-living animals it is part of the nearly rigid structure involving the spine; in dolphins it is greatly reduced in size.

Pinnipeds

An order of animals comprising three familes:
Otaridae: sea lions, furred seals;
Odobaenidae: walrus;
Phocidae: seals and elephant seals.

Port

The nautical term used to designate the left side of a vessel when one is facing forward toward the stem.

Red Mullet, or Surmullet

The red mullet, commonly known as the bearded mullet, is easily recognizable by its iridescent red and yellow scales and by its two "whiskers," which are actually exploratory and tactile organs.

Rorqual, or Blue Whale

The rorqual *Balaenoptera physalus* is a baleen whale which belongs to the *Balaenoptera* genus of the Balaenopteridae family. It takes its common name of "finback" from its large, well-developed dorsal fin. Its lower jaw projects beyond the upper, and its underside is marked by a number of parallel ventral furrows.

The Blue Whale, *Balaenoptera musculus,* may attain a length of between 60 and 75 feet and a weight of 50 to 100 tons. The largest specimen known was a hundred feet in length. "The Blue Rorqual," says Professor Budker, "holds a record which has never been beaten. It is the largest, the most massive, and the heaviest creature that has ever existed on land or in the sea."

(See Appendix II, "The Cetaceans.")

Scrotum

The external bag, or pouch, which, in most mammals, contains the testicles.

Seine

A seine is a large net used for fishing. The two ends of the net are maneuvered

The Blue Whale -- the largest living creature existing either on land or in the sea.

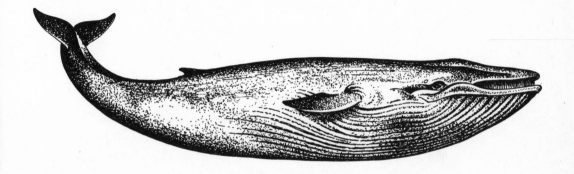

in such a way as to close gradually, shutting either the entire net or a section of it where the fishes have gathered.

Semantic

In language, that which is signified by a sign (or word). The study of such meanings is a function of the science of linquistics.

Sharks

The name "shark" is generally applied to fish belonging to the Elasmobranch, or Selachian, group.

Since sharks have no bones (their skeletons are composed entirely of cartilage), they are usually thought of as primitive animals. Yet, the nervous system of the shark is highly developed. There is a great variety in the ways in which various species reproduce, and some of these methods are especially well developed.

Among the Selachians, fertilization is internal, and there is a true mating. Professor Budker, an expert on sharks, writes: "So far as the mating of the species of large, pelagic sharks is concerned, it is impossible to formulate any hypotheses, since it is so difficult to observe such matings and the opportunity for such observation is so infrequent."

Among the smaller species, however, observation is possible, and we have more data. We know, for example, that the male dogfish swims in a tight circle near the female, while the latter remains stretched out and completely motionless.

Among the Carcharhinidae, especially, the young are always born live, and the foetus is connected to the mother's uterus by a kind of placenta. The number of sharks in a litter may vary from four to forty.

The heads and bodies of sharks are generously equipped with sensory organs — the "pit organs" described by Professor Budker in 1938 — which furnish them with an abundance of precise information on their environment. Work is currently under way to determine the roles of the different sensory organs which seem to make it possible for the shark to measure hydrostatic pressure, to perceive sonic and ultrasonic waves, to detect the chemical composition of water, etc. It is already known that a shark is able to perceive the presence of blood in the sea at a great distance, probably by means of its nostrils and the organs of taste with which the animal is equipped.

The shark enjoys the use of senses which man lacks, and thus it is much better equipped than a human diver for survival in the seas. This is particularly true at night, for the shark's eye, while it is not very effective in distinguishing the details or colors of a fixed object, is capable of perceiving and recognizing anything that moves in the water. Its field of vision is constant, even when the shark suddenly twists and turns in the water.

For more detailed information on the shark, and for a description of various experiments on the behavior of sharks, the reader is referred to *The Shark: Splendid Savage of the Sea*, by Jacques-Yves Cousteau and Philippe Cousteau, Doubleday & Co., Inc., and Cassell, 1970.

Sonar

"Sound Navigation Ranging" equipment, used in underwater detection and communication. It is analogous to radar and is based upon the reflection of sonic and supersonic waves.

Sphincter

A circular muscle surrounding, and able to contract or close, a natural opening or passage.

Spout

When a cetacean rises to the surface to breathe, it gives off, through one or two blowholes, a spout which is visible from a distance. It is a whitish spray, which cannot be attributed solely to the condensation of vapor in cold air, for it is visible even in tropical waters and climates.

As there is no passageway between its mouth and its blowhole, a whale cannot blow water out while exhaling.

Paul Portier, a French biologist, has offered the following hypothesis: the expansion in the open air of air which has been compressed in the thorax of a whale causes the condensation of the water vapor when the whale exhales.

F. C. Fraser and P. E. Purves have noted the presence in the whale's lungs of very small drops of oil and mucus, which may explain the visibility of its spout. This oil in the whale's respiratory tract may also play a part in the absorption of nitrogen.

Each species of whale has a distinctive spout. That of the blue whale and of the common rorqual is a single geyser that rises from eighteen to thirty feet above the surface. The right whale's spout is double. That of the sperm whale is single and emerges from the blowhole to the left of the whale and at a 45-degree angle.

The dolphin's spout, on the other hand, is barely visible above the water.

Squid

The squid is a cephalopod of the Loliginidae family, suborder Myopsida, order Teuthoidea, subclass Coleoidea.

The *Loligo vulgaris*, or common squid, is cigar-shaped and tapers to a point.

Squids have two triangular lateral fins and a horny, transparent internal element known as a "pen." They are common in the Atlantic, the North Sea, the Mediterranean, and the Red Sea. Most specimens of *Loligo vulgaris*, both in the Atlantic and in the Mediterranean, live to a probable age of between twenty-four and thirty months. The body of the male reaches a length of about eight inches. That of the female is of comparable length, but the arms of the male are longer. Certain species of squid, belonging to other genera, are true giants.

The *Loligo opalescens* has been the subject of a film made by the Cousteau team.

Stages of Ascent

Decompression accidents, during a diver's ascent to the surface, result from the diver's breathing of compressed air and from the gases that are dissolved in his system, by water pressure, during the ascent. The faster a diver rises, the larger are the air bubbles that may be generated. (The depth of the dive, and its duration, are also factors.) These bubbles block the circulatory system and may result in what is known as "gas embolism."

The diver's ascent is therefore slowed in order to allow these gases sufficient time to dissolve. Tables have been worked out which show the number and duration of the stops a diver must make during his ascent, in relation to the depth of the dive and the time spent at that depth. These mandatory stops are the "stages of ascent."

Starboard

The right side of a ship or boat, when one is looking forward, toward the stem.

Stays

Stays (also known as "shrouds" or "guys") are the lines of hemp or steel which run from the top of the masts of a ship to the hull. They serve to steady the masts. The term "to stay" or "to guy" means to steady a spar by means of lines.

Stem, or Stem Post

The specially sturdy piece to which sides of a ship or boat are secured in the bow. The prow.

Tuna

There are two commercial varieties of tuna: the white tuna (Thunnus, [or Germo] alalunga), and the red or true tuna (Thunnus thynnus). Both varieties are members of the Tunnidae family.

The giant tuna of Nova Scotia attains a length of thirteen feet and a weight of 1,500 pounds.

Undersea Houses

Captain Cousteau's first experiment with undersea houses (Conshelf I) took place in the Mediterranean, off Marseilles, in 1962, where two divers remained at a depth of 35 feet for eight days.

The second experiment (Conshelf II) was in the Red Sea, at Shab Rumi, in 1963. There, two oceanauts lived for a week at 80 feet, and eight others lived for a month at 37 feet.

The latest experiment took place in 1965 and was called Conshelf III. On that occasion, six divers remained at over 300 feet for three weeks, in an undersea house built in the open water off Cape Ferrat.

Bibliography

Alpers, Antony. *Dolphins, the Myth and the Mammal.* Boston, 1961.

Anthonioz, Raphaelle. "Les Imragen, pêcheurs nomades de Mauritanie". *Bulletin de l'IFAN.* t. XXIX (1967), t. XXX (1968).

Budker, Paul. "Dauphin," "La Mer," Encyclopedie Alpha, Paris, 1973.

Busnel, Rene-Guy, Moles, A., and Gilbert, M. "Un Cas de langue sifflee utilisee dans les Pyrenees francaise." *Logos,* V5-2, October 1962.

—————— "Le dauphin, nouvel animal de laboratoire," in *Sciences et Techniques,* III, 1966.

——————(ed.)*Les systemes sonars animaux.* Laboratoire de physiologie acoustique, Jouy-en-Josas, 1967.

—————— "Symbiotic Relationship between Man and Dolphins," *Meeting of the Section of Psychology,* N. Y. Academy of Sciences, 1972.

Caldwell, David K., and Melba C. *"World of the Bottle-Nosed Dolphin"* in *Sciences,* No. 108, 1966.

——————————. *The Ugly Dolphin.* St. Augustine, Florida.

——————————. *The World of the Bottlenosed Dolphin.* Philadelphia, 1972.

Classe, Andre. "L' Etrange language siffle des Iles Canaries," in *Courrier de l'Unesco.* Nov. 1957, No. 11.

Fraser, F. C. *British Whales, Dolphins and Porpoises.* London, 1966.

Green, R. E., Perrin, W. F., and Patrick, B. P. *The American Tuna Pure Seine Fishery.* London (n.d.)

Herald, Earl S. *Field and Aquarium Study of the Blind River Dolphin,* 1969.

Hershkovitz, P. *Catalog of Living Whales.* Washington, D.C., 1966.

Irvine, Blair. "Conditioning Marine Mammals to Work in the Sea," in *M. T. S. Journal,* Vol. 4, No. 3, May–June 1970.

Jonsgard, A., and Lyshoel, P. B. "A Contribution to the Knowledge of the Killer Whale," in *Nouveau Journal de Zoologie,* 1970.

Kellogg, W. N. *Porpoises and Sonar.* Phoenix, 1961.

Lilly, John C. *Man and Dolphin.* New York, 1961.

—————. *The Mind of the Dolphin: A Non-human Intelligence.* New York, 1967.

Matthews, L. H. *The Whale.* London, 1968.

McNeely, Richard L. "The Pure Seine Revolution in Tuna Fishing," in *Pacific Fisherman,* June, 1961.

Norris, Kenneth S. "Trained Porpoise Released in Open Sea." *Science,* 147 (3661), pp. 1048–50.

—————, ed. *Whales, Dolphins and Porpoises.* Berkeley and Los Angeles, 1966.

Perrin, William F. "Using Porpoise to Catch Tuna," in *World Fishing,* Vol. 18, No. 16 (1969).

Pilleri, G. *Observations on the Behavior of Platanista gangetica in the Indus and Brahmaputra rivers.* 1970.

Rice, D. W., and Scheffer, V. B. *A List of the Marine Mammals of the World.* Washington, D. C., 1968.

—————. *Recent Mammals of the World.* New York, 1967.

Riedman, Sarah R., and Gustafson, Elton T. *Home Is the Sea for Whales.* New York, 1966.

Slijper, E. J. *Whales.* London, 1962.

Index

Aegean civilization, 235-38
Airmen Against the Sea (Llano), 200
Albino whales, 24
Alinat, Commandant Jean, 44, 127
Alpers, Anthony, 108, 167
Amirante Island, 21-23
Anthonioz, Raphaelle, 206
Apollo (god), 237, 247
Arion (poet), 71
Aristotle, 146, 242, 265
Asbury, Jean, 73-75, 84, 85, 89, 154
Asbury family, 73-80

Backing down (fishing technique), 223-24
Baker, Jill, 93-94
Balaenidae, 268-70
Balaenopteridae, 270-71
Bassaget, Jean-Paul, 161-63
Bastian, J., 149-50
Bats, sonar abilities of, 142
Batteau, W., 157-58
Beck, Dr., 46, 52
Beluga whales, 24, 226-27, 262
Beps (dolphin), 53
Boissy, 45
Bonnici, Christian, 161
Bottlenosed Dolphin (*Tursiops truncatus*),
    40, 69, 95-103, 158, 219, 261; brain
    size, 165; gestation period, 109-10;
    length of, 135, 262; man's preference for,
    181-83; mating technique, 108; swim-
    ming depth of, 173. *See also* Dolphins
Bouchet, General du, 208
British Museum, 218
Budker, Paul, 172, 184, 261
Bullen, Frank T., 91
Bureau of Marine Research (France), 36
Busnel, Rene G., 21, 69, 87, 88, 118, 119,
    122, 125, 142, 148-49, 152, 156, 175, 178,
    184, 185, 186, 208, 218, 219

Caldwell, David K. and Melba C., 67, 76, 148,
    183, 184-85, 186, 192, 235, 265, 273
California Fisheries Bureau, 223
Calypso expeditions, 16, 17, 21-30, 31-32,
    87, 98, 227. *See also* Dolphin Project
Cape Verde Islands, 230
Cephalorhynchus, 262
Cetaceans: characteristics of, 265-66; order
    and species, 266; suborders of, 266-71
Chalazonitis, Dr., 48
Chauvin, 161-63
Christ the Saviour, symbol of, 247
Common dolphin (*Delphinus delphis*), 40, 41,
    113, 262
Common porpoise (*Phocaena phocaena*), 262

Cook Strait, 91-93
Corsica, 24, 36-37, 38
Cousteau, Philippe, 77, 80, 146, 196
Crete (ancient), 235-37, 242
Cuvier, Georges, 165

Delemotte, Bernard, 98, 126, 161
Deloire, Michel, 84, 213, 215
Delphi, ancient sanctuary of, 237
Delphinapterus leucas, 262
Delphinidae family, 183, 184; genera, 266;
    members of, 261-63
Delphinus leucas, 24
Democratic National Convention (1972), 85
Dimple (dolphin), 202
Dolly (dolphin), 71-89, 91, 99, 154, 234;
    background of, 75-76; *Calypso*'s acquaintance
    with, 77-81; in the Florida Keys, 73-75;
    relationship with Asbury family, 73-75, 80-82;
    social contacts and, 82-85; tricks learned by, 74-
    75, 81
Dolphin Project: behavioral research observations,
    161-80; problem of captivity, 158-60; purpose
    of, 159; researchers participating in, 118; sound
    and communication research, 137-60; use of
    U-shaped pincer, 118-19; in vicinity of Malaga
    and Gibraltar, 123-35; yellow (color) and, 114-
    15
Dolphins: abdominal cavity of, 202; acoustical
    system of, 168-69; association with tuna, 222-
    36; behavior of (in captivity), 184-85; bond
    between humans and, 26-28, 60, 71, 91-111,
    174-76, 177-80, 235-50; brain of, 164-65, 256;
    capturing of, 43-53, 183-84; children and, 88,
    93; directional sense of, 13-14; dominant types,
    66-69; education (in captivity), 181-202;
    experiments performed on, 189; first encounters
    with, 11-30; as fisherman's friend, 203-19; food
    and eating habits, 56, 63; future and, 253-56;
    games and love of play, 12, 20, 176-77;
    gestation period, 109-10; happiness and
    unhappiness of, 188-89; intelligence of, 164-67,
    177; land origins of, 118; life span of, 191; love
    life of, 103-11; mating activities, 64, 104-8;
    music sensitivity, 245; naval training of, 192-
    202; position (with respect to a ship), 12-13;
    respiratory rhythm, 172-73; schools of, 21, 25,
    44, 61, 103; sense of caution, 14-20; senses of,
    138, 167-69; skin sensitivity, 56-57, 84; sleeping
    time, 173-74; as a social animal, 57-60, 63-64;
    swimming depth and speed, 63, 116, 169-72,
    173; teeth of, 63; training process (U. S. Navy),
    192-202; vision of, 61-63, 138, 168; weight of,
    36, 60. *See also* names of species

Dolphins: The Myth and the Mammal (Alpers), 108
Dorado, Francois, 161
Dreher, Dr., 155
D.S.L. (deep scattering layer), 230, 232
Dufduf (dolphin), 49-52
Dumas, Frederic, 21, 23, 230
Dziedzic, Albin, 87, 118, 126, 130-31, 134, 142, 148, 151, 175, 176, 178

Echolocation system, 137-43; in blind dolphins, 168; clicking sounds, 139-41
Elie Monnier (ship), 13, 115, 227-30
Eschrichtiidae, 270
Espadon (trawler), 32-52, 60
Estruscans (ancient), 238
Euphronius cup, 238
Evans, W. E., 135, 195-98
Experimental research, 254-56; laboratories and centers for, 280-82

Falco, Albert "Bebert," 31-53, 60-63, 69, 113, 184, 211, 212-13; Dolphin Project, 118-19, 122-23, 125-27, 131, 134, 169; pincer device developed by, 55-56
Farquhar Islands, 33
Fish, Marie Poland, 143, 226
Fishermen, dolphins and, 203-19; in ancient times, 203-5, 221, 237; Imragen people of Mauretania, 205-18, 219; local collaboration, 219; in modern times, 221-34; tuna fishing, 222-36
Fitzgerald, S., 202
"Flipper" (TV series), 88
Florida Marine Studios, 68, 108, 109
FNRS II (bathyscaphe), 13, 227-28
Fox Trot (dolphin), 126
Franco, Francisco, 98
Francois, Joseph, 126, 127, 134
Fraser, F. C., 218, 265
Fresh-water dolphins, species of, 273-74

Gardner, Allen, 155
Gautheron, Bernard, 118, 126
Gilbert, Perry, 192, 202
Glotz, Gustave, 237
Grampus griseus, 91
Gray, Sir James, 172
Greece (ancient), 237-38, 242
Griffin, Edward I., 151
Gulf of Malaga, 69

Haig (dolphin), 202
Harbor Porpoise (Phocoena phocoena), 119, 142, 185, 261
Hawaii Research Center, 193
Hellion, Alain, 118
Homer, 242
Homosexuality, 110-11
Howe, Margaret, 110
Humpback whales, sounds of, 146

Imragen people, 205-18, 219
Indian Ocean, 16, 21-23, 33
Inia geoffrensis, 219
Irvine, Blair, 195

Kay, Leslie, 143
Kellogg, Remington, 110-11
Kellogg, Winthrop, 168
Key West, dolphin-training base at, 75-76

Kientzy, Canoe, 24, 41-42, 44, 45, 46
Kiki (dolphin), 43-53; capture of, 43-45; death of, 53; feeding of, 48-49
Killer whales, 181, 183, 195, 211-13, 215, 218, 226; acoustical system, 150-51; intelligence of, 262; length of, 262; mating technique, 108
Knossos, palace at, 235
Korianos, story of, 71-73
Kramer, Max O., 172

Laboratory of Acoustical Physiology of INRA, 21, 87, 118
La Corogna, Spain, 95-103, 246
Lagenorhynchus acutus, 262
Lagenorhynchus albirostris, 262
Lagorio, Eugene, 146
Lamb, F. B., 219
Leandri, Maurice, 41-42, 44
Legislative protection, 275-276
Lerner Laboratory (Bimini), 76-77
Lilly, John C., 110, 111, 148, 154, 155, 156-57, 177

Lipari Islands, 24
Llano, George, 200
Longhurst, W. M., 143
Lorenz, Konrad, 88

Marinelands and aquariums, 67-69, 77, 277-80
Marine Mammal Protection Act of 1972, 224
Matthews, Harrison, 265
Mauritania, 67, 205-18, 219
Medusa (ship), 206
Miami Seaquarium, 188, 202
Millet, Dr., 245
Mind of the Dolphin, The (Lilly), 111
Mona (dolphin), 109
Monodontidae, 266
Mote Marine Laboratory, 192
Myotis lucifugen, 142
Mystacoceti, families of, 268-271
Myth and symbolism, 235-50

Narragansett Laboratory, 143
Narwhals (Monodon monoceros), 234, 262-63
National Fishery Service, 224-26
Natural History (Pliny the Elder), 203-5, 243-45
Naval Registry (France), 221
Naval Undersea Research Center, 135, 195-98
New Zealand, 91-95, 246
Nino (dolphin), 95-103, 234, 246; monument to, 102-3
Nivelot, Dr., 24-25
Norris, Kenneth, S., 20, 66, 69, 265
Northern Bottlenosed Whale (Hyperoodon rostratus), 263

Oceanographic Institute of Hawaii (Honolulu), 192
Oceanographic Museum of Monaco, 31, 127; first dolphin in captivity, 43-53
Odontoceti, families of, 266-68
Omer, Yves, 98, 114, 115, 116, 126, 127, 211, 212-13, 215
Opo (dolphin), 93-95, 102, 246
Oppian (poet), 203
Orcella fluminalis, 219

Pacific White-sided Dolphins, mating technique, 108
Pedro (dolphin), 188
Pelorus Jack (dolphin), 91-93

304 DOLPHINS

Persian Gulf, 20-21
Peter (dolphin), 110
Phoenicians (ancient), 237
Phonetics Institute, 118
Physeteridae, 266-67
Piccard, Professor Auguste, 13, 227
Pilot whales, 67, 119, 175-76, 181, 191, 227-34, 263; mating technique, 108; suicide of, 232-34; taming and training of, 227
Pliny the Elder, 200, 203-5, 207, 243-46, 250
Pliny the Younger, 246
Plutarch, 71-73
Point Mugu (training center), 195, 198-202
Porpoise School of Florida, 189
Poseidon (god), 238
Premack, Professor, 155
Prezelin, Louis, 161, 245
Primauguet (cruiser), 11-13, 20

Racine, Jean Baptiste, 147
Red Sea, 16, 20, 163
Renoir, Jacques, 95-98, 102, 103, 110, 113, 131, 196, 208, 211, 213, 215
Riant, Jean-Clair, 215, 217
River dolphins (Platanistidae), 262, 266
Rome (ancient), 238
Rufus, Caninium, 246
Rumbaugh, Professor, 155

St. Thomas Laboratory, 111
Salleres, Luis, 96-98, 103
Santini, A. V., 183, 189
Saout, Captain Francois, 21
Sea lions, 195
Seattle Aquarium, 151
Sharks, dolphins and, 32-36, 200-2
Silent World, The (motion picture), 20-21
Sirot, Captain Philippe, 114
Smithsonian Institution, 232-34
Sound and communication system, 28-29, 126, 127, 130, 137-60; echolocation, 137-43, 168; night calls (when captured), 151-52; non-

Sound and communication system (continued) language signals, 152-60; signals of communication, 143-46; voices and vocabulary, 146-49; whistle sounds, 155-58
Sousa teuszi, 67, 219
Spallanzani, Lazzaro, 142
Sperm whales, 66-67
Spinner Dolphin (*Stenella longirostris*), 224
Spotted Dolphin (*Stenella graffmani*), 183, 224, 262
Spray (dolphin), 109
Steno, 119; mating technique, 108
Sub-Committee on Small Cetaceans of the International Whaling Commission, 263
Sugar (dolphin), 85

Taranto, Italy, 239
Taylor, Professor, 202
Telemachus (sone of Ulysses), 242
Theseus the Diver, 237-38
Toscano, Captain Jean, 44
Tuffy (dolphin), 76, 198-200
Tuna fishing, dolphins and, 222-36; association between species, 222-24; casualties, 224; Congressional legislation, 224-26
Twain, Mark, 91

University of Centerbury, 143
University of Oklahoma, 155

Vasquez, Jose Freire, 96, 103
Von Fritsch, Karl, 146
Voronine, L. G., 154

Walker, Ernest P., 265
Weddell seals, 146
Whistled languages, 156-57
World of the Bottle-Nosed Dolphin (Caldwell), 67, 76, 235
World War II, 200

Zero-syntax language, 154
Ziphiidae, 266